WITHDRAWN

Sociologists, Economists and Democracy

BRIAN BARRY

The University of Chicago Press
Chicago and London

The University of Chicago Press, Chicago 60637
The University of Chicago Press, Ltd., London

82 81 80 79 78 9 8 7 6 5 4 3 2 1
ISBN: 0–226–03823–8
LCN: 78–55039

Contents

Contents

Preface to the Phoenix Edition

This book was first published, in a manner of speaking, in 1970. There is no need to rehearse here the vicissitudes that underlie that qualification and resulted in the book's becoming, almost from the start, something of a collector's item. I am delighted that the University of Chicago Press is now making it available (and at a reasonable price), thus enabling me to wind up my role as lender of last resort. I leave the book distribution business without regrets and look forward, for the first time in eight years, to being able to attend a gathering of academics without having to anticipate that, at some stage, somebody is going to take the opportunity of complaining to me about the frustrations of trying to get hold of copies so as to assign it for a course.

Despite its quasi-*samizdat* status, *Sociologists, Economists and Democracy* has been referred to in a number of books and articles, and page references to the original edition will be correct for this one too, since it is reprinted unchanged. The only exceptions, apart from this Preface, which replaces the original one, are that some lines scrambled by the printer on page 65 are corrected, and that the last two paragraphs of the original bibliographical essay on pages 189–90 have been replaced by a new Postscript.

I should not, however, have agreed to let the book be reprinted unrevised if I thought subsequent developments called for substantial changes. But, after pondering the question at some length, I have concluded that, if I were writing the book today, I would use exactly the same canon of 'economists' and 'sociologists'.

It is always risky to pronounce a verdict of death on ideas, even after an extended period of apparent lifelessness, but I predict that we have seen the last of the 'sociologists' in political science. I cannot, of course, claim personal responsibility for the demise of the 'sociological' approach. Rather, I would take it that what has happened is that others too have penetrated the characteristically sloppy logic and flabby prose to discover the deeper problems of circularity and vacuousness inherent in the approach.

This is not to say that all the lines of thought entering into Parsons's 'action frame of reference' have been abandoned. Far from it: stocks in Max Weber have never stood at a higher level. One might even advance the hypothesis that among Anglo-American social scientists the condition for recognition of his true stature was his extraction from the Parsonian synthesis. What does seem defunct, at any rate in writing about politics, is the notion, introduced by Durkheim and elaborated by Parsons, that the way to explain some feature of a society is to show how it relates to other aspects of the society to form part of a functional whole—not to explore the way it came about or the reasons people have for maintaining it.

The story of the 'economic' approach is quite different. It has flourished quantitatively and qualitatively. Membership in the Public Choice society in the U.S.A. has grown dramatically and a similar society has recently been formed in Europe. In the two main areas that I treat in the book—collective action and the choice of candidate or party in an election—much work has been done in refining and extending the models discussed here. But, although this work is technically interesting, the books of Downs and Olson are still the best place to start, and I believe that all the important questions about the uses and limitations of the 'economic' approach can be raised by analysing them. There is only one subsequent book that I would feel tempted to say something about if I were starting from scratch today and that is Albert Hirschman's *Exit, Voice, and Loyalty* (Cambridge, Mass.: Harvard University Press, 1970). Hirschman's attempt to fit the concept of loyalty into an 'economic' framework does, I think, raise some interesting points. I have written a long review of Hirschman's book which relates it to themes developed here: 'Review Article: Exit, Voice, and Loyalty', *British Journal of Political Science*, 4 (1974), 79–107.

CHAPTER I

Introduction

1 THE STATE OF POLITICAL THEORY

In the past fifteen years or so, a remarkable thing has been happening to the academic study of politics: it has shown signs of starting to become a theoretical subject. Until fairly recently, political theory had for many years been regarded as something that had occurred in the past, but could hardly be expected to happen nowadays—rather like the Church of England's view of miracles. Indeed, the very term 'political theory' had become applied conventionally to the study, not of theoretical problems about politics, but of men who wrote about these problems in the past. Of course, this curiosity of linguistic usage, in which a historical study is called 'theory', did not arise accidentally. Two defences of the identification may be found. One, which takes a relativistic line, argues that there are a certain number of fundamental outlooks on politics, each of which has now been expressed by a writer of genius, and each of which will always be attractive to some people. The alternative line is far from relativistic. A common hostile characterisation is that 'it's all in Aristotle'; a more temperate description would be that the history of political thought from the seventeenth century on is one of decline rather than progress. Both issue in the conclusion that political theory has already been established about as well as it can be, so the study of past writers is properly to be called 'political theory'. Both stem from the conception of politics as the 'master science'—with the emphasis on 'master' rather than 'science'. That is to say, politics is regarded as a subject of such broad significance that questions of ends—the criteria of the 'good life' or of 'justice', for example—are inextricably bound up with it. And since, on the one view these questions are insoluble, while on the other view they are already solved, both schools of thought can happily concur in the conclusion

1

that (to quote Hume) 'new discoveries are not to be expected in these matters'.

It may be allowed that the field of 'political theory' must include somewhere within it explicit consideration of ends. It may also be allowed that, even where apparently empirical claims are made, they may, if they are at a high level of generality, involve assumptions about human behaviour which cannot be directly tested. But it does not follow that new developments in political theory are impossible. Although theories about the workings of politics usually have ethical implications, this does not preclude the possibility of saying that a particular theory is true or false. And rival conceptions of 'human nature' can give rise to testable theories, which means that in the long run the plausibility of these conceptions is capable of being either dented or enhanced.

There is no intention of suggesting that the theoretical work to be examined below has no intellectual antecedents; in fact, I shall shortly trace two main lines of contemporary theory to their roots in opposing nineteenth-century ideologies, and this process could be carried further back. There is nothing unusual in this; indeed, it would be extraordinary if it were not so. At the same time, the work we shall be looking at is recognisably new.

There are three main external sources of innovation in political theory. First, there are developments in other disciplines, which suggest possible parallels to be exploited in the study of politics. Economics, physiology and information theory are examples. Second, there are changes in the actual phenomena of politics, which inevitably drive theorising on politics in new directions. Three obvious post-war illustrations are nuclear weapons, new states created out of colonial territories, and the growth of mass communications. Lastly, there are changes in the amount and kind of information about politics that is available. As with physical scientists, it is no doubt true of political scientists that at least half of those there have ever been are alive at the moment. This enormously increases the amount of information available and, by facilitating the division of labour, its minuteness of detail. Equally important are new kinds of information, especially those yielded by sample surveys, and new techniques for analysing information which would have been impracticable before the development of high speed computers. In the long run, this third kind of development probably constitutes the most important pressure towards innovation, but so far political theory has not really risen to its challenge. Herbert Spencer's idea of a tragedy—a beautiful hypothesis destroyed by an inconvenient fact—is so appallingly likely to be the fate of any non-vacuous theory produced today that it is easy to grow fainthearted and avoid ever saying anything liable to empirical check. Not all the 'theory' to be looked at in this book avoids that fate.

A full-scale attempt to test the theories to be discussed would represent a programme of work for a number of research institutes, and would indeed be inseparable from a great development in the precision and sophistication of the theories themselves. This book will therefore concentrate mainly on expounding the theories themselves, and examining the evidence that has been offered for them. But, where possible, I shall suggest areas in which research would help determine the correctness of the theories. And I shall endeavour always to keep in the forefront the question whether a theory is at least *testable*, even if it has not actually been tested satisfactorily.

2 THE TWO APPROACHES OUTLINED

As I have already implied at several points, contemporary political theory should not be imagined as a monolithic 'movement'. On the contrary, it has been remarked sourly that 'there are many approaches but few arrivals'. It is not my intention to offer a general review of these developments, a task that has in any case been admirably performed by others.[1] The discussion in this book is deliberately limited in scope so as to permit the examination of some ideas in depth. It is focused on two kinds of theory, which differ in a number of ways. One type is axiomatic, economic, mechanical, mathematical; the other is discursive, sociological, organismic, literary. They differ in the questions they ask and the answers they give. They rest on different ideas about the most fruitful

[1] Section 1 of the Bibliography is designed to offer guidance to readers who would like to pursue any of several kinds of interests in contemporary political theory.

ways of abstracting from the overwhelming particularities of 'reality', and on different assumptions about the nature of the scientific enterprise itself. They come out of sharply contrasted ideological traditions. It will be my object to articulate these two approaches and show them at work on the analysis of democratic politics.

Why concentrate on democratic countries? One reason is that this provides a more manageable field: even as it is, it will be possible only to cover selected topics and discuss some of the more significant and controversial writers. Another reason is that the 'economic' approach has as yet been applied relatively little outside democratic countries. I say 'as yet', but a critic might argue that this limitation of scope is no accident but reflects a limitation in the method itself. Its defenders might retort that the enthusiasm with which the 'sociological' approach has been picked up by writers on the so-called 'developing areas' illustrates only its utility in concealing an almost total lack of hard information to work from. We shall return to this question at the end, when we should be in a position to compare the two.

The two approaches referred to will be called 'economic' and 'sociological'. These terms are not arbitrarily applied and are to some degree sanctioned by usage. But it would be as well to issue a caution at the outset against reading too much into our labels. It is only certain features of orthodox economic theory that are drawn on to provide the specification for our 'economic approach', and much sociological work lies entirely outside the framework of our 'sociological approach'.

To most people the most noticeable feature of economics as a discipline is its subject matter: economists deal with the production, distribution and consumption of goods and services, with money, and so on. But when we speak of the 'economic approach' we are not referring to this feature of economics at all. We are not singling out the effects of political decisions on the production and distribution of goods and services, nor the effect of these on politics, interesting as these subjects are. Rather, we are picking out certain characteristic ways of tackling problems that until now have been found especially among economists. When an economist wants to estimate what is likely to happen in a situation of a certain kind, his first step will often be to construct what he will probably nowadays call a model. (We need not pause to ask whether he should call it a model, since all we are interested in at the moment is describing what he actually does.) The model will be a deliberate simplification of the kind of situation he wants to think about. He will postulate the existence of a number of individual actors, with certain ends (such as maximising their incomes), and will then try to work out deductively how they will act in a situation of a kind which presents certain alternatives to them, on the assumption that they pursue their goals rationally.[2] It is this characteristic method of analysis that has led some economists to argue that their discipline should be defined not in terms of subject-matter (goods and services, etc.), but as 'the logic of choice'.

'Economic theory is, indeed, relevant whenever actors have determinate wants or objectives and at the same time do not have such an abundance of the means needed to achieve these ends that all of their desires are satisfied. The ends in question may be social status or political power, and the means will be anything that is in fact conducive to the attainment of the ends, whether or not these means can fetch a price on the market. This means that economic (or more precisely micro-economic) theory is in a fundamental

[2] 'Economic analysis as such is merely a process of logical deduction whereby one says: "Given certain assumptions about economic and social institutions, about the nature and size of economic resources, and about the way in which individuals react in given situations, then such-and-such a change at such-and-such a point in the system will have such-and-such effects upon other variables in the system" . . .

'Any economic system constitutes a very complicated set of relationships. . . . It is this complexity which above all constitutes the essential difficulty for economic analysis. How then can one proceed? The author of this work can think of only one method. One must construct a simple model which isolates one or two features of a possible real world; one must study their implications in this simple setting and then progressively elaborate and expand the model by making the assumptions less and less restrictive. But on each occasion there will soon come a point at which further elaboration will make the model too complicated for it to be of any more use than the real world itself in helping one to comprehend the forces actually at work. Then one must begin again with another simple model which isolates another set of relevant features of the real world and start the whole process of gradual elaborations over again.' (Meade, 1965, pages 13 and 22.)

sense more nearly a theory of rational behaviour than a theory of material goods.' (Olson, 1967, page 9.)

One of the purest examples of the 'economic approach' is not in fact part of the traditional discipline of economics at all. The theory of games studies in general terms the strategies that rational actors would follow in situations where (in various ways) decisions are interdependent—in other words, where each party's outcome depends jointly on how he acts and how the other parties act. (See Section 3 of the Bibliography.)

The 'sociological approach' cannot be set off in a neat point-by-point contrast with the 'economic approach'. Nevertheless, it is very different. Taking Talcott Parsons as the representative figure, we can begin by pointing out that the characteristic aim is in one way more ambitious in that it eschews the advantages of a simplified or schematic psychology. In place of rational maximisers with set goals, the sociological approach can allow for the development and change of motives, which themselves can be treated in a more complex way than simply as 'goals'. (Perhaps all this should be qualified by 'in principle', since it has been maintained that in practice the psychology employed is equally crude, though different.) But the sociological approach, as developed so far, is less ambitious in that no claim is made for the development of a theory which will deduce propositions from premises. The word 'theory' *is* used in relation to the sociological approach, but tends to mean only the elaboration of concepts.

There are other differences. The talk tends to be of whole societies or even all societies. And though, in the Parsonian system, the economic-sounding term 'exchange' frequently crops up, this refers not to exchanges between people but to exchanges between abstract entities, such as the integrative sub-system of the adaptive sub-system and the goal-attainment sub-system of the integrative sub-system. Moreover, the sociological approach is occupied heavily with a particular kind of question: how does this system manage to maintain itself in existence, in spite of constant threats from its environment? The economic approach, by contrast, tends to ask how certain initial conditions will work themselves out, rather than to ask under what conditions a certain result will be effected. And the conceptions of 'system' and 'equilibrium' which are required to make sense of the question about system-maintenance are foreign to the economic approach.

3 IDEOLOGICAL ORIGINS: SOCIOLOGICAL APPROACH

A full discussion of the differences between the two approaches is best postponed until we have seen them both at work. In the last chapter most of the points touched on in the previous section will be taken up again in the light of the detailed analyses of particular pieces of work which make up the bulk of the book. But anyone who is troubled by not having a map of the territory spread out for him in advance is urged to forget scruples derived from reading detective novels and turn at once to the first two sections of Chapter VIII which are devoted to the different conceptions of theory, system and equilibrium held by representatives of the two approaches. It should be possible to get the gist of this discussion even though the illustrative references to the body of the text will not, of course, have much meaning.

There is, however, one point made in the previous section which can be discussed adequately without any need to refer in detail to the contemporary literature. In this section I shall sketch the origins of the two approaches in rival ideologies. Some people may feel that this helps them to 'place' the two approaches, but I should emphasise that it is not my intention to suggest that the two contemporary schools of political theory are no more than expressions of ideology. In the final chapter I shall take up explicitly the question of the logical connection, if any, between alternative evaluations and alternative lines of analysis, and the conclusion arrived at is that the connection is in fact a fairly loose one.

If we are to look for the intellectual roots of the two approaches, we first have to decide at what point in time to start looking. It would not be fanciful to say that we can find many of the contrasts in a comparison between Plato and Aristotle. But we shall eschew such speculations and pick up the story at a point in time when the foundations of the modern disciplines of sociology and economics were being laid: the late eighteenth and early nineteenth centuries. We shall begin with the sociological approach.

In the period following the French Revolution, there arose

in Europe a number of thinkers who rejected the premises on which they believed the Revolution had been based. That the political involvement of the ordinary members of a society leads to despotism; that men are moved largely by irrational forces; and that there are distinct, relatively unalterable 'national characters' which explain much of what happens in history—these were prominent among the items of the new orthodoxy.[3] Out of this intellectual matrix developed the new discipline of sociology.[4]

The period following the Second World War, and especially the nineteen-fifties, saw a rather similar movement of thought, this time centred on the U.S.A. Although the Cold War, in which many intellectuals saw themselves as front-line defenders of the 'Free World', must have played some part, there were a number of specific factors that were probably more significant. The earlier collapse of democracy, almost undefended, in Germany and Italy; the failure of successor states in Asia and Africa to operate their new constitutions in the way envisaged by the drafting experts of the departing colonial power; the increasingly unavoidable conclusion that the Russian Revolution had led to an oppressive and barbarous régime; and the phenomenon of McCarthyism right on the doorstep: all these things contributed to the revival of conservative thought in the intellectual community. This revival took many forms. For example, a new generation of social and economic historians looked critically at the work of their predecessors, who had tended to have radical sympathies.[5] And just as sociology grew out of the previous wave, so the fullest manifestation of the new one was the rise of a

[3] See *The Works of Joseph de Maistre* (de Maistre, 1965). Hegel may stand for the phenomenon in Germany and Coleridge in England. John Stuart Mill's essay on Coleridge and his *Autobiography* both contain succinct statements of the truths which he claimed French and German writers had discovered: for the former, see Mill, 1859, page 99; for the latter, Mill, 1873, pages 136–46. Preceding these writers we may mention Burke and Montesquieu; following them, Saint-Simon, Comte and de Tocqueville.

[4] See Leon Bramson, 1961, for a discussion of the connection. H. Stuart Hughes, 1959, is an easily read account of the 'founding fathers' of sociology in the period 1880–1920. A recent treatment of the key ideas in this sociological tradition is Nisbet, 1966.

[5] For the concept of 'revisionist' history, used in the present way, see Moore, 1966, Appendix.

new subject: political sociology. Here all the leading conceptions of the earlier period found a home, with new names,
new forms of evidence, and a new framework almost as im-
pressively complex as that of Hegel himself. The tendency of
popular participation to lead to absolutism became the 'theory
of mass society', and 'national character' re-emerged in the
guise of 'political culture'. New evidence of irrationality was
found in survey data. Parsons provided a framework within
which the central question was the classical conservative one,
'How can social order be maintained?' and in which much of the
answer was said to lie in the existence of common value-systems
among the members of a society—precisely the factors, such as
religion, by which the earlier conservatives had set such store.

4 IDEOLOGICAL ORIGINS: ECONOMIC APPROACH

In 1840, John Stuart Mill wrote of Bentham and Coleridge:

'They employed, indeed, for the most part, different
materials; but as the materials of both were real observations, the genuine product of experience—the results will
in the end be found not hostile, but supplementary, to one
another. Of their methods of philosophising the same thing
may be said: they were different, yet both were legitimate
logical processes. In every respect the two men are each
other's "completing counterpart"; the strong points of each
correspond to the weak points of the other. Whoever could
master the premises and combine the methods of both,
would possess the entire English philosophy of his age.'
(Mill, 1859, page 123.)

Coleridge, here, stands for the entire movement of European
conservatism referred to above, and Bentham for the kind
of thinking against which it was a reaction. Our present
interest is limited to the continued vitality of Mill's two
schools of social thought; we shall take up in the final chapter
the prospects and desirability of a synthesis between the
theories that are their descendants.

What then, are the salient characteristics of the Benthamite
analysis? Its most important assumptions are: that men tend
to act rationally in the pursuit of their ends; that most men

in all societies want power, status and economic goods; and that internalised restraints on the pursuit of these are less significant than sanctions which make use of them (public disapproval, legal punishments, etc.). Its characteristic method of proceeding is to work out how men rationally pursuing power, status and economic goods would behave in a certain set-up, and then to suggest that men in the real world behave sufficiently similarly to make the conclusions applicable.[6]

The intellectual heirs of Bentham are not hard to recognise. Just as the counter-revolutionary tradition found a cultural 'carrier' in the discipline of sociology, so the Benthamite tradition continued to live in the discipline of economics.[7] And, just as sociological theory has had a big impact on the study of politics since the Second World War, so has economic theory. In explaining the influence of sociological modes of thought we resorted to one common phenomenon in the history of ideas: the congruence of a theory on one hand and the social and political context on the other. To explain the rise of economic modes of thought in the analysis of politics, we shall appeal mainly to another common phenomenon: the way in which methods and concepts which are successful in one area tend to be applied in other areas in the hope that they will give results there, too. Thus Newtonian mechanics and Darwinian natural selection provided for certain generations models of explanation and sets of concepts which exercised a wide sway in many spheres of thought. Cybernetics is perhaps the nearest contemporary equivalent, though it is a good deal less striking.

The powerful attraction which economics holds for the

[6] Of all Bentham's works, the *Constitutional Code* and the pamphlet *Emancipate your Colonies* are perhaps the best exemplars of these assumptions and methods. (Bentham, 1843, Vol. 9, and Vol. 4, pages 407–18. The *Essay on Government* by James Mill (1828) is, however, the best illustration: as a cruder and more doctrinaire disciple, Mill exemplifies more clearly the basic approach. On the movement of which Bentham was the most noted member, Halévy, 1928, is standard.

[7] It should perhaps be emphasised that the point being made here is not that utilitarian principles of evaluation were held by most classical and neo-classical economists, though this is in fact the case. The continuity being referred to is in methods and assumptions. Among contemporary economists, the best examples are perhaps the 'Chicago school', notably Milton Friedman (1953 and 1962), and in Britain, the economists associated with the Institute of Economic Affairs. But the continuity is by no means lacking in the mainstream of economic analysis.

other social sciences is not hard to understand on this basis, since it has for so long possessed a theoretical structure much more impressive than theirs. The question should perhaps be posed rather in the form: why was the attempt to apply economics so long postponed? The original utilitarians— Bentham and James Mill especially—were just as happy applying their methods to politics as to economics. The results may appear somewhat crude, but it seems to me a serious question whether James Mill's political theory is any more of an over-simplification than, say, Ricardo's economics. The difference is, of course, that Ricardo's ideas were refined by subsequent theorists, whereas James Mill's *Essay on Government* had no successors until the last decade or so.

We can trace, if not in any real sense explain, the collapse of the characteristic utilitarian methods in the study of politics. John Stuart Mill maintained in his *System of Logic* (1843) that the techniques used by Bentham and his father were appropriate only in economics. Outside this area, a new science of 'ethology', the inductive study of variation in 'national character' (or, as it would now be called, 'culture') was necessary. However, Mill never succeeded in creating 'ethology', which left his various political recommendations resting on a void.[8] The growth of 'political science' or 'government' as academic subjects led to a tendency to drop the sermonising aspect of Mill without taking up the hopes for 'ethology', so that the subjects developed on a purely descriptive basis.[9] One way of viewing the contemporary political theory with which we have been concerned is as a reaction against this tradition.

5 SUBJECTS TO BE COVERED

It would, of course, be convenient for the purpose of this book if the adherents of our two schools took up the same topics and merely differed in what they said on them. We could

[8] Thus, in *Considerations on Representative Government* (Mill, 1861) he opposed the secret ballot and the payment of M.P.s, and proposed a voting system which would in effect have made the country one constituency with several thousand candidates. But he simply did not have a theoretical basis from which he could talk sensibly about the likely results of doing what he suggested. For a recent work of a similar kind, see Crick, 1964.

[9] For a history of American academic political studies, see Easton, 1953. There is no similar work on Britain.

B

then, taking each topic in turn, lay the two treatments side by side and try to form a judgment on their relative merits. But, in fact, the questions tackled within one framework have only a very limited overlap with those to which the adherents of the other framework address themselves. Since the main task of this book is to look at the actual work that has been done by the adherents of the two approaches (though we shall sometimes suggest modifications or extensions) it is necessary to follow along the paths they have chosen to go down. The primary basis for evaluation, then, will be how successful our theorists are in coping with the problems they set themselves. But, after these detailed discussions, the more general comparison will be broached in the final chapter.

We begin with an extended discussion (Chapter II) of the 'economic' theory of political participation. As well as being a topic of obvious theoretical and practical importance, this also provides a good chance for raising, in a context which shows that it is no mere verbal quibble, the question what precisely is to be understood by words such as 'rational' and 'economic'. After this we proceed to a fairly detailed consideration of a number of books on politics whose authors have a more or less 'sociological' perspective (Chapter III). The question which we shall follow through is one which is again of undeniable importance, namely the conditions under which a democratic form of government flourishes. The answers, it will be seen, place a heavy emphasis on the role of 'values', and in the following Chapter (IV) the whole question of using values as explanations will be discussed. The next chapter (Chapter V) shows the economic approach at work on the logic of party competition. It is largely devoted to an exposition and critique of Anthony Downs's stimulating book *An Economic Theory of Democracy* (Downs, 1957). The last two substantive chapters (VI and VII) are concerned with the working and (to some extent) the justification of democratic politics. We shall ask how far the kinds of assumption made by Downs are realistic, and then draw a contrast between the 'economic' image of democracy and the 'sociological' one. To conclude the book (Chapter VIII) there is a discussion of the methodological presuppositions of the two approaches and their prospects for future development, separately or in combination.

CHAPTER II

Political Participation as Rational Action

1 THE DECISION TO VOTE: DOWNS AND RIKER

Let us begin by examining the 'economic' approach to a simple question: why do people involve themselves in political activity? There are three advantages in studying this question. First, it is hardly possible to deny its importance for the understanding of politics. Second, an 'economic' style of analysis is able to show that the question is not as easy to answer as one might at first glance suppose, and that some answers which appeal to common sense are fallacious. Thus, the power of the 'economic' approach to clarify thought can be illustrated, even though its claims to produce interesting deductions that are also true must be judged more dubious. And, third, in following the attempts of economic theorists to answer the question 'why participate?', we can see in a relatively clear form some of the conceptual difficulties about the definition and scope of the 'economic' approach that have up to this point been skated over.

Two treatments of the question will be discussed in this chapter: first, Anthony Downs's analysis of the decision to vote (as against not voting) in his book *An Economic Theory of Democracy* (1957), and then Mancur Olson's more general theory of rational participation in 'collective action', as set out in his book *The Logic of Collective Action* (1965). We shall be returning to Downs in Chapter V in order to examine in detail his theory of the workings of party competition. All we need do now, therefore, is present the minimum outline necessary to make intelligible our discussion of the decision to vote.

Downs constructs a theory of politics in which there are,

basically, only two kinds of actor. There are the parties, and there are the voters. The internal processes of the parties are abstracted from by the assumption that they consist of single-minded teams, and a further assumption is that they are dedicated to only one object, namely winning elections. 'The politicians in our model never seek office as a means of carrying out particular policies; their only goal is to reap the rewards of holding office *per se*' (Downs, page 28). There is a clear analogy with the conception of the profit-maximising entrepreneur of classical economic theory. The voters correspond to the consumers. But, whereas there is not much point in asking why consumers do *anything* with their money (as against throwing it away), it is a perfectly serious question why voters should use their vote.[1] For one has to make some effort in order to cast a vote, yet what is the benefit to be derived from so doing? If we wish to apply an 'economic' analysis, an obvious line to take is that with which Downs begins: the value of voting is the value of the expected effect it would have in changing what would otherwise happen.

But what are the components of this calculation? When there are only two parties, the matter is fairly simple. The citizen faced with the question whether it is worth voting or not first computes his 'party differential', that is, how much better off he would be (not necessarily in purely financial terms) if his preferred party won the election, and he then multiplies it by the probability that his vote for that party will change the result of the election so that his party wins instead of losing. Obviously, this means that he has to reckon the probability of the election's turning on a single vote, and in an electorate of millions this probability is so small that the value of voting will be infinitesimal, even for someone who has a large party differential.[2] Thus, it seems to follow that

[1] Of course, a consumer may decide to defer expenditure on consumption and save money instead, but this course is not open to a voter. If you fail to vote in one election you have lost that vote for ever—you do not get an extra vote next time.

[2] Even if we relax the assumption of a single national electorate, and allow for constituencies, the citizen still has to guess (i) what is the chance of his constituency being won by a single vote, and (ii) even if it were, how likely it is that a single seat more for his party would make any great difference. Of course, we could suppose that politicians are sensitive to the narrowness of their majority in popular votes as

rational citizens would not vote if there are costs involved—
and it always takes time and energy to cast a vote. But in fact
it is notorious that many people do vote. Even low turnouts
of, say, 25% are, on this analysis, clearly inconsistent with
rationality.

In a recent article, Riker has criticised Downs as if this were
his last word on the subject. He says that 'it is certainly no
explanation to assign a sizeable part of politics to the mysterious and inexplicable world of the irrational' (Riker, 1968,
page 25). And he then proposes an amendment to the theory.
But the 'amendment' is in essence the same as one put forward by Downs himself, though Downs describes it as a factor
increasing the reward of voting and Riker counts it as a
reduction of the cost.[3] Riker says that this reward consists of
satisfactions such as 'compliance with the ethic of voting',
'affirming allegiance to the political system', 'affirming a
partisan preference', 'deciding, going to the polls etc.', and
'affirming one's efficacy in the political system' (Riker, page
28).

Now it may well be true that much voting can be accounted
for in this way, and one can of course formally fit it into an
'economic' framework by saying that people get certain
'rewards' from voting. But this *is* purely formal.[4] And it forces
us to ask what really is the point and value of the whole
'economic' approach. It is no trick to restate all behaviour
in terms of 'rewards' and 'costs'; it may for some purposes be
a useful conceptual device, but it does not in itself provide
anything more than a set of empty boxes waiting to be filled.
The power of the 'economic' method is that, in appropriate

---

such (and this was apparently true of Churchill in 1951 and Kennedy
in 1960) but even so, one vote is still not likely to make a noticeable
difference (cf. Riker, 1968, pages 40–2).

[3] Another point which Riker presents as original is that a rational
voter's decision will be partly a function of how close he expects the
election to be, and not simply of the size of the electorate. In fact,
Downs makes this observation quite explicitly on page 244. Riker also
describes the idea as 'non-obvious' (page 38). Its non-obviousness is
not, perhaps, obvious.

[4] Insofar as it includes voting as a purely expressive act, not undertaken with any expectation of changing the state of the world, it fails
to fit the minimum requirements of the means-end model of rational
behaviour.

kinds of situation, it enables us, operating with simple premises concerning rational behaviour, to deduce by logic and mathematics interesting conclusions about what will happen. Whether a situation is 'appropriate' or not depends on the extent to which other factors can safely be ignored.

Thus, the classical model of 'competitive equilibrium' in a market does approximate what happens in various 'real world' situations especially where profit-maximising traders make a living by dealing in some homogeneous commodity. But in a situation where, for example, all the participants believe in a 'just price' which is independent of supply and demand, the 'competitive equilibrium' model of price-determination will have no application. Again, we can bring this formally within the 'economic' framework by saying that the people get 'satisfaction' from keeping to the 'just price', or we can simply say that they are maximising subject to a 'constraint'. (Government controls are often dealt with in this way in economic analysis.) But neither of these devices helps very much. The point is that explanatory attention must shift to the question how people came to believe in a 'just price', how the belief is transmitted and maintained, and what determines the level of price which is believed right for each commodity. In other words, there are no interesting deductions to be drawn from the interaction of given 'tastes' in a market; the price can simply be read off from the universal 'taste' for a certain price. The question is how that taste arises, and this is a question that cannot be answered within the 'economic' framework.

The relevance of this example to voting decisions will, I hope, be clear. Riker says that people vote because they derive satisfaction from voting for reasons entirely divorced from the hope that it will bring about desired results. This may well be true but it does not leave any scope for an economic model to come between the premises and the phenomenon to be explained. Instead, the question shifts back to: 'Why do some people have this kind of motivation more strongly than others?'

Obviously, the utility of an 'economic' model in a given situation is not an all-or-nothing question. Thus, we might find that expectations about the closeness of the election result and beliefs about the importance of one party winning rather than another had a fairly big effect on the probability of a man's voting (though this itself would be hard to explain in 'economic' terms), and that the sheer satisfaction in voting as such was somewhat less important. But some data given by Riker suggest that this is not so. He presents a table showing, for the U.S. Presidential elections in 1952, 1956 and 1960, what proportion of respondents voted of those who were, for example, high on 'citizen duty', low on expecting the result to be close, and high on thinking it important who won. If we average the three sets of observations, we get the following:

	'Citizen Duty' Score					
	HIGH		*MEDIUM*		*LOW*	
Expected closeness of election result	*High P.D.*	*Low P.D.*	*High P.D.*	*Low P.D.*	*High P.D.*	*Low P.D.*
Close	91%	83%	85%	71%	63%	44%
Not close	86%	74%	77%	71%	62%	39%

(P.D. = party differential, i.e. how much difference the respondent thought it made which side won)

The percentages give the proportion who voted in each category. Calculated from Riker, 1968, Table 3, page 38.

Now the only thing Riker extracts from the table is the fact that, holding the other two factors constant each time, the proportion in a category of respondents is higher the more close they expect the result to be, the more they 'care' about the result, and the higher they score on a scale measuring a sense of 'citizen duty'. He does not bother to ask what is the relative *weight* of these three factors in determining the probability that a given person will vote. Yet this can be easily done, even though the combination of a trichotomous division with dichotomous divisions makes precise comparison tricky. The most elementary and intuitive sort of multivariate analysis (consisting simply of comparing the distances in percentage points between the 'highs' and the 'lows' on any one factor for a given combination of the other two factors) is enough to show that 'citizen duty' has the most important effect, and that the expected closeness of the contest has rather little effect. This is not just an artifact of the three-way division of the 'citizen duty' factor, for the distance in scores just between 'medium' and 'low' is greater on the average than the spread shown by either of the other (dichotomously divided) factors between 'high' and 'low'.

A closer look shows that there is clearly an interaction effect among two of the variables: when 'citizen duty' is medium or high, 'party differential' makes only a modest difference to voting levels, but among those with a low score on 'citizen duty' (who presumably have little reason to vote just for the sake of voting) 'party differential' makes a difference of around twenty percentage points. Thus a 'Downsian' type of analysis, reasonably enough one might think, applies much better when a low sense of 'citizen duty' gives it a chance to come through. But is it so reasonable? It hardly seems possible to make out that it is 'rational' in the terms set out by Downs. Can we really imagine anyone for whom the product of party differential and probability of swinging the election could be other than infinitesimal?[5]

Thus, paradoxically, the result of an 'economic' analysis is to suggest that, even if the empirically found relationships go in the predicted direction, the 'rational' explanation (in terms of a computation of 'party differential' multiplied by the probability of being decisive) cannot be correct. 'Common sense' might well support an 'economic' interpretation of the statistics, which, on a more careful 'economic' analysis, cannot be sustained. Thus, for example, Angus Campbell, in his paper on 'The Passive Citizen', writes:

> 'If we consider only those attributes of the election situa-
> tion which influence the level of interest or passivity of the
> electorate, disregarding those forces which create partisan
> reaction, we may conclude that the major variable dis-

[5] Riker suggests that electors may hold grossly inflated notions of their chances of altering the result, based on the occasional dramatic case, and that their party differentials may be far higher than is normally supposed (Riker, pages 38–9). This seems to me a pretty desperate salvage attempt. Moreover, it is doubtful whether the first point can be accommodated within the *rational* theory that Riker claims to have constructed. It is true that one does not wish to include the possession of correct information in the criteria of rationality, but this is more a question of elementary estimation based on a figure—how many elections are tied or won by one vote—that must be roughly known to many. This is, incidentally, something on which light could be thrown by survey techniques: when people say 'close', how close do they mean?

tinguishing different elections is the size of the differential which the electorate thinks likely to result from the choice of one or the other of the alternatives open to it. *We would take it as a self-evident proposition that the motivating force of the electoral situation will be proportional to the perceived probability that a vote for one alternative rather than others will make some significant difference to the voter'* (Campbell, 1962, pages 208–9).

And he then cites Chapter 3 of Downs. In fact, in his discussion he lumps together, under the heading 'expected differential', both Downs's 'party differential' *and* the factor by which it is to be multiplied, namely the chance of one's vote altering the election result. But the trouble is that the 'expected differential' in this wide sense is, as we have seen, almost certain to be negligible. So the 'self-evident proposition' put forward by Campbell does not help much in explaining variations in turnout. The perceived probability that one's vote will alter the result significantly *may* of course be quite irrationally high, as Riker suggests, but I seriously doubt whether the answer lies in this direction.

2 THE DECISION TO VOTE: LIMITS OF THE ECONOMIC APPROACH

As mentioned above, Downs himself allows for people getting a satisfaction from voting which does not depend on the possibility that their vote will alter the result of the election, though one would gain a contrary impression from Riker. But whereas Riker leaves the phenomenon unexplained, Downs boldly tries to cover it from within his economic model. His attempt is, I think, ultimately unsuccessful, but its failure is itself interesting, because it turns on the criterion for rational behaviour. According to Downs, the citizens in a democracy always consider that they benefit heavily from the continuance of the system, as against its replacement by some other; but the system must collapse if too few people vote. Therefore at least some people will incur a 'short-run' cost (voting) in order to help to secure the 'long-run' gain of the continuance of the system (Downs, 1957, pages 266–71).

But to say that what we have here is a question of

short-run versus long-run benefits for any given individual is
a misleading way of putting the matter. It is quite fair to say
that 'rational men accept limitations on their ability to make
short-run gains in order to procure greater gains in the long-
run' (page 268). But the long-run gains must depend *for a
given individual* on himself foregoing the short-run gain.
Such is not the case here, as Downs himself admits: 'of course,
he will actually get this reward [living in a democracy] even
if he himself does not vote as long as a sufficient number of
other citizens do' (page 270). And, by the same token, if the
system is going to collapse because too few people vote, his
one additional ballot-paper is unlikely to prevent it. But, in
the next sentence, Downs commits a common fallacy in social
thought which most of the book turns on his avoiding, when
he adds that our citizen 'is willing to bear certain short-run
costs he could avoid in order to do his share in providing long-
run benefits' (page 270). 'Doing his share' is a concept foreign
to the kind of 'economic' rationality with which Downs is
working. It requires our citizen to reason that since the benefits he gets depend on the efforts of others, he should contribute too. This may be good ethics, but it is not consistent
with the assumptions of the model, which require the citizen
to compute the advantage that accrues to him from his doing
x rather than *y*; not the advantage that would accrue to him
from *himself and others* doing *x* rather than *y*, unless, of
course, his doing it is a necessary and sufficient condition of
the others doing it.[6]

Downs might reformulate his argument (and there are
hints of this in his text) by saying simply that the gains to
any given individual from the continuation of democracy
rather than its collapse are so great that it may well be worth
his while to incur a small cost in voting even when he does
discount the value of saving democracy by the very low prob-

[6] A precisely analogous problem about rationality arises in the
analysis of the 'prisoners' dilemma', where if both actors pursue their
individual self-interest they both finish up with a worse outcome than
they could have achieved by behaving differently. Rapoport (1960), in
his discussion of this, suggests that they should adopt a different criterion of rationality which requires that one should be happy to see
others act on the same principle. But the trouble is that, whatever the
other person does, an actor who follows the self-interest criterion of
rationality will do better than one who follows Rapoport's.

ability that his single vote will make a difference to its fortunes. And we might then explain the pronounced tendency for higher-status people to feel a stronger sense of 'citizen duty' by saying that they are, after all, the greatest beneficiaries from the *status quo*.

Any such line of argument, however, raises in an acute form the question of 'realism'. Downs, like other exponents of the 'economic' approach, adopts the view that the test of a theory lies not in the plausibility of its premises but in the testability of its conclusions. To some extent, this seems correct. For example, an economist may start from the assumption that businessmen act so as to maximise profits and then work out how they would behave if they did. If he could predict what businessmen would do, he would probably not be deterred by the fact that the businessmen themselves claimed (perhaps truly) that they followed various rules of thumb, for he could easily imagine that these rules of thumb had gradually been selected out because they 'worked'. Similarly, in our voting case, if we could get evidence about the amount democracy was worth to each person and the chance he thought his vote would have of preserving it, and found that these multiplied together and compared with the cost of voting enabled us to predict whether he voted or not, we could feel happy with our 'explanation', even if nobody actually gave such an explanation of how he made up his mind. But it seems doubtful that sensible answers to these questions could be extracted—no doubt because people don't in fact think that way—so we can establish the values only by inference from observed behaviour. But three unknowns and only one observation present us with an impossible problem of identification. We can easily *invent* values which will give the observed result in each case, but there is an infinite number of possible triplets of values for each person, and no way of choosing between them.

It looks, then, as if we have to abandon as unfruitful the attempt to explain the decision to vote as the unfolding of 'economic' rationality, because its most important component cannot usefully be discussed in those terms. Does this mean that the whole discussion up to this point has been a waste of time? I would say not, and adduce two kinds of understanding that we can carry away from it: substantive and methodological. In terms of substance, our main result, although in negative form, is surely not without considerable interest. Especially when we add a parallel analysis of the decision to vote for one party rather than another (Chapters V and VI) we have an idea which is disturbing for the normative theorist of democracy in that it calls into question the foundations of the edifice. Nor is it true to say that the demonstration of non-rationality is without significance for those who wish to explain political phenomena, for it makes a great difference to the range of possible explanations if a whole family of them, namely those in terms of rational 'economic' behaviour, are dismissed.

There is a further point of importance. The crucial point in the demonstration—the infinitesimal 'expected value' of voting—can itself, as Downs himself points out (page 266), help to explain various features of electoral turnout such as its susceptibility to the weather, small poll-taxes, the average distance from the polling stations, and so on. Nobody would let such things deter him from doing something he really thought important, yet such factors can make a big difference to the numbers who vote. There is also evidence from people's own mouths which supports the view that variations in the cost make more difference to turnout than variations in the (suitably discounted) benefits expected. Thus, in a survey carried out in Britain in 1964 into reasons for non-voting, 9% of abstainers said that 'the result was obvious in their constituency' (low expectation of closeness), 5% said there was no Liberal standing (low party differential, presumably), but 50% of abstainers (out of 66% who answered the question) talked about the inconveniences in which, for one reason or another, voting would involve them (Butler, 1965, page 294).

In spite of our mainly negative results, we have gained some insight into the way the 'economic' mode of analysis operates. And we have learned the crucial importance of always relating the costs and benefits of any action to each individual actor. It is of cardinal importance to hold fast to this conclusion as we move into areas of greater complexity. Note, however, what is *not* being said. There is no intention of denying that we will sometimes want to allow for the possibility that a given actor's costs and benefits are partially constituted by the happiness or unhappiness of other people whose interests he has at heart. We insist only that they must still figure explicitly as *his* costs and benefits. And when we do allow for this sort of altruism, we must recognize that we weaken the deductive power of our 'economic' model. Thus, we could have said that voters took direct account of the interests of others in deciding to vote, and this increased the reward of voting. But to do that would not be very different from saying that they felt guilty if they didn't vote and this was a cost of not voting. Even so, there is still a big difference between slurring over the difference between self-interest and collective interest by saying they coincide in the same action for a given individual, and saying that a person may prefer to follow the collective interest rather than his own self-interest.

We can also begin to surmise something about the limitations of an analysis of behaviour in terms of economic rationality. It may well be that both the costs and the (suitably discounted) benefits of voting are so low that it is simply not worth being 'rational' about it. Thus habit, self-expression, duty and other things have plenty of room to make themselves felt. Might we not reasonably expect better luck in analysing situations where more is at stake, and perhaps especially situations of a kind which recur frequently for a given individual and where he gets some feedback from each decision he takes, that is to say, situations where we may expect adaptive learning to take place? Let us turn to a more general formulation of the economic logic of participation, and see whether the 'economic' method of analysis can explain more of the details of behaviour in some other kinds of decisions about participation.

3 THE BASIC LOGIC OF OLSON'S THEORY

We have examined a two-sector model (political entrepreneurs and ordinary citizens) in connection with a specific form of political activity, voting. We shall now move to an assumption of one sector, in other words an undifferentiated population, though we shall ask later what difference, if any, would be made to the system by the introduction of entrepreneurs (Section 7). We shall also leave for the present the relatively trivial action (from the point of view of the ordinary citizen's psychic economy) of casting a vote in an election and consider more costly activities, in time and money, such as contributing money or energy to an organization devoted to altering the state policy on some matters. We shall take this up by following the argument of *The Logic of Collective Action* by Mancur Olson, Jr. (1965). This is the only book fit to rank with Downs' *Economic Theory of Democracy*, as an exemplar of the virtues of the 'economic' approach to political analysis. Both books, as may be expected in pioneering works, suffer from obscurities and ambiguities which become apparent on close examination. But it is greatly to their advantage that, unlike so many books on political and sociological theory, they stimulate and repay this degree of careful attention.

The discussion so far will enable us to present Olson's central point very quickly, for it is essentially a generalization of the idea that the reward of voting (in rational 'economic' terms) is the party differential times the probability that one vote will alter the outcome of the election. Olson's argument is intended to apply wherever what is at stake is a 'public good', that is, a benefit which cannot be deliberately restricted to certain people, such as those who helped bring it into existence. A potential beneficiary's calculation, when deciding whether to contribute to the provision of such a benefit, must take the form of seeing what the benefit would be to him and discounting it by the probability that his contribution would make the difference between the provision and the non-provision of the benefit. Where there are large numbers of potential beneficiaries, and especially when none of them stands to gain a lot, Olson argues that the total contribution made to the provision of the benefit will be much less than it would be if the beneficiaries were all rolled into one person who did the best possible for himself. In many cases, he suggests, there will simply be no contributions at all.

An excellent example of a 'public good' is a state policy—for instance, a particular piece of legislation on tariffs or the labelling of consumer goods. Someone who stands to be benefited by this legislation will not automatically be advantaged by paying to support a lobby in its favour. He has to ask not whether an extra pound spent on campaigning will bring in more than a pound's worth of benefit to the potential beneficiaries taken all together, but whether an extra pound contributed by him will bring in more than a pound's worth of benefit to him. And on this basis he often will not contribute. He will not reason: 'If everyone fails to contribute, we'll all be worse off than if we all contribute, so I'll contribute'. For whether all, some or none of the others contribute will not be affected by whether or not he does, and it is therefore irrelevant to ask what would happen if they all acted on the same principle as himself.

Of course, where the beneficiaries form a small group in close contact with one another, the assumption that the decisions are independent of one another cannot be upheld. The members of the group can say to one another 'I won't contribute unless everyone else does', and, by making mutual threats of this kind, get the rate of contributions above what it would otherwise be. Even in quite small groups, however, this round of threats may be pretty hollow if some of the potential beneficiaries obviously could not afford *not* to contribute because they stand to gain so much. So the basic logic of self-interest may still show through. Thus, Olson has argued (Olson, 1966) that, insofar as N.A.T.O. can be regarded as providing a 'public good' to the member countries—defence against 'Communist aggression'—one would expect from the theory that the bigger countries (especially the U.S.A.) would contribute more than in proportion to their G.N.P., and the smallest countries less than in proportion, and this is in fact the case.

There are, then, two general results if people apply an individually rational calculation to the decision whether to contribute to the provision of a public good. First, the total contribution will be 'too low'; and, second, the contribution of the greatest beneficiaries will be disproportionately high. The latter will tend to come about in conditions of independent decision as well as in the interdependent case discussed. Suppose the total benefit is £1,000, and that one potential beneficiary stands to gain £100 while 90 others stand to gain £10 each. The first man should think it worth spending £25 on promoting the benefit even if nobody else co-operates, provided he thinks that this expenditure has a better than one in four chance of bringing about the benefit. But it would not pay any of the others to contribute £2 10s.

unless he thought that £2 10s. had one chance in four of bringing the benefit about.[7]

4 APPLICATION OF OLSON'S THEORY

The bulk of Olson's short book consists of applications of the basic ideas to various kinds of social organization. His analysis has a destructive and a constructive side. The destructive part consists of pointing out that a common explanation of organizations providing 'public goods' to the members is fallacious. This is the explanation that it pays them to belong because by contributing to it they help it to succeed and thus increase the benefits to themselves. The question is whether the contribution that the individual makes increases the benefit *he* gets enough to make it worth while, and where there are many beneficiaries the discounted pay-off from the organisation's success is unlikely to be significant. The fallacy arises from treating 'the beneficiaries' as if they were a single individual deciding how to allocate his resources to the best advantage. Thus one must reject all conventional explanations of the existence of trade unions or pressure groups in terms of the self-interest of members stemming directly from the collective benefits provided. Similarly, if Marx's theory of class was intended to move from an assumption of individual self-interest to the 'rationality' of pursuing one's *class* interests once one realises what they are, then, Olson argues, it breaks down in precisely the same way.

The constructive side of Olson's work lies in his insistence that wherever we do find an organisation providing a public

[7] As it stands, this analysis is somewhat weak in that it argues from the amount that each actor would contribute if he were the only contributor to the amount he would actually contribute. But of course the question a potential beneficiary must ask is what his contribution would do at the margin. But in order to know where the margin is he has to know the decisions of everyone else, and their decisions in turn depend on everyone else's. So the answer is strictly indeterminate. But we can say that, if campaign funds (etc.) bring decreasing returns, the amount each person would contribute if he were the only contributor gives us the *maximum* total contribution possible. We can also say that if the biggest beneficiary commits himself first, then the next biggest, and so on, the tendency for the biggest beneficiaries to pay disproportionately will be increased. It must be admitted, though, that Olson does not seem to appreciate the way in which assumptions of this kind are needed to make his 'proof' work.

good and supported by the beneficiaries we must look for, and will normally find, motives other than the provision of the public good keeping people contributing to the organisation. Olson calls these 'selective incentives': that is to say, they are benefits which (unlike the public good) can be provided for members and effectively withheld from non-members, thus providing a particular gain to offset the cost of belonging.[8] Olson suggests that trade unions do not gain members by preaching their advantages to the working class as a whole, or even to all the workers in a particular industry, but by providing selective incentives. These may in the earlier stages be such things as sickness and death benefits but, once established, the union may succeed in getting a 'closed shop' (i.e. make union membership a condition of employment enforced by the firm) or bring about the same result by informal social pressures. Another possibility is that the function of representing individual workers who have grievances against management may be to some degree a selective incentive offered by the union to its members. Again, Olson argues that pressure groups do not rely for membership on showing that they are doing a good job in promoting measures to benefit all members (since these would equally well benefit potential members who do not join) but, as predicted by his theory, their staffs tend to devote a great deal of energy to providing specific benefits—information and other services—on an individual basis to members.

How convincing are these applications of the basic idea? Let us divide this into two questions, one involving its application to the arguments of other writers, and the other involving its use in explaining actual social phenomena. It seems to me quite clear that Olson has succeeded in finding arguments in various writers which make sense only if one supplies the premise that it is in an individual's interest to support collective action that would be to his interests. Thus, D. B. Truman, in his influential book *The Governmental Process* (Truman, 1951), really does seem to claim that

[8] The word 'benefits', here, as normally in economic analysis, includes the absence of costs. Thus, for example, if a man would be ostracised or physically molested for not joining a trade union, we can say that belonging to the union provides the benefit of *not* having these unpleasant things happen.

c

wherever there is a common interest among people similar
in some respect we have what he calls a latent group, and
this group will be transformed from latency to actuality if
its common interests are infringed. This is, of course, a very
comforting notion for one who supports a group-dominated
polity (as does Truman) because it suggests that if there are interests with no organisation this must show that they are being
adequately catered for already. Olson is surely right to argue
against this that 'latent groups' are latent not because there
is no collective action that would advance the interest but
because conditions are unpropitious for getting it organised.[9]

The difficulty which a highly intelligent man can have in
extricating himself from the fallacy attacked by Olson—
moving from collective interest to individual interest without specifying selective sanctions—may be illustrated by referring to a recent lecture by the German sociologist, Ralf
Dahrendorf (1967). In this, he repudiates what he claims to
have been his earlier assumption that quasi-groups (defined
as a category of person with a shared interest in something's
happening) have a natural tendency to become actual, organised groups. I am not at all sure that his earlier theory
(in Dahrendorf, 1959) was definite enough to have committed
him to this (or to anything else) but that is not the present
point. What I wish to show is that Dahrendorf fails, in the
lecture, to free himself from the fallacy exposed by Olson.

The idea he puts forward is that, starting from an axiom
of self-interest, we can deduce the circumstances under which
energy will be put into collective action, namely that it will
be at a maximum when there is little scope for advancement
by individual action. Collective action among the working
class has declined, Dahrendorf asserts, and the explanation
is that it is now possible to find self-fulfilment by, say, taking
a holiday in Italy. But, on Olson's analysis, it is doubtful
whether joining in collective action aimed at the benefit of
the working class as a whole would ever be in the interests
of an individual, if we are thinking (as Dahrendorf apparently
is) of the benefit as simply the value to the individual of the

[9] For a development of this argument at a theoretical level, see Barry,
1965, Chapters 14 and 15. A full-scale treatment of the theme, with much
supporting evidence drawn from the history of the U.S.A. is McConnell,
1966.

result of the collective action. Dahrendorf would probably have been on a better tack had he argued that the *selective* incentives offered by being a prominent member of an organisation have declined in value because other sources of gratification have become available and also because the status gained in a local community from being, say, a Chapel Elder or a Labour Party officer, has less currency in a more mobile society with a more centralised status-hierarchy.

Turning to Olson's examples of successful and unsuccessful organisations, I think one has to say that he tends to pick the cases which support his thesis rather than start by sampling the universe of organisations of a certain type within certain spatio-temporal boundaries. This is especially significant in the matter of explaining the levels of success of different organisations. Olson seems on fairly safe ground when he suggests (with examples) that an organisation which starts offering selective incentives at a certain point in its history will find that recruitment increases. But can we hope to explain the generally higher levels of unionism in Britain than in the U.S.A. by saying that there are more selective incentives? Can we explain the variations in union member-ship between industries by selective incentives? And can we explain the rise of mass unionism in Britain in the 1880s and the decline in union membership after 1926 by this means? On the face of it, these seem more related to such things as the perceived prospects for the success of collective action: the 'new unionism' was reinforced by successful industrial action, while the fiasco of the General Strike led to disillusionment. Likewise, the more similar the positions of a large number of workers are, the more they are likely to see a chance for collective betterment by unionism (Lockwood, 1958). Yet these are precisely the kinds of consideration that are ruled out by Olson, on the grounds that it is not rational for anyone to incur a cost where the increased amount of a public good that will thereby come to him personally is negligible.

5 PARTICIPATION IN COLLECTIVE ACTION: SOME EXPLANATIONS

We thus arrive at a somewhat curious position. Downs tri..
to argue for the discounted value of the additional collective

benefit (in this case the prospect of averting the collapse of the system) as an adequate explanation of voting. Olson, on the other hand, in accounting for membership of trade unions and pressure groups, dismisses the extra bit of collective benefit as an inadequate motive and insists on 'selective incentives'. The actual situation seems to be the same in both cases. In neither case would the marginal bit of collective benefit normally be sufficient to motivate an economically 'rational' person. Here Downs is wrong and Olson right. But, equally, in both cases a belief in the efficacy of the process does look as if it is related to participation, though not necessarily via an ill-calculated judgment of private self-interest. Whatever the reason why a person may attach himself to a cause, more enthusiasm for its pursuit is likely to be elicited if it looks as if it has a chance of succeeding than if it appears to be a forlorn hope. Nobody likes to feel that he is wasting his time, and that feeling may be induced by contributing to a campaign which never looks as if it has a chance.[10] Thus, it has been suggested that extreme right-wing political groups flourish in California and certain other states not so much because the sentiments are so much commoner as because the political structure (especially the weakness of party organisations) makes it more likely that intervention will produce results (Wolfinger, 1964). In a similar vein, Banfield has argued that the fragmented decision-making structure in Chicago makes it easier for citizen groups to modify policy and thus encourages their activity (Banfield, 1961).

Finally, a 'sense of duty' appears to be an important factor in voting, and perhaps it is in some voluntary associations too. To take a pure case, it is difficult to see what 'selective incentive' or personal benefit comes about from sending a cheque to Oxfam. It is, of course, true and important that organisations providing selective incentives (e.g. shops) and those raising money coercively to provide public goods (e.g. the government) succeed in getting hold of a lot more of our

[10] There is, of course, in addition to this the combative satisfaction of being on the winning side, but this takes on a high value only if one previously had doubts about one's own side winning. So this reinforces the tendency for cases where the issue is in doubt to produce more activity, though it would lead us to expect a bias towards the side with the better chances.

incomes. But the example shows that other factors must be allowed for somewhere.

Now, as we have already seen, we can fit anything into a loosely 'economic' framework, if we are sufficiently hospitable to different kinds of 'reward' and 'cost'. Thus, we could say that the sense of guilt at not contributing to some altruistic organisation provides a 'selective incentive', since the guilt is obviously not incurred if one contributes. Or, where an organisation is expected to provide collective benefits for its members (but, by definition, not exclusively to its members), a man might be said to feel the pangs of conscience if he shares in the benefits without contributing time or money to the organisation himself. It is interesting to notice that this is a moral position, in that it does not reflect pure self-interest, though at the same time it depends on the belief that one will benefit personally from the activities of the organisation.[11] A difficulty here is that sentiments of reciprocity are probably most likely to arise in face-to-face groups, and it is in these that social sanctions (a straightforward selective incentive) are most likely to be applied and to be effective. This implies that behaviour alone will often not enable us to infer the actor's motivation. But there are still two kinds of evidence. One is what people say, and the other is how they act when the non-co-operative move would remove them from the reach of the group's available sanctions. Examples, from armies in the Second World War, may be found for both. Thus, survey data on soldiers' attitudes for the U.S.A. and information on desertion rates in the closing stages of the war for Germany both bear out the point. (See Stouffer, 1949, and Shils, 1948.) In both cases it can be concluded that unwillingness to let down 'buddies' seems to be a

[11] Goldthorpe *et al.* seem to me to neglect this point in their discussion of the motives for joining a trade union. They contrast 'moral conviction' with a belief that 'union membership pays', but the latter belief needs to be broken down into conceptions of individual and collective benefit (Goldthorpe, 1968, page 98; Table 39 on page 97). Notice that this is not just a matter of finding out more exactly what people think, but of having, as an observer, a clear idea of the structure of the situation and its implications for distinguishing between self-interested behaviour and 'principled' or altruistic behaviour. The informant might not think of his behaviour explicitly as altruistic, though objectively it is.

large component of 'morale', that is to say preparedness for fighting.

An alternative 'moral' position which might lead to participation in collective action would be a simple utilitarian one. On this basis someone might argue in a certain instance that the increment of benefits (or incremental probability of benefit) produced by his contribution would be greater than the cost incurred by himself, so there would be a net benefit (not to himself, of course, but to the human race as a whole) if he contributed. Olson himself argues, contrary to this, that even if a man's intentions were wholly altruistic it would not be rational to join an organisation producing collective benefits. 'Even if the member of a large group were to neglect his own interests entirely, he still would not rationally contribute toward the provision of any collective or public good, since his own contribution would not be perceptible' (Olson, 1956, page 64). This is surely absurd. If each contribution is literally 'imperceptible' how can all the contributions together add up to anything? Conversely, if a hundred thousand members count for something, then each one contributes on the average a hundred-thousandth. If it is rational for workers in an industry to wish for a closed shop, thus coercing everyone to join the union, this must mean that the total benefits brought by the union are greater than its total costs. (Otherwise it would be better not to have the union.) But if this is so, it must mean that anyone who wished purely to maximise the gains of workers in the industry would join the union voluntarily.

It should be clear that this is not inconsistent with the basic point of Olson's that we have accepted. Suppose, for example, that (up to some point) for every pound spent on a public good a thousand people will derive ten pounds'-worth of benefit each. An altruist (who might or might not be one of the potential beneficiaries) would clearly find a good use for his funds here. But it would not *pay* one of the potential beneficiaries to contribute, because the benefit *to him* from giving a pound would be only one new penny (ten pounds divided by a thousand).[12]

---

[12] It may be noted that the same analysis can be applied to Downs's calculus of voting. If someone adopts a utilitarian position he may well

6 SELECTIVE INCENTIVES AS EXPLANATIONS

Obviously, the constant danger of 'economic' theories is that they can come to 'explain' everything merely by redescribing it. They then fail to be any use in predicting that one thing will happen rather than another. Thus, if an organisation maintains itself, we say 'It must have provided selective incentives'; and this is bound to be true since whatever motives people had for supporting it are called 'selective incentives'. Olson himself recognises that a 'selective incentive' can be *anything* that constitutes a benefit contingent on contributing to the organisation: 'In addition to monetary and social incentives [social status and social acceptance], there are also erotic incentives, psychological incentives, moral incentives, and so on' (Olson 1965, page 61, footnote 17). He adds: 'The adherence to a moral code that demands the sacrifices needed to obtain a collective good therefore need not contradict any of the analyses of this study; indeed, this analysis shows the need for such a moral code or for some other selective incentive.' Nevertheless, he says that he does not intend to make use of such incentives because they are untestable, unnecessary, and unlikely to be of importance in the kinds of organised pressure group to be discussed. It is this restriction on the 'selective incentives' to be acknowledged that gives Olson's theory some real predictive bite, but in this form it does not seem capable of giving an explanation of all the relevant phenomena.

Suppose, however, that we fall back on making the theory a tautology. It is still a quite potent tautology, because it can be combined with empirical assertions to produce significant implications. Thus, it is possible to say, as Olson does, that many 'latent groups' (people with common interests in a certain kind of collective good) will not turn into organised groups because of the difficulty of getting selective incentives to operate. Consumer protection by law is to everyone's benefit, but organisations pressing for such legislation cannot count on economic rewards and sanctions, social pressure or moral principle to attract members in the millions. The most

---

think it worth voting, either to increase the chance of one party winning or to protect the system. (Cf. Barry, 1965, pages 328–30.)

successful organisation is, as we would expect, one which is able to offer a selective incentive for membership, namely the Consumers' Association, with its reports on marketed goods. Similarly, churches (especially if they claim that attendance and obedience are necessary and sufficient conditions of salvation) are obviously in a better position to act as pressure groups, because of their command over selective incentives, than humanist or secular groups which have little to offer except the 'cause' itself.[13]

Again, it is an important fact that, in the absence of economic or social 'selective incentives' which might make it 'pay' to join an organisation providing a public good, the reason for joining *has* to be altruistic. This surely throws light on the notorious difficulty of organising the poor and generally socially disadvantaged to press for improvements in their lot. Sometimes this is described as 'apathy' and regarded as something irrational, which might be expected to disappear with more information and more self-confidence. But since it is not rational from a self-interested point of view to contribute to a widespread collective improvement, one way of looking at this 'apathy' would be to say that the poor cannot afford the *luxury* of collective action.[14]

It is not my intention to deny that malnutrition and debilitating diseases, which are often associated with poverty, must play a part; nor that lack of leisure, unfamiliarity with the routines of organisation and, in many societies, illiteracy are important factors inhibiting collective action. But I think it makes a difference to the way we look at collective action if we recognise that the collective betterment which might result from action cannot, at the individual level, be offset

[13] For an approach to the study of organisations which starts from the tautology that an organisation must offer adequate incentives if it is to persist, see Clark, 1961. Organisational incentives are divided into three kinds: 'material' (monetary returns), 'solidary' (satisfactions derived from participation itself, such as status, honour, or the intrinsic rewards of the activity) and, finally, 'purposive' (attractions deriving from the goals of the organisation, such as its stands on public issues). This scheme has proved useful in books by Wilson (1962) and Banfield (1961).

[14] Compare Sjoberg on pre-industrial societies: 'Where the primary concern of most persons is sheer survival, the horizons of expectation for these persons are narrow indeed. In their incessant preoccupation with survival, the poor have little time or inclination for seeking to change the system . . .' (Sjoberg, 1960).

as a material benefit against the material cost of taking the action.

To put essentially the same point another way, we would expect to find a fairly direct relation between the costs of collective action for a category of people and the probability of collective action among them. (These costs might indeed be negative for the leisured and gregarious people who form a large element in the American and to some degree the British upper middle class.) But we would not by the same token expect to find any close connection between the potential collective benefits to be gained from political action and its probability, since it is (from the point of view of the individual) altruistic anyway. In fact, a good deal of upper middle class collective action is not directed towards the material benefit of the upper middle class, but towards such objects as the poor, people in other countries (once mainly their spiritual welfare, now more their material welfare), or, especially in Britain, animals.

Among the poor, the question to be asked is what can provide the incentives sufficient to overbalance the costs of collective action. One possibility is to arrange selective incentives.[15] Thus, it is highly illuminating in this context to contrast the political 'machine' in American cities, with its relatively low-status clientele and provision of individual benefits (jobs, money, 'fixing' things) and the new style politics of the upper middle class, who 'come to party work not so much in search of a patronage job or some other form of political preference, but out of a combination of ideological and social purposes.'[16]

In the absence of selective incentives, such as the old-style American city 'machine' dispensed (not, it should be said, in

[15] There are, of course, in almost any organisation, some advantages to running it, and these can obviously be enjoyed only by belonging to the organisation. We are not, therefore, regarding the recruitment of leaders as a problem, but we are asking how the rank-and-file are to be got to join and then kept loyal.

[16] Sorauf, 1967, page 42. See also Wilson, 1962. An early example, discussed by Wilson, was the overthrow of the ailing Tammany machine in New York by the Democratic 'clubs'. The activists who secured the Republican nomination for Senator Goldwater in 1964, and those who confounded the commentators who wrote off the campaign of Senator Eugene McCarthy in 1968, are good examples of these 'amateurs'.

order to build support for collective benefits), what remains? An important answer that has been given is 'class consciousness', and Olson devotes a chapter to refuting Marx's theory of class. He argues (pages 105–10) that Marx's theory falls into the fallacy he has exposed, for Marx believes that the self-interest of the workers will lead them to join in political action once they understand their common interest with other members of the working class in bringing about socialism.

Now, if 'class consciousness' is purely an intellectual recognition of a *class* interest, and in capitalist society everyone pursues his *individual* interest, Olson is right and the theory is inconsistent. But does 'class consciousness' mean something more subtle than this, for example a feeling of 'solidarity' with a class, such that one actually identifies with its fortunes? This would fill the bill better, if we are looking for adequate motivation, though it needs to be supplemented by the proposition that one feels one ought to join in advancing the interests of the class. 'Identification' by itself would not be sufficient to provide motivation, unless it amounted to a dedication so absolute that one's private interests were virtually eliminated as a force. Otherwise it would still run into a variant of Olson's basic argument. For, suppose we allow that the success of the movement is worth more to someone if his sympathies or identifications are broad enough to make him value it for more than the prospective change in his own circumstances. We still have to recognise that the movement's success is unlikely to be worth so much to him *when discounted by the difference his own efforts would make* as to outweigh the cost to him of advancing the cause. Thus, some sort of anti-free-rider sentiment is still needed.[17]

It is not clear whether Marx himself believed that 'class consciousness' could provide an adequate motivation for revolutionary action if it were simply an intellectual appreciation that one had interests in common with those in a similar class situation. Although, as Olson points out, Marx regarded self-interest as a dominant motive in capitalist society, he may have thought that the members of the working class were less

[17] Compare the comments below (in Section 8 of this chapter) on Coleman's 'investment' theory of support for the State.

exposed to its corrosive effects than were the capitalists.[18] And his emphasis on close communications and other ties between the members of a class as a condition for the development of class-consciousness suggests that he may have had in mind something more like solidarity.[19]

7 LEADERSHIP AND COLLECTIVE ACTION

The relevance of the economic line of analysis is twofold. First, it shows that in certain circumstances the pursuit of collective interest cannot be explained in terms of individual interest; so, in as far as the pursuit of collective interests does occur in such circumstances, the explanation must require that some other motive be invoked. And, second, an 'economic' analysis suggests that if 'class consciousness' (or, more generally, 'group consciousness') requires an identification sufficiently intense to enable it to overcome the cost to each individual of participation, it may not be easy to sustain over a long haul. Self-interest can operate quietly, but mass altruism tends to require a succession of dramatic and well-publicised events to keep it going. Severe action against some members of the movement outside a context of extreme and general repression may, for example, keep the rest of the following in a militant mood, thus bearing out the general relevance of the saying that the blood of the martyrs is the seeds of the Church.

Thus, in any organisation that lasts long, we tend to find leaders who are held by selective incentives such as money, power or status. This still leaves the followers outside the theory. If selective incentives are out, we cannot in general expect the followers to incur severe costs for a long haul, but they can be got to contribute smaller ones. Thus, the introduction of leadership into the picture (the return of a two-sector model) does not mean that the economic approach can be completely rehabilitated, as one writer has enthusiastically suggested (Wagner, 1966). Wagner argues that, with a division of labour between the political entrepreneurs and their

[18] This still leaves the question of class action by the capitalists to be accounted for. Perhaps (especially at the local level) Marx could hold that there were few enough to avert the 'Olson problem.

[19] See his explanation of the failure of the peasants to organise as a class despite their common interests: they 'do not enter into manifold relations with one another' (Marx, 1869).

customers, we can solve the 'Olson problem', since the would-be leaders get their 'selective incentives' as a consequence of success in competing for the support of the ordinary citizens. Unfortunately, however, this simply evades the question how, if the only benefits they have to offer are collective goods, the leaders can get followers to provide cash and compliance for themselves.[20] Perhaps Olson does tend in his opening chapter to suggest that unless there is a large beneficiary there will be nobody to get an organisation started, even if there are a number of people who would find it worth contributing a limited amount. But there is nothing in the theory itself or in his subsequent application of it to rule out the possibility that an organisation will be run (if the support can be obtained) by someone who is himself indifferent to the collective good in question—a professional political entrepreneur. What Olson concentrates on is whether there would be any way of getting the support, even if there were no rigidities in turning potential support into organisation.[21]

What this attempted amendment of Olson's theory in fact does is inadvertently to reinforce the impossibility of explaining various phenomena of group activity on the basis of any 'economic' calculation. For the prime examples that Wagner gives as counter-examples to Olson's conclusions are unaccountable on his premises too. These are the success of relatively unorganised categories of voters (such as old people, or consumers) in getting any legislation at all which favours them.[22] The answer, as Wagner points out, lies in the fact that these are interests which can be expressed in voting, and

[20] If it were postulated that the leaders could offer selective incentives, this would not be a distinctive solution to the Olson problem, since it is, of course, the solution that Olson proposes himself.

[21] Such rigidities may, however, be a factor, as Schelling points out: 'If a drainage ditch at the back of one house will protect both houses, and if it costs $1,000 and is worth $800 to each homeowner, neither would undertake it separately; but we nevertheless usually assume that they will get together and see that this project worth $1,600 to the two of them gets carried out. But if it costs 10 hours a week to be scoutmaster, and each considers it worth 8 hours of his time to have a scout troop but one man must do the whole job; it is far from certain that the neighbours will reach a deal according to which one puts 10 hours on the job and the other pays him cash or does 5 hours' gardening for him' (Schelling, 1960, page 32).

[22] One might still say that they do not do as well as those who are

politicians therefore have an incentive to offer legislation which will further them. But they are still collective goods, so we are thrown back to our old question why people vote, and it is now surely clear that an 'economic' analysis cannot explain it.[23]

An important point is brought out by the failure of the 'two-sector' model of collective action to plug the gaps in the Olson version. In so far as leadership *is* necessary for the success of collective action, it presumably cannot simply consist of pointing out how a collective good can be obtained by providing support. For even if this were believed, it would not in general provide an adequate motive for giving support. Leadership may, of course, involve arranging some selective incentives, but, as we have seen, these are not in fact found in all movements. An alternative or supplementary method is to make people feel they want the cause to succeed enough to contribute to it. 'It is the professional business of politicians, as of other promoters and organisers, to find in the electorate or other constituency organisable blocs who will shift their allegiance to them, who will respond with passion in the midst of indifference, and with identification in the midst of diffuse and plural ties' (Bell, 1955, page 113). This normally seems to involve at least two things. The first is the creation of an ideology, by which is meant here a set of beliefs attributing to the movement some significance over and above the self-interest of the participants.[24] The second

---

strongly organised, and this is something Olson can explain. But the question is whether he can explain why their interests are regarded by politicians at all.

[23] Olson himself recognises this and even goes so far as to say that the 'group theory of politics' would work well enough for the case of voting, as against that of pressure groups (page 164).

[24] Daniel Lerner has pointed out the contrast between the need for ideologues in making a revolution and their relative superfluity once coercive power has been established: 'Each totalitarian régime began with its variant of an "intelligentsia" at or near the apex of the new élite. . . . Once power was seized . . . the role of the intelligentsia, the specialists in persuasion, rapidly diminished; the power of the specialists on coercion rapidly increased. . . . Trotsky survived the assassin's axe just long enough to witness the process [in the U.S.S.R.] and reach back to the French Revolution for a historical parallel. The "Thermidorean Reaction" supplied the lesson' (Lasswell, 1965, page 461). Underground resistance movements are clear instances of the rule that in the absence

is the dissemination of the idea that the movement is near success, so that only a short (though hard) push will be needed to produce spectacular results.[25]

8 CONDITIONS OF ECONOMIC RATIONALITY

Is it possible to carry any further forward the question raised earlier in the chapter: when is the 'economic' approach likely to work and when isn't it? The best lead in still seems to be the one mooted then, that the size of the cost is crucial. Olson himself suggests that 'there is a "threshold" above which costs and returns influence a person's action and below which they do not' (page 164). But he apparently places the threshold very low: he contrasts voting for a union shop (below) with paying dues to a trade union (above). Where the threshold comes, if indeed there is one, must, of course, be an empirical matter.

Perhaps, rather than saying there is a threshold below which calculation has no place, we might suggest that where the cost is low it will take little to overcome it. Due to the opportunities for idiosyncrasy to operate, this may make it more difficult to predict whether action will be taken or not. But we can at least make the prediction that inertia will be a powerful force. Thus, when a positive effort is needed to

---

of selective incentives an ideology is essential: 'All men are volunteers, they can desert almost whenever they desire. Moral elements of the underground army are therefore of primary significance. . . . Monter [acting commander of the Warsaw uprising of 1944] understands the primary significance of ideology in the formation of an underground army. Without an ideology which does not appeal to underground soldiers, an underground army is hardly possible' (Gross, 1958, pages 354–5).

[25] 'The task of the intellectual consists in maintaining the freshness and vigour of the workers in their movement towards their great goal and elucidating for them the social relationships which make the approaching victory of the proletariat a certainty' (Mehring, quoted by Lerner in Lasswell, 1965, page 461). Marxism, of course, provides both cosmic significance and inevitable success for the movement. Again, the case of underground armies provides an extreme instance: 'Hope is an important psychological factor, for hopeless struggle can scarcely attract a large following. Hope that change will come *soon* is an important driving force of an underground movement, and that is constantly stressed in underground publications. . . . When the terminal point was distant, the [Russian] revolutionary movement was small: it was a secret society. When the chances of revolution increase—the secret society expanded into a real revolutionary party and mass movements' (Gross, 1958, pages 355–6).

join—sending off money, for example—organisations offering collective benefits may be expected to enjoy little success. But as soon as action is required to avoid joining, inertia will tend to work the other way. An excellent example of this is the 'political levy' which many trade unionists pay unless they contract out. The big increase in the numbers paying this levy when the basis was changed in 1946 from contracting in to contracting out is a vivid illustration of the fact that inertia is itself a powerful factor.[26]

It might be argued that asking to contract out invites social sanctions from fellow-workers, and this may sometimes be so; but failure to contract in might equally do so. In any case, this argument merely invites us to push the question further back, for a work-group is itself too small a unit to benefit *collectively* from the increased probability of union control over the Labour party and/or electoral success of the Labour party. In other words, we cannot say that it would pay the work-group to institute a tax on itself, and that social sanctions are a substitute. (This might be true at the level of the union as a whole, if it is a large union, but it is not the union as a whole that exercises social sanctions.)

We might suggest that the main relevance of 'economic' reasoning here is to explain why it should matter so little to a Conservative trade unionist that he is paying a political levy to support the Labour party, as many apparently do. Just as it is not worth contributing if it involves a cost, neither is it worth not contributing if that involves a cost.[27] Another slightly less obvious example is the lack of protests by shareholders against proposals by the directors to pay sums of

[26] In 1964 contracting *out* ran at 21%; before the change in 1947 contracting *in* ran at 55%. On the basis of this, Rose has said (apparently not recognising that a lot of assumptions are involved in drawing the conclusion), 'Thus, approximately 25 per cent of trade unionists are indifferent as to whether they pay a political levy averaging 2s. 9d. [per annum] in 1964' (Rose, 1967, page 251). See Harrison, 1960.

[27] We can strike a further Downsian note here by adding that, in view of the small sums involved, it is not even worth making an effort to find out about the political levy. The realism of this conclusion is confirmed in a study of Luton workers: 'it would appear that in all groups except the craftsmen from a third to a half are making their contribution without realising this; that is to say, either they do not think they pay the levy but have not contracted out or they admit to having no knowledge of the levy at all' (Goldthorpe, 1968, page 111; see also Table 48 on page 110).

money to the Conservative party or satellites of it, or to engage directly in political advertising. This is in effect a charge
on the shareholders from which there can be no contracting
out (except by selling the shares) but the cost to each is negligible. This is not, of course, a pure 'Olson' situation, in that
it might be rational to vote as a shareholder for a compulsory
political levy on all shareholders while it would not be rational
to contribute to a political campaign as an individual. But the
chance of a single company's efforts making a difference is still
too low to make it worthwhile from the shareholders' collective
viewpoint to try.[28] And there is the thought-provoking case of
the steel companies in the 1966 election: the shareholders of
many companies stood to gain if renationalisation took place
on the terms proposed by the Labour government.[29]

Individual membership of a political party, as against
inertial contribution to one, requires that one should take the
initiative in joining or at least allow oneself to be recruited.
Thus, in Britain, individual membership of both major parties
is much lower than the 'affiliated' membership of the Labour
party; and the one with more 'selective incentives' (Conservative clubs and business contacts, and, of course, the heavily
social emphasis of the Young Conservatives) has many more
members (Blondel, 1963). But we cannot avoid the recognition
that many individual members cannot be explained in terms
of 'selective incentives' unless we stretch the concept so as to
lose any distinctive meaning and include sentiments ranging
from fairly unreflective party loyalty to an elaborated set of

[28] Rose compares the prospective loss to the 'steel industry' which
might arise in being nationalised as a result of the 1964 election, with
the amount that 'the industry' spent in propaganda. He concludes that,
since the prospective loss might have been expected to be £600 million,
while the amount spent on campaigning was £1.3 million, this 'was
reasonable if the chance of such propaganda decisively and positively
influencing the result was at least about 1 in 450' (Rose, 1967, page 146).
This as it stands obviously commits the fallacy of treating 'the industry'
as a collectivity: on the face of it the relevant calculation is the cost
and prospective benefit to *each company*. Perhaps steel companies are a
small enough group to overcome this 'Olson problem' at least to the
extent of, say, N.A.T.O.; but Rose's own account does not suggest much
in the way of mutual coercion—or even co-ordination.

[29] See Rose, 1967, page 280. It was, of course, still rational for the
directors to spend (mainly) other people's money in an attempt to retain
their own very desirable jobs.

political beliefs. And, if this point is weakened by the existence of face-to-face contacts in a local party, let us consider
the phenomenon of Americans sending money through the
post to the 'party of their choice'. (See Heard, 1960, pages
41–7.) Although this is a minority practice, it involves many
millions of U.S. voters and seems to fall as far outside the
'economic' model as the contributions to famine relief or
other charities mentioned earlier.[30]

When the cost is small, it does appear that, though the
economic model can account for some variations, its prediction
of total failure for an organisation can be falsified rather easily
either by 'selective incentives' (such as inertia) which are
rather dubious, or by the 'moral' considerations which, in
order to give the theory any teeth at all, we have decided to
exclude. But can we say that, when the cost is great, the
economic approach comes into its own? There is a certain
amount of truth in this, in that the role of selective incentives
tends to be much clearer in inducing participation.

Thus membership of a union may in some cases be pretty
automatic; but attending meetings is rather more demanding
than paying a subscription and, in the absence of selective
incentives, few members go.[31] Strikes, finally, may well involve

[30] Olson himself writes that 'the average person will not be willing
... to contribute to the party coffers ...' (page 164). Those with personal
ambitions or desires for favours in return may do so, but not those for
whom the only motive is the 'collective good' of victory for the party
they support. But if Olson's theory were as strong as he often implies,
there should be no contributions from such people. The theory may
explain why these contributions are not more or bigger, but it cannot
explain how they occur at all. On the other hand, it is highly relevant
to our theme to note that *large* contributions in the U.S.A. come from
'people interested primarily in government policy' (Schlesinger, 1958,
page 771). This 'interest' is not in the *collective* benefits of government
policy but in decisions which can act as selective incentives: 'Individuals
with a direct stake in the organization's victory, such as candidates and
public employees dependent upon them, can be expected to contribute,
as can businessmen such as contractors or others needing licences from
the state' (Schlesinger, 1958, page 786).

[31] Those that do are disproportionately made up of those motivated
by ideological zeal, who thus fall outside the model. This again illustrates
that it may be possible to give an 'economic' explanation of a *difference*
in numbers (why x has a smaller membership than y) by adducing selective incentives, even though these cannot account for every feature of
the situation (why x has any members at all).

D

a substantial sacrifice by the worker and his family. But here 'selective incentives' come fully into play: ostracism and violence, verbal or even physical, may well be inflicted on the blackleg.[32] It is easy to see that these are essential to overcome the fact that it would otherwise pay any individual employee to continue work, even though he stands to gain if the strike is successful.

Nationalist movements which are banned by the government concerned provide an interesting parallel: the government often argues that if the movement finds it necessary to use 'terrorism' on those whom it claims to represent, this shows that they do not really support it. Governments who employ this line of reasoning should reflect that exactly the same case could be made against them insofar as they find it necessary to resort to penal sanctions in order to raise taxes, enforce laws and conscript an army. In fact, the argument is equally fallacious in both instances. As Baumol pointed out, in a book which in some ways anticipates Olson (Baumol, 1952), it is rational to support the coercion of ourselves along with others to finance the state, even if we would not contribute the same amount voluntarily. In exactly the same way, a man might welcome 'terrorism' aimed at providing a counter-sanction to those in the hands of the forces of 'law and order', just because he is aware that he and many others would not otherwise have an adequate incentive for supporting the opposition organisation.

These examples, however, raise in an acute form the question whether it is really true that where the costs are high the 'economic' mode of analysis comes into its own. Are not nation states and nationalist movements precisely the sorts of thing that are capable of eliciting action which incurs a substantial risk of very high cost without the presence of 'selective incentives'? I think the answer is that this is so, but that the qualifications already made apply here too. First, selective incentives still make a difference, though their absence (or at least their apparent inadequacy to offset the costs involved) does not reduce activity to zero. In Britain during the First World War the number of eligible men

---

[32] The employer's optimal response, if he decides to try to break the strike, as few do nowadays, is to recruit from outside the community, ideally among people who do not speak the same language as the strikers.

who volunteered to join the army was quite large; and, even if one recognises that many of the volunteers (especially in the earliest stages) did not expect to be killed and that there were social sanctions at work, we probably need to bring in other motives. However, it is significant that conscription was introduced later and that the selective incentives of penal sanctions did produce more men. Similarly with revolutionary movements: the amount of voluntary joining is above that explicable in terms of selective incentives, but tends to be only a minority of those who could participate. Again, coercion is often used to aid recruitment.[33]

The second point is that not all ways of serving a state or movement are equally far outside the 'economic' calculus. Fighting, hardly surprisingly, is the furthest away, but at the other end economic dealings (in the ordinary sense of the word) are apparently difficult to dislodge from it. Even in wartime, states continue to rely on taxation rather than voluntary contributions for fiscal support, even if they can do without conscription for their armed forces; revolutionaries too seem to find food more difficult to obtain than men.[34]

An attempt has been made (Coleman, 1966) to get the sense of national identification into the 'economic' style of analysis, by showing that it can be expressed in terms of self-interest, but I do not think the attempt is successful. National identification does, in my view, lead to certain kinds of action outside the 'economic' framework, and the most useful thing is to work out the circumstances and areas in which it does.

[33] See, for an 'economic' analysis of revolutionary movements, Ireland, 1967. The author develops an analysis of 'nationally'-motivated participation on orthodox Downs/Olson lines: 'In choosing his course of action, the individual will calculate the differential between expected utility streams under the existing and revolutionary arrangements. . . . This differential is then discounted in the individual's mind by the probability that he personally will change the chances for the success of the revolution. . . . This discounted value is then compared to costs of action. . . . The individual participates if his discounted expected utility for supporting the revolution exceeds the expected costs of participation . . .' (Ireland, 1967, pages 52–3). Unfortunately, the author does not attempt to relate his model to the facts of any revolution, so he does not have to face the question whether it actually works.

[34] See Etzioni, 1961, for the view that normative appeals are unlikely to be successful in economic matters. The 'spirit of Dunkirk' cannot usefully be invoked in a balance of payments crisis.

Coleman's attempt is, however, interesting in that it falls
down on the same confusion between individual and collective benefit that undermined Downs's demonstration of the
economic rationality of voting. Just as Downs suggested that
a democratic form of political system might be regarded as
an investment, yielding a steady stream of utility but needing
to be kept going by period acts of voting, so Coleman suggests
that one might regard the whole country as something in
which one has a certain investment, again requiring sacrifices
(money at least, and perhaps more) from the investors to keep
it going. The fallacy is the same in both cases (and Downs
inconsistently admits the point), namely that the condition
of the investment is so little affected by the actions of one
ordinary person that it would not pay to contribute anything
to its upkeep.

Coleman's idea of an individual's 'optimum' division of resources between public and private use, based on self-interest
but taking into account his 'investment' in the nation, is use-
less because the 'optimum' level of public contribution would
be zero, exactly as deduced by Olson. And the analogy that
Coleman draws between a citizen's 'investing' in the nation
and one firm's investing liquid funds in another firm breaks
down at the crucial point, for the profits of the company
invested in are *not* a public good but go to the shareholders.
If the state, like the firm, simply provided services in proportion to the taxes paid, the analogy would hold; but on
that assumption the distinctive feature of the state, that it
provides collective goods (including policies such as income
redistribution), would be lost and with it the whole problem.

In this chapter I have tended to emphasise the things
Olson's theory cannot explain. When a theory is so simple
and the claims advanced for it are so sweeping this may be
unavoidable. But it should not be allowed to conceal the fact
that, for such a simple theory, Olson's does explain a great
deal. Although not all variations in strength between organisations can be accounted for by the theory (including the fact
that certain organisations exist at all), much of the pattern of
effective organisation over the long term in a society does
seem broadly to correspond with the predictions we would
draw from Olson. This is no mean achievement for the
'economic' approach.

CHAPTER III

Values and Stable Democracy: Three Theories

1 INTRODUCTION

This chapter and the next will be devoted to work carried out by men belonging to what, in terms of our preliminary discussion, may be called the 'sociological' school. We shall follow through their treatment of a particular question, the conditions of stable democracy. And we shall ask whether their characteristic type of answer, in terms of the prevalence of certain 'values' in the population, carries conviction.

Concern for the viability of democratic forms of government is not central to the work of our economic theorists, Downs and Olson. Downs worries about the prospect of a rational electorate deciding to a man (and woman) not to vote. Olson points out that much of the conventional 'pluralist' defence of democracy—as a way of registering the results of a struggle among pressure groups—rests on a fallacious assumption that any significant shared interest is likely to give rise to a pressure group whose strength will in some sense be proportional to the aggregate strength of the interests affected. But for neither author is the viability of democratic institutions a central preoccupation around which the whole discussion is organised, whereas this is precisely the position it holds for the writers whose ideas we are to examine in this chapter.

An even clearer distinction emerges if we turn from the question posed to the kind of answer offered. For, insofar as 'economic' writers address themselves directly to the question of how a state maintains itself in existence, the answer they give is, naturally enough, couched in terms of the 'selective incentives' it can call upon. In particular, of course, a state can refrain selectively from inflicting punishments. (See especially Baumol, 1952; also Olson, 1965.) Against this, our 'sociological' theorists emphasise the importance of internalised, normative constraints. These norms are said to form part of the 'political culture', and the main way in which actors acquire them is by a process of 'political socialisation'.

2 ALMOND AND VERBA

The rest of the present chapter will be devoted to an analysis of three pieces of work which ask what are the conditions of stable democracy within a country, and give an answer couched primarily in terms of values that must be held by the people who live in the country in question. The first study to be discussed is *The Civic Culture*, by Gabriel Almond and Sidney Verba. Their book (Almond, 1963) is subtitled *Political Attitudes and Democracy in Five Nations*, but although it provides a wealth of fascinating survey data on political attitudes, there is very little attempt made to provide evidence about the relation between these attitudes and the working of a country's actual political system. The structure of the book is as follows. First, the authors consider the possible attitudes or 'orientations' that people might have towards their country as a whole and to various political institutions within it (parties, branches of government, and so on). They suggest in the course of this discussion that a certain combination of such attitudes is conducive to the maintenance of a democratic political system. Then, using this as a guiding thread, they examine how far the combination of attitudes postulated as favourable to democracy is actually found in the five countries where their survey was carried out, namely, Britain, the U.S.A., Italy, Germany and Mexico.

The combination of attitudes which the authors believe to be most supportive of democratic government they call the 'civic culture'. Summarising drastically, it might be described as a judicious mixture of respect for authority and sturdy independence. The ideal democratic citizen, according to this, would believe in the legitimacy and the general competence and goodwill of the political authorities while at the same time believing that he has the right (or even the duty) and also the ability to exert influence on what they do, so as to secure redress of grievances for example. These two components are called 'subject competence' and 'citizen competence' respectively.

From the armchair, this all sounds fairly plausible. Almond and Verba, unfortunately, do not get us any further than the armchair, in spite of their wealth of survey data. They conclude, on the basis of this, that, of their five countries, Britain comes nearest to approximating the ideal balance constituting the 'civic culture'. The U.S.A. follows, marginally stronger on 'citizen competence' but deficient, apparently, in respect for government. The other three countries are not ranked, but all deviate from the assumed norm in different ways. Germans have no shortage of deference for authority, but do not have much belief in the right, duty or possibility of political action by ordinary people. Mexicans have more belief that participation is desirable, but less belief that it might succeed and not much confidence in the government, civil servants or police. Italians just seem pretty generally disaffected from their political system. But what is the connection between attitudes such as these and the existence of democratic politics in a country?

To get the beginnings of an answer, we should need three things. We should first need an hypothesis relating the prevalence in a country's population of the 'civic culture' (to a specified extent) with the existence in that country of (a certain amount of) democracy. (The criteria of 'democracy' would, of course, have to be spelt out.) Then we should have to test this hypothesis by seeing whether the two kinds of variable—'cultural' and 'institutional'—were related in the data in the way required by the hypothesis. And, finally, we should have at least to face the question of causality. To put it crudely, even if the relationship does exist, is this because the 'culture' influences the working of the 'institutions', or is it merely that it reflects them?

We look in vain to Almond and Verba for any of these items. The nearest approach to a hypothesis is the question: 'Is there a democratic political culture—a pattern of political attitudes that fosters democratic stability, that in some way "fits" the democratic political system?' (Almond 1963, page 473). Now, 'fits' says so little that the statement that a certain culture fits a certain system might be interpreted as immune to empirical disproof. In that case even the vague words such as 'support' or 'conducive' that I have been using to summarise the claimed relationship are too strong. But I think it is fairly clear that Almond and Verba do mean that certain attitudes actually affect the attainment or maintenance of democracy. Beyond that, though, it would be hard to go. Assertions of various kinds might be made: some level of 'civic culture' could be held to be a necessary condition for the possession of a certain degree of 'democracy', or a sufficient condition, or a necessary and sufficient condition.[1] Or it could simply be said that, other things being equal, a country with more 'civic culture' is more likely to be democratic than one with less; and this would imply that, unless there were special reasons to the contrary, the 'other things' should tend to cancel out, leaving a positive correlation between the amount of 'civic culture' and the amount of 'democracy'.

These hypotheses would require, in order to be tested, that we should have either a criterion for the presence of relevant amounts of 'civic culture' and 'democracy', or a scale for them on which at least ordinal positions could be established. As we have noted, Almond and Verba do make it clear that they think the order of their five countries in 'civic culture' is led by Britain and the U.S.A., but that is all. As for the other side of the relationship, it is an extraordinary fact that they do not address themselves to the question how 'democratic' their five countries are. Nor would this be easy without taking a lot of rather arbitrary decisions: to mention one obvious example, it would make a big difference whether or not one went back beyond 1945. If 'civic culture' is an independent causal factor it would surely be one that could hardly be expected to change very fast, since it would depend on such things as socialisation through family decision-making, and this would suggest taking a long time-span for the determination of 'democracy'.

But this raises the final question, of the direction of

---

[1] In the two last cases, the other things that could vary would have to be stated, and, to make it at all plausible, some limits would have to be placed on the range within which they could vary and 'civic culture' still be a sufficient condition of 'democracy'—but then would it be the limitations on the ranges of the other variables that were really carrying the strain?

causality, which Almond and Verba discuss only incidentally, as when they occasionally remark that a certain attitude may reflect something in the history of the country in question. Suppose that some hypothesis or other connecting 'civic culture' and 'democracy' is confirmed for the five cases studied —and it is at any rate plausible to say that Britain and the U.S.A. would head both lists—would we be much further ahead? Might one not argue that a 'democratic' political culture—such as the 'civic culture'—is the *effect* of 'democratic' institutions? The *prima facie* case for saying this is not without force. If you ask people whether they expect to get fair treatment from civil servants or whether they think they could do anything about changing an unjust government regulation, it is possible that their replies add up to a fairly realistic assessment of the actual state of affairs, rather than, say, projections onto political life of childhood conclaves about the best place for a picnic.[2] This interpretation of the data has some support, in that many differences in response from one category of person to another look as if they could be accounted for as accurate perceptions of reality. For example, men tended to be much more confident of their ability to operate politically, whereas women were almost as confident about getting a fair deal from the police; and the better educated, reasonably enough, fancied their chances more against the civil service. Of course, all this could be 'explained' as the result of selective exposure to the dominant 'political culture', or in terms of the dissemination of several different 'subcultural' outlooks; but the alternative explanation that the differences express reasonable expectations founded on common experience has the great virtue of parsimony.

Obviously, if this interpretation is correct, there are no grounds for saying that the correlation arises from the conduciveness of the 'civic culture' to 'democracy', but rather for

[2] More precisely, it could be argued that, although the actual proportion saying 'yes' and 'no' to any particular attitude question has no great significance in itself, the differences between proportions in different countries are significant and may well reflect different political conditions. No doubt, for any given objective situation, some people would be more discontented or more sanguine than others, but between countries such personality differences might be hoped to be distributed in roughly the same way.

the unexciting conclusion that 'democracy' produces the 'civic culture'. But this interpretation can no more be established from data for a single point in time than can the other. The naturally-occurring 'crucial experiment' is, of course, a change in régime. If the 'political culture' alters *afterwards* (e.g in Germany after 1945, towards a 'civic culture' type), this strongly supports the view that it is a more or less accurate reflection of the current political reality. If, on the other hand, it does not change, then this interpretation of the basis of 'political culture' collapses; and if, some time *before* the change in régime, a change in 'political culture' in the right direction were observed, this would provide good evidence for the view which attributes to it causal efficacy. To acquire information for answering these questions, it would be necessary to pick the cases for study in the light of their relevance to the questions—an obvious point but one often overlooked. (Almond and Verba do not explain the rationale of their choice of countries for study.) It would be difficult to get systematic data for the past about the 'political culture', and there is always the difficulty that undemocratic régimes may be hostile to surveys which ask people what they think of their rulers, but whatever could be established would at any rate have a direct bearing on a major theoretical question.

3 ECKSTEIN

Our second study is entitled *Division and Cohesion in Democracy*, and is addressed squarely to the problem we have chosen to discuss. But it has the same limitation as the Almond and Verba work in that it does not have a time dimension. That is to say, it does not follow the form of a 'natural experiment' by correlating changes in the dependent variable ('stable democracy') with changes in other variables (the alleged 'conditions' of it). It is also based on only one country, Norway. The author, Professor Harry Eckstein, tells us that Norway was chosen partly because he hoped that it would support his *Theory of Stable Democracy* which was published some years before. (It is now reprinted with the study of Norway, as Eckstein, 1966, pages 225–88.) Since Eckstein tells us that he still stands by the earlier monograph, both will be dealt with together.

In two important respects, Eckstein marks an advance over Almond and Verba. He recognises the need for an explicit definition of 'democracy' (or in his case 'stable democracy') and the desirability of stating the relationship that is claimed between dependent and independent variables in less evasive terms than 'fit'. The execution is less happy. 'Stable democracy' is presumably a sub-class of 'democracy' but, rather curiously, Eckstein discusses the concept of stability almost to the exclusion of any attention to the concept of democracy.

In the work on Norway, he interweaves his definitional material with a demonstration that Norway fits the definition. But that Norway is a democracy is simply taken for granted, and the discussion centres on its stability. Eckstein takes stability to be constituted by three things: durability (sheer longevity), legitimacy (absence of serious challenges) and effectiveness (governmental output adapted to conditions) (Eckstein, 1966, pages 11–20). The relation between these three criteria is not stated. It might be thought that legitimacy and effectiveness are to be thought of simply as means to durability, which is itself on the face of it the key criterion. But, since Eckstein says that he intends 'to use the terms "stable", "effective" and "successful" as virtually interchangeable' (page 11), what we have is presumably a three-item definition.

The earlier *Theory of Stable Democracy* is a little more illuminating on this question, though also different in detail. The endurance of a régime is, Eckstein says, part of the concept of 'stability', but only a part, since a régime might continue for a long time by a series of lucky accidents, an example being (he maintains) the Third French Republic. But, since political science can deal with general conditions rather than historical accidents, this sort of case must be ruled out (Eckstein, pages 227–8). It would seem reasonable, though Eckstein does not make the point, to extend this in the other direction and say that a régime might be 'stable' even if, due to exceptionally bad luck (e.g. an invasion) it collapsed. Indeed, since Eckstein wants to call Norway a 'stable democracy' in spite of the wartime Quisling government, he must presumably be committed to this view. The difficulty, of course, which is equally acute for 'good luck' and 'bad luck', is defining the terms with sufficient precision to allow different scholars to classify countries in the same way.

Eckstein does not face this crucial problem, but goes off on a different tack. Having said that longevity is not enough to define 'stability', he now says that stability also implies 'effective decision-making . . . in the basic sense of action itself, any sort of action, in pursuit of shared political goals or in adjustment to changing conditions' (page 228). This is tantamount in the context to putting forward the theory that 'effectiveness' so defined is a necessary and sufficient condition of 'stability'—an interesting idea, also pursued by Lipset, but not in fact the one that Eckstein speaks of as his 'theory of stable democracy'. In fact, Eckstein argues that 'a government must govern, . . . otherwise it is not a government at all' (page 229), but it is hard to believe that he really wants to make 'effectiveness' in this sense part of the definition of 'government'. On the whole, then, the attempt to specify the further conditions of 'stability' ('effectiveness' in this version; 'effectiveness' and 'legitimacy' in the other) seems a mistake. 'The capacity for non-accidental survival' might be the best interpretation of 'stability', though this would admittedly leave 'stable' régimes difficult to identify.

Eckstein adds a third criterion to 'durability' and 'effectiveness', in the *Theory of Stable Democracy*, namely 'authenticity'. This means that the régime must be 'genuinely "democratic" '. Two criteria for this are stated: first, 'democratic structures must not be mere façades for actual government by non-democratic structures', and, second, 'elections in such systems must decide, in some basic way, the outcome of the competition for power and policies' (page 229). The second criterion is surely the fundamental one. For the first presupposes that we already possess a criterion for a 'democratic structure'. If, in the light of the second criterion, we say that a democratic structure is one in which elections play a large part in determining what happens, then the first criterion simply becomes redundant.

The main trouble with the second criterion is the difficulty of applying it: it could mean a lot or a little. Eckstein wants it to mean a lot, since he rules out the Third French Republic under this head. He also rules it out under his first criterion.[3]

---

[3] It is curious that Eckstein devotes such labour to showing that the Third Republic, though long-lived, was not stable, since apparently it is in any case not an example of democracy.

But even if it were true that 'elections decided very little' in the Third Republic, this may reflect the limited variation in election results. It does not entail that the same things would have happened had the electorate voted quite differently. Surely, rather than try to force a division here between France and the countries counted as 'democratic', it would be better to assume, as does Moore (1966), that the right kind of question is: why were Britain, France and the U.S.A. different from Germany, Russia and Japan? In other words, is it really sensible to lump Third Republican France in with Hitler's Germany and Stalin's Russia in the 'non-democratic' category?

I would suggest that a *weak* version of Eckstein's second condition would be quite appropriate, namely one in which the emphasis was on the possibility of everyone voting, and the possibility of changing power and policy outcomes by voting one way rather than another. This becomes close to the definition which Lipset (1959) adopts from Schumpeter (1950), that democracy is 'a competitive struggle for the people's vote'. The emphasis on voting as a criterion of democracy might, of course, be challenged, but all we need to do here is note what is being proposed.

Let us assume that we now have a rough definition of 'stable democracy' as the non-fortuitous maintenance of institutions in which power and policy outcomes are affected by mass voting. The next question is: what relation is asserted to exist between this state of affairs and some other conditions, and what are these conditions? Unfortunately, this is a difficult question, not because Eckstein fails to state any hypotheses, but because he states a number of them, each several times in different ways. From all this we may pick out two themes. How these themes are themselves inter-related, though, is quite unclear. The first theme, which occupies much of the book on Norway (it does not occur in the earlier monograph on 'Stable Democracy') we shall call the theme of 'solidarity'. The other theme, which is in fact the basic idea of the *Theory of Stable Democracy* and also appears in the book on Norway, we shall call the 'congruence' theme.

The 'solidarity' theme is introduced through a discussion of Almond and Verba, among others. According to Eckstein, there is a prevalent view that political divisions make for

instability, especially where they are strongly felt and important, where the same lines of division occur for a number of
issues, or where there is 'division over general social identifications or broad cultural norms' (Eckstein, 1966, page 37).
This view is stated in terms of stable democracy requiring the
absence or low level of such divisions. In other words their
absence or low level is a necessary condition of stable democracy.

Eckstein then maintains that Norway provides a counter-
example, and that a reformulation of the proposition is in
order. He introduces it by citing Almond and Verba. 'In *The
Civic Culture* Almond and Verba suggest that political
divisions . . . can be "managed" by a certain "inconsistency
between norms and behaviour". More specifically, competitive political "behaviour" may substantially coincide with the
social or cultural segments of society, but this somehow need
not destroy the cohesion of a polity if there exists in it a norm
that this *ought not* to be so, emanating from "some higher,
over-arching attitudes of solidarity" ' (Eckstein, page 76).

It is difficult to see what could be meant by talking here
about an *inconsistency* between norms and behaviour. The
situation depicted is one in which there is a norm to the effect
that 'divisions' should not destroy 'the cohesion of the polity',
and apparently this norm is acted on to such good effect that
'the cohesion of the polity' is not destroyed. It is also puzzling
in what way Eckstein thinks this quotation, which he says is
'squarely on the track we will follow in the rest of this essay',
really contradicts the 'orthodox' view to which it is placed in
apposition.[4] Surely, the most one could say is that Eckstein
has switched from necessary conditions to sufficient conditions
(though it is doubtful whether the 'received view' is generally
thought of in terms so precise), and that he has switched the
emphasis somewhat from the absence of division to the presence
of solidarity. This is not a change in the kind of explanation
offered, for it says in effect that you can have divisions so long
as the 'division over general social identifications or broad

[4] Especially curious in this context is the fact that exactly the same
passage about 'higher over-arching attitudes of solidarity' as a sufficient
condition of stability is quoted by Eckstein in a footnote to his earlier
discussion, devoted to illustrating that the position he is describing as
the received view is actually held by various writers. (Eckstein, page 37,
footnote).

cultural norms' does not exclude a commitment to the integrity of the state boundaries and the form of government. But once the notion is expressed in this way, we must ask whether it is very different from the 'legitimacy' which is part of the definition of a 'stable' polity? Are we simply left with the tautology that a régime is legitimate when there is a widely accepted norm to the effect that its nature and geographical extent are acceptable?

The answer is, I fear, that this is so. But there is still a subsidiary proposition that is not merely definitional, namely that the 'norm' is sustained by 'solidarity'. This, of course, could be trivial if the existence of the norm were taken to be the evidence for, or criterion of, the presence of 'solidarity'. But in fact Eckstein argues independently for its presence in Norway. He cites in support (i) the distaste for defining what are elsewhere purely economic relationships in such neutral and limited terms, (ii) the prevalence of the notion that the community as a whole has a responsibility for the unfortunate, as evinced in the high standard of welfare services, and (iii) the fact that more Norwegians think other people behave decently than do survey respondents elsewhere.

The relation between sentiments such as these and the legitimacy of the régime is a genuinely contingent one, but it is to the same degree a questionable one. Since the whole analysis is presented as a contrast with other countries (including other 'stable democracies'), we can hardly be dealing with necessary conditions, and Eckstein suggests rather that these are sufficient conditions. This is a bold claim, though it may still be correct. It implies that, whatever other conditions obtained, attitudes of 'solidarity' would guarantee the stability of the régime. To test this, we would need to look at all countries which manifested a high level of solidarity, and see if they had in common the characteristic of stability. But what countries are these?

Eckstein does not give us any answer, and it is difficult to know how to get one. This is partly because it is not clear whether the three features of Norway which are cited by Eckstein have to be present elsewhere before we can say there is a high level of 'solidarity'. Or is 'solidarity' a condition which may be manifested in many different ways, the three cited for Norway being simply the ways it shows itself there?

If it is the former, the difficulty arises that there may well be no other country which satisfies the three conditions,[5] in which case the proposition that they are jointly sufficient for stable democracy must be regarded as unverifiable. If it is the latter, we need some more general criterion for 'solidarity' —perhaps a sense of having a lot in common, as in a family. But then is it very plausible that this should be a sufficient condition of political stability? Families can be riven by feuds, made all the more intense by the closeness of the members.[6]

It is hard to know how one would test for 'solidarity'. (Even Eckstein's statement about non-economic relationships was challenged by Norwegian readers.) Possibly a strong widely spread sense of nationalism could be identified, but it seems doubtful that countries scoring high on nationalism would be found to be unusually stable. No doubt, in an era in which nationality is regarded by many as the only legitimate foundation of statehood, one would be safe in saying that, other things being equal, a state within whose borders a strong national sentiment was found would be more stable than otherwise. But this is a long way from saying that solidarity (if nationalism can be taken as a species of solidarity) will overcome any other divisions and bring about political stability single-handed. As for the particular case of Norway, nothing that Eckstein says really convinces me that the linguistic and regional conflicts which he depicts have been remarkable for their intensity or irreconcilability.

The second theme in Eckstein's work is that of 'congruence'. This comes out especially clearly in the *Theory of Stable Democracy* (in fact, it *is* the theory, in that monograph). How this theme relates to that of solidarity is not, as far as I can see, ever stated by Eckstein. Perhaps one condition brings about the other, though this seems implausible. If, on the other hand, they are independent, we have the problem that, since solidarity is a sufficient condition of stability, con-

[5] 'Welfare states', in any precise sense of highly bureaucratic social security measures, are found only in industrial societies, whereas the tendency not to reduce relationships to the 'cash nexus' is, of course, characteristic of non-industrial societies, as Eckstein himself points out.

[6] Of course, someone might make the move here of saying 'If it is *really* close, the members can't possibly quarrel violently.' But that would be to leave us with a tautology: stability is produced by solidarity and part of the meaning of 'solidarity' is stability.

gruence is superfluous as an explanation of the stable history of Norway. I shall not pursue this problem any further, simply taking it that congruence is in some way held to tend to induce stability.[7]

The congruence in question is between the central governmental institutions of a society and those of other associations and organisations within it, such as families, clubs, schools, trade unions or local levels of government. As Eckstein recognises, this idea has certain points of contact with the 'pluralist' theory of democracy.[8] But, whereas the point of this theory is to emphasise the importance of independent bases of power, the 'congruence' theory rests on the notion that a form of government is legitimised by familiarity with it in other spheres. It is thus closely related to the 'moral education' conception of democratic politics held by J. S. Mill, who indeed wrote in the *Political Economy* that '. . . a democratic constitution, not supported by democratic institutions in detail, but confined to the central government, not only is not political freedom, but often creates a spirit precisely the reverse' (Mill, 1848, page 444). Thus, although Eckstein contrasts the explanation in terms of forms with 'cultural' explanations of stable democracy in Norway, the 'forms' operate not directly but via an effect of creating or reinforcing appropriate norms and values.[9]

[7] Eckstein himself does, however, say at various points that congruence is necessary (pages 186–9 and 240–1) and that it is sufficient (pages 234 and 239–40), for stability.

[8] Perhaps one should say: the 'pluralist' theory of constitutional government. (This is sometimes called 'liberal democracy' by American writers, but it has more liberalism than democracy in it.) See Kornhauser, 1959, for an influential recent statement; forerunners include Montesquieu (1949) and de Tocqueville (1946). See also Crick (1962), who confusingly calls the same phenomenon 'politics'.

[9] This at any rate seems the most plausible interpretation of what Eckstein says, and I cannot find any alternative possibility canvassed in the book. At the same time, I have to confess that I find it hard to understand a passage in which Eckstein says that in the Weimar Republic a democratic ideology was fervently accepted, attributes the collapse of the Republic to a lack of congruence between it and other institutions, and regards this as supporting his theory. If the other institutions were not congruent with a democratic constitution, how could there be fervent support for a democratic ideology? Perhaps the answer is that he considers an 'ideology' as something highly abstract, whereas the supportive values and norms produced by democratic forms

E

There are many difficulties involved in the congruence thesis, as it is stated and defended by Eckstein. The first difficulty involves what appears to be an incoherence in Eckstein's argument. A large part of the *Theory of Stable Democracy* is devoted to the idea that there should be congruence between the different branches of the central government itself. On the basis of this idea, Eckstein suggests that, since the actual impact of the government on the citizens is always inevitably going to be somewhat 'authoritarian', it would be well for stability if the rest of the political system also avoided being too democratic. As his illustrations of what happens when the 'input' side (political parties and parliament) gets out of line with the 'output' side, Eckstein mentions the Weimar Republic and the French Third and Fourth Republics. But in *Division and Cohesion* he describes the internal party structures, the electoral system and the working of the Storting (parliament) in Norway as being highly democratic; yet it is, of course, central to the analysis that Norway should be accepted as a 'stable democracy', whatever else is or is not.[10]

Eckstein points out that the conclusion to be drawn from this part of his thesis is that 'stable democracies' cannot be too democratic; but surely the logical conclusion would be that 'stable democracies' are impossible, since the rest of the system should match the 'authoritarian' structure by which rules are applied in individual cases, by civil servants, magistrates, etc. Perhaps such a conclusion should make us ask whether the thesis, in this form, has any particular plausibility. It is difficult to see it. The traditional view of democratic theorists has been, I suppose, that the unavoidably 'authoritarian' aspect of rule-application in a large state is made more acceptable, not less, by the fact that the rules themselves come about by

---

of institution operate in more concrete terms. The problem is, in any case, not in any serious sense one about the Weimar Republic, because the premise—fervent support for a democratic ideology—is so absurd. The opponents of democratic ideology may have been a minority but they were a large minority and included important élite groups.

[10] Another example of something that is also presumably a 'stable democracy', combined with proportional representation of the most theoretically perfect kind, enabling electors to pick and choose within party lists, is the Republic of Eire. Even monarchy, which Eckstein regards as an institution giving a suitably 'authoritarian' cast to politics, is lacking in Ireland, and the Presidency is not a powerful office either.

processes which allow for discussion and for the intervention of interested parties at various points.[11] It does not seem to me that we have as yet any evidence on which to reject this view.

There is another way in which it is difficult to see how Eckstein's thesis, in the form just discussed, is supported by the example of Norway. He suggests that the 'forms' of the political system are made more acceptable because they are imitated in precise detail by the 'forms' of other organisations, such as trade unions, local authorities and even clubs. But if these organisations have a 'bureaucratic' component, they presumably suffer from the same internal incongruence as the state itself, while, if they do not, they surely make the incongruence between the different organs of the state even more apparent. I do not wish to press this point or the previous one as reasons for rejecting the entire thesis. Perhaps they could be met by a more careful formulation of the 'congruence' proposition when applied to different parts of the same institution. Since, however, I cannot myself see how this reformulation might be carried out without virtually giving up the idea, the best thing seems to be to ignore this aspect of the thesis as far as possible in discussing the rest.

Taking 'congruence', then, to refer to similarities of structure among different institutions, let us consider two problems of evidence. Both also arose in connection with the work of Almond and Verba. This is not surprising since the two problems are surely among the main stumbling blocks to be met by any theory about the cultural conditions of certain kinds of polity. The first is whether régimes that have changed dramatically in their politics have changed in the other ways postulated sufficiently sharply to provide an explanation. Germany again provides an interesting case. Eckstein describes the post-war German Federal Republic as 'hyper-stable'. He does not explain in what way this differs from just

[11] It is no doubt true that if these processes allow so much room for objectors to operate as to make it impossible for tolerably coherent policies to be put into effect, this 'output failure' may in the long run induce disaffection. But the causal mechanism involved here would simply run from the failure of government to the disaffection with the political system. It would not be necessary to postulate any independent contribution from 'incongruence'.

being 'stable', but let us simply take it to mean 'very stable'. The Weimar Republic, by contrast, is declared to have been 'unstable'; while the Nazi period, not being democratic, is not appraised in terms of stability either. How far is the post-war stability associated with greater congruence than the period of the Weimar Republic? Presumably, if Eckstein were to discuss this (as he does not in the book) he would argue that there has been a convergence from both sides: the polity is less democratic and the other institutions more democratic. This is probably true, but are the changes sufficiently great to account for the difference between Weimar and Bonn? My impression would be that it is not, but perhaps what this emphasises is the crying need for some sort of measurement.

The same lesson would emerge if almost exclusive weight were placed on the change in the régime, thus giving the argument the form of an assertion that the régime had now been brought into line with the other institutions. One would have to look for rather precise criteria of a régime's being 'democratic' before agreeing that the Weimar Republic was, in fact, extremely democratic. There appears to be a great danger of the same features of Weimar being adduced as evidence for its being highly democratic as were adduced for its being unstable. If this were so, then there would of course be a link between the two, but it would not require to be mediated by any reference to other institutions.

The other problem, which is again a quite general one, is that of inferring causation from correlation. Suppose we find in a society (Norway, Britain) that there is in various respects a correspondence between certain features of the central political institutions and those of other institutions. Eckstein would maintain that the correspondence works so as to enhance the acceptability of the central political institutions, but might not the flow run in the other direction?[12] The

---

[12] This, of course, all presupposes that the correlation is found. There is, however, at least one case where state and non-state institutions have remained incongruent for a long time, yet the regime has been quite stable. This is the Republic of Eire, which has (as already pointed out) a quite democratic political system while at the same time the bulk of the population gives its allegiance to one of the most illiberal branches of an (in any case) hierarchical institution, the Roman Catholic Church, which also runs most of the schools. Perhaps this can only be dealt with by saying that the proposition about congruence is to be under-

prestige of the Oxford Union probably depends more on the prestige of parliament than vice versa—perhaps the only causative factor going the other way is the tendency for politicians to acquire mannerisms in the Oxford Union which then help to increase the level of disaffection from parliamentary institutions. And perhaps the modelling of other institutions in Norway on those of the parliament reflects esteem for the parliament more than it reinforces it. But it may well be that de Tocqueville and Mill were right in saying that familiarity with a procedure in everyday matters produces respect for it where it operates at a distance.

Surely though, it would be odd to suppose that familiarity with a certain type of institution would by itself produce favourable attitudes to similar institutions. In other words, can 'congruence' between non-state and state structures plausibly be regarded as a factor supporting state institutions unless we know the person's attitude to the non-state institution? Surely something on the lines of 'balance theory' is called for (Cartwright, 1956). The hypothesis should be that if institutions A and B have the same form, and there is satisfaction with A, this lends some support to the form of B; but if there is dissatisfaction with A, this detracts from the appeal of B. Conversely, if there is dissimilarity of form between A and B, satisfaction with A will tend to weaken B, and dissatisfaction with A to strengthen B. For example, autocratic German or French universities may, if there is in any case dissatisfaction with their performance, produce demands among students for political participation generally. But for anything stated to the contrary, Eckstein is committed to the view that autocratic non-governmental institutions automatically lend support to autocratic governmental institutions.

4 LIPSET

Let us now look at a third and last example in which 'cultural' explanations are offered for the incidence of democracy. This is the work of the well-known political sociologist, S. M. Lipset. Lipset has not provided a book-length treatment of the theme, but a chapter in each of his books, *Political Man*

---

stood as referring to a tendency only, and that a few exceptions do not therefore disprove it.

(1959) and *The First New Nation* (1964), deals with it, and
his views are summarised in his contribution to the introductory textbook edited by Smelser (Lipset, 1967). Lipset's is
in many ways the most serious attempt to relate 'values' and
'institutions' that has been made. He has a definition of 'stable
democracy' which is on the whole workable: he defines
'democracy' in Schumpeter's terms as a 'competitive struggle
for the people's votes' and defines a 'stable democracy' as a
country where (i) this state of affairs has existed uninter-
ruptedly since World War I, and (ii) there is no major
political movement which challenges this kind of political
order (Lipset, 1967, page 443). In terms of this definition he
presents a list of countries which qualify as 'stable democracies'. In 1959 these were listed as Great Britain, Sweden,
Norway, Denmark, the Netherlands, Belgium, Luxembourg,
Australia, Canada, New Zealand, the United States, Switzer-
land and Uruguay (Lipset, 1959, pages 78–9). In 1967, the
same list was presented except that the status of the last had
been reduced to '. . . and possibly Uruguay' (Lipset, 1967,
page 443). Like Eckstein, who speaks of Norway as a democracy for thirty years, Lipset seems curiously amnesiac about
the period of the Second World War, which certainly 'inter-
rupted' the course of 'political democracy' in all of his eight
European countries except Britain, Sweden and Switzer-
land.[13] I would not regard this as too much of a problem—
presumably an exception could be introduced to cover the
case of foreign occupation. But if one has to make exceptions,
what about the case of the Republic of Eire? As we shall see,
Eire runs counter to many of Lipset's propositions, as it did
to some of Eckstein's. Since it came into existence in 1922, it
does not technically belong in Lipset's list, because the
criterion is uninterrupted democracy since the First World
War. But if we are to ignore up to five years of interruption
in the Second World War, we should hardly worry about
starting four years late.

The thing to be explained is why the countries in the
'stable democracy' list are there and others are not. In various
places, Lipset has advanced a number of different kinds of

[13] Indeed, since the general election due in 1940 was never held, and
there was no 'competitive struggle for the people's vote' over an eleven-
year period, one might query the case of Britain, too.

explanation, including the level and rate of industrialisation and the division of the 'founding fathers' into rival factions at an early stage in the country's history. How these are related to one another and to explanations in terms of 'values' he does not make clear. But it is on explanations of the latter kind that I shall concentrate, in accordance with the scheme of this chapter.

Lipset's basic idea is very simple and seems to make a good deal of sense, as far as it goes; but this is not perhaps very far. He suggests that there are two sources of support for a régime: a belief in its legitimacy and a belief in its efficiency.[14] Logically, these beliefs can occur independently of one another, though it is claimed that they are to some degree causally linked. We can pair them so as to yield four possible combinations: high on both, low on both, high legitimacy plus low effectiveness and vice versa (Lipset, 1964, page 81; 1967, page 446). Those societies 'which are high on both . . . have stable political systems, as have the United States, Sweden and Britain'. Those which are low on both 'are unstable and liable to break down, unless they are dictatorships maintained by force, such as some of the governments of Eastern Europe, whose authority rests on the actual or latent presence of the Russian army' (1967, page 446). Lipset does not quote any contemporary example of a society high in legitimacy and low in effectiveness, but maintains that there were a number in the 1930s—in fact probably all the countries which are described by him as 'stable democracies', since all had serious unemployment problems.[15]

High effectiveness and low legitimacy apparently marked the German and Austrian régimes of the 1920s, which 're-mained stable as long as they were reasonably effective economically' (Lipset, 1967, page 446). In the contemporary

[14] Note that for Lipset, unlike (in one version) Eckstein, legitimacy is not a part of the definition of 'stability'; here it is asserted to be a cause of it.

[15] He writes: 'When the effectiveness of various governments broke down in the 1930s, those European politics that were high in legitimacy remained democratic, while countries such as Germany, Austria and Spain lost their freedom, and France narrowly escaped a similar fate' (1967, page 447). Lipset also mentions the U.S.A. as another high legitimacy–low effectiveness combination in the 1930s, but the same could be said of the other non-European examples of 'stable democracy'.

world, many countries low on legitimacy 'repeatedly face effectiveness crises'. Perhaps this means that they swing between high and low effectiveness, or perhaps it means that they are always low, but this periodically results in coups. Examples are to be found in Latin America, East Asia, the Arab areas, and Africa south of the Sahara. Lipset says that 'the political stability of those few Afro-Asian nations with traditional legitimacy, such as Ethiopia and Thailand, stands out in sharp contrast to the situation in nearby former colonial territories' (1967, page 447), but he does not say whether these two cases are to be regarded as effective and legitimate or ineffective and legitimate.[16]

Unfortunately, no attempt is made to draw the discussion together in terms of necessary or sufficient conditions. From what has been quoted, however, it would appear that *either* legitimacy *or* effectiveness is a sufficient condition of stability, though neither is a necessary condition, as the Eastern European example mentioned by Lipset brings home. In practice, however, effectiveness is bound sooner or later to break down. This being so, we can surmise that any stable régime lasting a long time without external military support *must* be legitimate though it *may or may not* be effective. Thus the really crucial variable in accounting for long-term stability in democratic countries (which by definition cannot be under foreign occupation) is legitimacy.

So far so good, but how far is it? We now know that régimes are stable if they are viewed by those who live under them as either right in themselves or valuable in so far as they are the means to some end. We also know that the former motive is more reliable than the latter because the means–end relationship is always liable to break down. Perhaps this is not exactly tautologous, but it is hardly news. Indeed, if we make it more precise it becomes even nearer tautology, for we need to add that the people who must think the régime legitimate or effective (or both) are those who would otherwise have the power to overthrow it. In other words, the proposition should read: it is a sufficient condition of a régime's being

---

[16] In connection with Latin America he says, curiously, that states have lacked 'economic or symbolic effectiveness' and have thus 'failed to achieve legitimacy'. How 'symbolic effectiveness' differs conceptually from 'legitimacy' is rather puzzling.

stable that there is no group with power to overthrow it whose members believe that it is illegitimate.[17]

Lipset comes nearest to recognising this point explicitly in his most recent discussion, in which he places heavy emphasis on the importance of the army's believing the régime to be legitimate (1967, pages 447–8). But the point has ramifications extending into a great deal of his work on the conditions of democratic stability. Lipset has devoted much attention to threats from the left: he has written at length on the danger of working class authoritarianism (1959, Chapter 4) and the need to restrain populistic excesses (1964, Part I). Yet there is no case I can think of in which an operative democratic régime has been overthrown by an indigenous mass movement of the 'left', as against dozens of cases of successful army coups.[18]

Assuming it is accepted that one is not saying much when one has said that legitimacy in the eyes of the appropriate people is a sufficient condition of stability, the next question is obviously: what brings about the belief that a régime is legitimate? Lipset's most elaborate discussion of this question occurs in Chapter 6 of *The First New Nation*, entitled 'Values and Democratic Stability'. This discussion is based on certain of the Parsonian 'pattern variables' (or 'orientations to action'), especially the contrasting values of 'ascription' and 'achievement', that is to say, the contrast between being treated in a certain way in virtue of some relatively unchanging quality such as skin colour or parental class, and having one's rights, privileges and advantages related in some way to what one has actually done.

It would take too long to analyse the whole of this extensive and complicated discussion, but the final section of the chapter, on 'Social Change and Political Stability' is manageable (Lipset, 1964, pages 239–47). This section begins as follows: 'One problem faced by all developing societies is that the legitimacy of the existing distribution of resources and

[17] Compare James Harrington's statement that a form of government is stable when 'no man or men in or under it can have the interest or, having the interest, can have the power to disturb it with sedition' (Harrington, 1965, page 68).

[18] Italian Fascism and German Nazism might be regarded with some justification as mass movements, though of the 'right'; and even then a jointly sufficient condition of their triumph was élite connivance.

privileges, and of the political decision-making process itself, comes under severe tension' (1964, page 239). In the discussion a good deal of use is made of the 'pattern-variable' vocabulary, but it is a serious question how much explanatory weight it can really bear. According to Lipset, the 'ascriptive élite' may meet the challenge of a new economic class in either of two ways: 'incorporative' or 'insulative'. The 'incorporative' process is one in which the new class is absorbed into the ascriptive élite (page 239). An alternative formulation has it that the leaders (whose position is achieved) of the new class are absorbed (pages 240–1). Britain is said to be an example of this process.

The 'insulative' response occurs when 'the social system' adjusts by 'insulating the old ascriptive élites from the new ones (for example, by reserving for the old élite certain privileged positions, often in government, the military, religion and education)' (page 239). France is described as an example of this. According to Lipset, 'the *ancien régime* provided virtually no institutional access for the rising bourgeoisie to political decision making, much less incorporation into the ranks of the decision makers' (page 241). This led to the French Revolution, in which the bourgeoisie came out on top, and the aristocracy presumably 'insulated' themselves, though all Lipset says is that they formed a 'new and durable counter-élite of the right'. The bourgeoisie, however, in turn adopted what Lipset calls an 'insulative' attitude toward 'aspiring labor élites'. In support of this statement he says that they were prone 'not to feel responsible for the welfare of the lower orders just at a time when those classes were undergoing severe material deprivation and social dislocation', and thus the 'lower classes' became 'increasingly alienated from the system'. In Germany, too, the response was 'insulative' in that German businessmen were not incorporated (i.e. fully assimilated socially) into the aristocracy, nor were the workers' leaders 'incorporated into the political process' (page 242).

It is difficult to make anything out of this farrago because of the way in which Lipset confuses, first, political access with social assimilation, and, second, élites risen from (and/or representing) classes with classes themselves. Thus, the 'interesting phenomenon of the Labour peer' is no more peculiar than the Socialist or Communist Senator (or Deputy) in France. It is surely clear that political access in *this* sense is equally open to representatives of the working class in both countries. And the indifference of the French bourgeoisie to the condition of the working class has little to do with their adopting an 'insulative attitude toward aspiring labor élites'. Conversely, it seems highly doubtful that the idea of the 'aristocratic embrace', useful as it is in accounting for the behaviour of certain individuals, can be used as an explanation of the absence of a big anti-parliamentary working class movement in Britain.

The main questions, however, concern the role of values in this sort of explanatory account. To begin with, what is the gain from attaching the term 'ascriptive' to the term 'élite'? As far as I can see, there is a great disadvantage, in that the question whether the élite is 'ascriptive' or not is irrelevant. The French bourgeoisie was presumably much less 'ascriptive' than the aristocracy it displaced, in that being a bourgeois was not a status acquired at birth; yet, according to Lipset, the bourgeoisie too behaved in an 'insulative' fashion, even though this is defined as a reaction of an *ascriptive* élite.

We may also ask whether there is any point in Lipset's claiming that he is explaining legitimacy, as against support. In other words, is 'legitimacy' a genuine intervening variable which helps to explain the level of support for a régime, or is it merely a *synonym* for 'support'? These may be separable concepts, but it is difficult to see that 'legitimacy' is carrying much weight here. Perhaps it does mean something distinctive in the case of Britain, where the argument is apparently that the willingness to absorb new élites socially served to prevent a break in traditional legitimacy as symbolised by the monarchy. But the argument in the case of the French working class seems to be simply that its members were badly treated and turned against the system. (Lipset does not make it clear, incidentally, to what period he is referring—it could be anything from the 1790s to the 1920s.) Perhaps 'ineffectiveness' (unsatisfactory output) and 'illegitimacy' (rejection of the system) could still be distinguished by saying that the first leads, after some time, to the other. But one is bound to say that the utility of this way of putting it is not obvious.

Lipset says, shortly after the passages quoted, that 'up to

this point the discussion has focused on the way in which ascriptive values have been handled in establishing who should have the right to rule in a political democracy' (1964, page 245). One may wonder whether the Germany of Bismarck or the France of, say, Louis Philippe, were 'political democracies'. As we have seen, it may also be doubted whether the discussion is of ascriptive élites or whether it is simply of élites and classes which are challenged by other élites and classes.

In any case, it seems very odd to say that these conflicts are best described in terms of 'the way ascriptive values have been handled'. But the continuation of the text makes it clearer what Lipset thinks he has shown. There is, he says, an alternative to ascription as a 'basis of gaining support for a new system: effectiveness, or demonstrated and successful achievements. But as a sole foundation for legitimacy it is tenuous. Any government can become involved in crises; major groupings will oppose specific policies, sometimes to the point of alienation. Consequently, any government which persists must have ascriptive grounds of support—i.e. a sense of traditional legitimacy. Where a polity does not have such legitimacy to begin with, as in the case of new states or postrevolutionary governments, it is inherently unstable. If the basic value pattern of the society includes a strong emphasis on ascription, new governments will find it difficult to rule by any means except force. Only where the value pattern stresses achievement (as in the U.S.A.) will the political system, like other institutions and positions, be evaluated by achievement criteria. . . . These analyses suggest that the persistence of ascriptive and particularistic norms is compatible with democracy only in societies which have retained ascriptive legitimacy for their polity, that is, in monarchies. Where such traditional support is missing, the only way to create a legitimate régime is through long-term effectiveness, that is achievement' (Lipset, 1964, page 245).

The context of the word 'legitimacy' in the early part of this quotation shows that the term is being treated purely as a synonym for 'support'. If crises in performance can be said to produce *ipso facto* a collapse in legitimacy, then 'legitimacy' is not being used here in a sense which would enable it to be distinguished conceptually from efficiency as a basis of support. Legitimacy, in the sense in which it can be said to be a basis of support independent of efficiency, has now become 'ascriptive legitimacy'; and it comes about by only one means, namely, the survival of the régime (or some salient features of it) for a long time.

The two sentences just quoted from Lipset are in fact riddled with confusions and *non sequiturs*. This is brought about by his attempt to drag in ascriptive and achievement values at every turn, as we shall try to show by the inelegant but economical method of listing six objections:

(1) If, as Lipset suggests, a régime which is effective produces stability at least while it is effective, and if (as he also suggests) the duration of a régime eventually induces sentiments ascribing to it legitimacy, then the orientation of the citizens (achievement or ascription) is irrelevant. If, for example, the post-1918 régimes of Germany and Austria had continued to be even moderately effective (i.e. but for the slump) they would have become legitimate in time, since they were adequately supported until then.

(2) In any case, there is no reason for assuming that if achievement is the basis for evaluating people it will also be the basis for evaluating régimes, or that one could not evaluate régimes on achievement while evaluating people on ascription. Even worse, if the two *did* match up, the results would not be what Lipset supposes. For in a truly achievement-oriented society, such as the 'meritocracy' depicted by Michael Young (Young, 1958), status goes strictly with *current* achievements. Once your achievements slip you lose status. Yet the whole idea in the case of types of régime is that after a time achievement produces legitimacy. And what this means is precisely that the régime can rest on its laurels: its achievements in the past will enable it to ride out with relatively undiminished support failures to achieve in the present. There is thus something of a paradox at the heart of Lipset's analysis.

(3) There is a kernel of truth in what Lipset says, namely, that almost any régime will attract certain people to it by ties of sentiment and/or interest to such a degree that if it is replaced by another they will be disaffected. This point is just as relevant to the establishment of the U.S.A. as to any other abrupt change of régime, but the U.S.A. was fortunate

in avoiding much of the problem. In accounting for the fairly easy time the new régime had in establishing legitimacy (at least until the Civil War!) we must remember the great exodus of the Tories (those who opposed the Revolution) to Canada. It is very rare that a new régime has such a convenient opportunity of exporting its malcontents to a contiguous, relatively unpopulated country with exactly the sort of government favoured by them.

(4) Let us return to the case of the nineteenth-century French bourgeoisie. Lipset's discussion of them seems to me to present problems of coherence. On the theory he expounds, it is clear that they were not the 'ascriptive' rulers—those had been overthrown by the Revolution—so how is it that Lipset speaks as if they *lost* working class support by their callous attitude to the hardships of the working class during industrialization? This suggests, surely, that their support might have been *retained* by the bourgeoisie had they been more sympathetic. Yet Lipset maintains that France is an 'ascriptive' society. It ought to follow from this that the bourgeoisie could not have attracted working class support *whatever* they did—however efficient', in other words, they made the system.

(5) At a more fundamental level, we must ask how, on Lipset's theory, political change can ever come about in an ascriptive society? Yet come about it certainly does. An ascriptive society is, for Lipset, one in which there is 'value consensus' on the proposition that the traditional form of rule is right. But somehow traditional rule has almost disappeared from the face of the earth (and even where pseudo-traditional rule continues, as in Ethiopia, it is not without challenge). How can we explain this? Obviously a theory which starts from the assumption that societies are 'under constant pressure' to bring their institutions into line with their 'central value system' (Lipset, 1964, page 7) is not much use here. We might follow Edmund Burke, an earlier theorist of ascription (except that he called it 'prescription'), and put down to collective frenzy stirred up by wicked men out of a sheer delight in destruction. It seems more plausible to allow that most people are at any rate rational enough to come in out of the rain (Homans, 1961, page 82) and to suppose that they may sometimes consult their interests in deciding how

to act. It is the inclusion of interests in the scheme that enables us to explain how, in spite of 'socialisation' and all the rest, social change can occur.

It is worth noting that Lipset does covertly accept this: an example of Homans's charge that sociologists tend to keep explanations in terms of rewards and costs under the table for emergency use, while officially promoting theories of some other kind (Homans, 1961, page 14). For example, Lipset does not bother to try to explain why the bourgeoisie supported the French Revolution. He simply takes this for granted. Yet the whole idea of a 'rising class' is inconsistent with his theory. For, if everyone was adequately deferential to the power-holders of the existing order, why should a social group want to challenge this exercise of power just because they start to get more money? The case against 'values' as explanations can indeed be pushed further. For, if frustrated interests can help explain upheaval, it is surely only the other side of the coin to say that satisfied interests can help explain the absence of upheaval.[19]

(6) Finally, for light relief, we may consider briefly Lipset's ideas about the great importance of monarchy. It seems ludicrous to treat the presence of monarchy as a *cause* of stability, in the way Lipset does. Would it really shake New Zealand, Canada, Australia, Sweden, Norway, Denmark (or even Britain!) to the core politically not to be monarchies? Surely this is a perfect example of moving from a correlation to a cause in the wrong direction. It would be more true to say that stability causes (the retention of) monarchy, than that the abolition of monarchy causes instability. If a country gets in a big enough political upheaval the monarchy will probably go, and the country may well later be unstable, for reasons such as those given under heading (3). Conversely, if a country has a relatively tranquil political development, there may well never build up a sufficient head of steam to abolish the monarchy.

Even at the level of correlation, however, Lipset leaves out one conspicuous counter-example, the Republic of Eire, a

---

[19] I take issue on this point with David Lockwood's perceptive critique of Parsons's *The Social System* (Lockwood, 1956) in which he appears to suggest that 'values' explain one set of phenomena, (consensus) and 'interests' another (conflict). See also Dahrendorf, 1958.

country which has shown on the whole a remarkably high level of political stability since its inception in 1922. It might be argued that, until 1948, it had a tenuous constitutional connection with the British crown, and should thus be classified with Lipset's 'monarchies' of the British Commonwealth. But, if so, it raises an even more acute problem: how can we explain the lack of political trauma subsequent to the severance of the link in 1948? Even worse, it seems hard to deny that, if we have to call societies either 'achievement' or 'ascription' oriented, we must put Ireland in the 'ascriptive' box. How else could one describe a society in which, for most men, the means to an improvement in social status is to 'step into the old man's shoes'—in other words, take over the farm (Arensberg, 1940).[20] Ireland is, incidentally, a counter-example to another value-based hypothesis of Lipset's: that Roman Catholicism is inconsistent with democracy because of its authoritarian belief-system. Perhaps the religious homogeneity of Eire suggests the alternative hypothesis that religious *divisions* are conducive to political instability, which in turn makes the continuation of democracy more hazardous.

[20] Of course, not every son could inherit. But the traditional route for the 'achievement-oriented' was out of the country.

CHAPTER IV

Values and Democratic Stability: The Setting and the Problems

1 INTRODUCTION

In this chapter, we shall be looking somewhat more generally at the use of 'values' as explanations of social phenomena. In the first half, we shall take up some arguments put forward by the influential American sociologist Talcott Parsons in an attempt to demonstrate the primacy of values and the inadequacy of any approach (such as the 'economic' one) which does not recognise this primacy. Having cast doubt on Parsons's more sweeping claims, we shall suggest that the biggest problem lies in formulating testable hypotheses about the relations between particular values and certain other things such as 'stable democracy'. After this, in the remainder of the chapter, we shall switch to the opposite tack and defend our position against the view that explanations in terms of 'values' are either tautological or inherently unsatisfactory in some other way.

There are three reasons for beginning the chapter by discussing Parsons. First, he is just about the purest example of a 'sociological' writer, in the sense in which the word is being used in this book. Studying his writings thus helps to put flesh on the rather skeletal description of the 'sociological approach' that has so far been given. Second, Parsons has been immensely influential not just on people usually thought of as sociologists but also on (among others) political scientists. Specifically, the influence of Parsons on the writers discussed in the previous chapter is very clear. And, third, Parsons has the advantage, from our point of view, of having explicitly made the contrast between the 'sociological' and 'economic' approaches.

F

It should be emphasised at the outset that what follows is not an attempt to 'cover' Parsons. There are a number of versions of 'potted Parsons' on the market, and Parsons himself has attempted to do the job (not, it must be admitted, in a way very accessible to a neophyte) on several occasions.[1] The selection is, in fact, imposed by the three reasons for discussing Parsons that were mentioned above; all three point towards our concentrating mainly on some themes from Parsons's first book, *The Structure of Social Action* (1937). The 'sociological' features emerge clearly, unobscured by the increasing later fascination with system-building and conceptual elaboration. It is, obviously, this early work rather than the most recent which had a formative influence on political scientists now in their fifties such as Almond and Eckstein. And it is in *The Structure of Social Action* that we get by far the most extended discussion of the 'sociological' approach in relation to the 'economic' approach.

2 PARSONS ON THE 'HOBBESIAN PROBLEM'

The starting point of *The Structure of Social Action* is what Parsons terms the 'Hobbesian problem', namely 'How is social order possible?' We can regard the problem of the conditions of democratic stability as an offshoot of this general problem; and, as we shall see, the answers analysed in the previous chapter are akin to that offered by Parsons to his 'Hobbesian problem'. Parsons rejects what he believes to be Hobbes's own answer, that social order is maintained purely by means of coercion exercised by a political authority. And the answer he himself offers is in terms of internalised normative constraints based on common values. The question is, he suggests, wrongly put by Hobbes as one of stopping people from doing what they want. The real question is how it comes about that their wants are compatible with social order.[2]

It is a curious fact that, even though the later writings of Parsons have attracted much adverse comment, it usually seems to be supposed (either tacitly or explicitly) that at any

[1] See Section 4 of the bibliography for suggested reading.

[2] In Parsons, 1937, a section of one of the chapters on Durkheim (pages 378–90) is especially relevant. A more recent essay on Durkheim, which brings out the same points, is Parsons, 1967, pages 3–34. See also, for a sympathetic exposition, Devereux, 1961.

rate *The Structure of Social Action* is a monument of careful and exact scholarship. Parsons himself claims (1937, page 697): 'The propositions set forth have been based upon facts, and direct references to the sources for these facts have been given throughout in footnotes. That the phenomena with which the study has been concerned happen to be the theories that certain writers have held about other phenomena does not alter matters.' But, though the 'action frame of reference' associated with Parsons requires the analyst to look at things through the eyes of the actor, candour compels a degree of dissent from Parsons's self-estimation. For, while the heroes, the proto-Parsonians such as Durkheim and Weber, are well-documented, the villains are not. Yet the argument of the book requires that their villainy be thoroughly established so that we can fully appreciate the rescue of distressed social theory from their clutches by the heroes.

Thus, Parsons's treatment of Hobbes, whose 'problem' provides the 'main thread' (page 91) for the whole book, is far from satisfactory. When the point arrives at which Parsons might logically be expected to say what Hobbes's own 'solution' is, and to show in what ways it is defective, he is remarkably evasive. He merely says that it 'is not the solution in which the present study will be interested' and that 'a genuine solution of it has never been attained on a strictly utilitarian basis' (page 93). From a later footnote (page 97), it appears that Parsons believes there is for Hobbes no 'element of normative order' other than 'fear of governmental coercion'. But in fact Hobbes held that men might be motivated by a quite refined moral code (Thomas, 1965, Goldsmith, 1966, pages 79–82, and Oakeshott, 1962, pages 288–94). What he did insist on is that no society can rely solely on restraints of this kind, and therefore centralized coercion is a necessary (though not sufficient condition) of social peace (Barry, 1968). As far as I know, this conclusion was not challenged by Pareto, Durkheim or Weber for the kind of large-scale society with which Hobbes was concerned.[3]

[3] For recent quasi-deductive statements of a Hobbesian position see Hart, 1961, pages 189–95, and Lucas, 1966, pages 1–10. Empirical evidence abounds, the Congo after the departure of the Belgians being the clearest modern example. It is perhaps worth emphasising this: when Hobbes said that in the absence of government the life of man would

Parsons himself believes that it is not a necessary condition. He describes as a 'correct insight' the view that he attributes to Locke, that 'most societies would not dissolve into chaos on the breakdown of government' (page 97, fn. 1). This is, of course, an enormously revealing comment, for it places Parsons on the extreme 'tender' side of the 'tough–tender' continuum (Eysenck, 1954) with anarchists such as William Godwin and William Morris.[4]

It would be difficult to over-emphasise the importance of Parsons's predilections in this matter for the development of modern sociology, including political sociology. The manifest content of *The Structure of Social Action* is: 'Some people (the "utilitarians" especially) have implied that values and norms don't matter. Others (notably Pareto, Durkheim and Weber) have said that they do; and I agree with them.' But, though logically there is a big gap between saying values and norms have some effect and saying they have a dominant effect, psychologically Parsons and those whom he has influenced always seem to have found it imperceptibly small.

Indeed, in an extraordinary passage, Parsons writes: 'A normative orientation is fundamental to the schema of action in the same sense that space is fundamental to that of classical mechanics; in terms of the given conceptual scheme there is no such thing as action except as effort to conform with norms just as there is no such thing as motion except as change of location in space. In both cases the propositions are definitions or logical corollories of definitions' (page 77). He goes on to say that he is not raising 'the question whether human behaviour is "really" normatively oriented', and in his Conclusion he claims only that 'the action frame of reference is certainly one of those in which certain of the facts of human action can be for certain scientific purposes adequately

---

be 'poor, nasty, brutish and short' he was referring not just to actual violence but to the probability that uncertainty would discourage investment (Hobbes, 1946, Chapter 13). Thus, as recent African cases illustrate, one of the commonest results of the breakdown of government is famine a year later, due to non-planting of crops.

[4] Locke himself always emphasised the great 'inconveniences' of an absence of government, and said it was an 'ill condition'. Moreover, he relied, for its not being worse than it was, not so much on internalized restraints but on a primitive informal system of punishment (Locke, 1960, Chapter 2).

described. It is not the only one of which this is true, but the critical results of this study show that, for certain purposes, which cannot but be considered scientifically legitimate, it is more adequate than any of the alternative frames of reference which have been considered here, such as the natural science schema of space-time and the idealistic schema' (Parsons, 1937, page 756).

But the victory over the 'utilitarian' schema is an empty one, because Parsons's 'utilitarians' are men of straw. Utilitarianism is usually understood to be the doctrine that actions, laws, institutions etc. are to be evaluated according to the goodness of the state of affairs they bring about, or, more specifically, according to their tendency to bring about a greater net amount of pleasure or happiness than any feasible alternative. Parsons does not adopt this usage (on which, incidentally, Hobbes would not be a utilitarian) but treats 'utilitarianism' as a psychological theory, according to which human action consists of the 'rational' pursuit of 'random' ends. Unfortunately, Parsons never succeeds in making it clear what he means, by giving detailed examples.[5] 'Rationality' apparently means the application of the best available scientific knowledge to the pursuit of one's ends. However, it is not clear who Parsons believes ever held this 'objective' view of rationality, except ironically, Pareto with his conception of 'logical' action. Certainly, the concept of rationality employed by our 'economic' theorists does not entail that an actor's information be correct.

More mysterious, though, is the second notion, of 'random' ends. Parsons writes (page 59): 'If the concrete system be considered as analysable exclusively into rational unit acts it follows that though the conception of action as consisting in the pursuit of ends is fundamental, there is nothing in the theory dealing with the relations of the ends to each other, but only with the character of the means–end relationship. If the conceptual scheme is not consciously "abstract" but is held to be literally descriptive of concrete reality, at least so far as the latter is "important", this gap is of great significance. For the failure to state anything positive about the relations

[5] See Parsons, 1937, pages 51–60 and 86–107. For a recent treatment in essay form, which contains much the same ideas, see Parsons, 1967, pages 166–91.

of ends to each other can have only one meaning—that there are no significant relations, that is, that ends are random in the statistical sense'; or, again, that ends 'varied at random relative to the means–end relationship and its central component, the actor's knowledge of his situation' (page 63). The nearest we get to an example is the comment that 'Hobbes' system of social theory is almost a pure case of utilitarianism. . . . The basis of human action lies in the "passions". These are discrete, randomly variant ends of action, "There is no common-rule of good and evil to be taken from the nature of the objects themselves". In the pursuit of these ends men act rationally, choosing, within the limitations of the situation, the most efficient means. But this rationality is strictly limited; reason is the "servant of the passions"; it is concerned only with questions of ways and means' (page 91).

This is unpromisingly vague and poorly expressed; but, through the mists, I think several points emerge, some better than others. First, Parsons is right to insist on the difference between a deliberate over-simplification (often, as we have seen, called a 'model' by economists) and a purported 'complete description'.[6] Most 'economic' theories exclude factors which may in fact be important, and Parsons himself, as we have noted, claims only that the 'action frame of reference' enables *some* social phenomena to be stated. The constant danger is, of course, that the factors excluded by the theory will tend to be discounted when explanations are given of real-life events. Thus, for example, we have seen that Olson underestimates the modifications to his 'economic' theory that would be required before we would have an adequate explanation of the prevalence and intensity of action directed to collective goals.

By the same token, it must be said that Parsons has not subsequently heeded his own good advice. When he writes articles about actual social phenomena (voting, stratification,

[6] We need not worry here about the philosophical question whether any description can be 'complete'. There are plenty of cases where someone leaves out of a theoretical construction some factor that he knows perfectly well plays some part in the working of the phenomenon he is trying to analyse, because he thinks it would complicate things too much to include it. A physical example would be the exclusion of atmospheric drag from the calculation of free fall of objects to earth.

power, McCarthyism and so on) he often says that he is doing so from the standpoint of the theory of action, but this qualification (if such it is conceived as) does not lead him to indicate that the 'theory of action', with its built-in assumption that all human behaviour is normatively regulated, may happen to be capable of capturing only a tiny part of the phenomenon in question.[7]

Parsons's followers have tended to follow his practice rather than his theory, without expressing even the ritualistic *caveat* that a 'frame of reference' is a long way from a universal truth. This is particularly interesting in the case of the hybrid subject, political sociology. In his Conclusion (page 768) Parsons writes that 'the solution of the power question, as well as of a plurality of other complex features of social action systems, involves a common reference to the fact of individuals with reference to [*sic*] a common value system, manifested in the legitimacy of institutional norms, in the common ultimate ends of action, in ritual and in various modes of expression. . . . "[C]ommon-value integration" . . . is a clearly marked emergent property readily distinguishable from both the economic and the political. If this property is designated the sociological, sociology may then be defined as "the science which attempts to develop an analytical theory of social action systems in so far as these systems can be understood in terms of the property of common-value integration." ' This would presumably make political sociology the study of political phenomena in so far as they can be understood in terms of common-value integration. Much contemporary political sociology does indeed make a great deal of play with common-value integration, or consensus. But the idea that this is a partial study only, and that 'in so far' may not be very far, is not found.

Returning to the quotation about 'utilitarianism', there is another point which is valid, but not in the form stated by Parsons. It is quite true that economists and, for some purposes of political analysis, utilitarians such as Bentham, often take wants as given, and concentrate on the consequences of people's attempting to satisfy these wants. But Parsons then

[7] See, for more detailed critiques of Parsons on this point, Dahrendorf, 1958, Dahrendorf, 1959, pages 159–65, Lockwood, 1956, Wrong, 1961, and Rex, 1961, pages 103–12.

comments that 'if the conceptual scheme is not consciously "abstract" . . .' it is in trouble; and he seems to assume that 'economists' do meet the conditions set in the 'if' clause. I doubt whether this has in fact been at all frequent; but, in any case, even if some writers have (like Parsons himself) fallen into the 'fallacy of misplaced concreteness', what relevance has this kind of personal failing for the adequacy of the 'utilitarian' conceptual scheme? Consider the 'utilitarian' position as a deliberate abstraction, in which wants (or 'ends') are taken as given. The corpus of economic theory based on this is, in my view, much more impressive in its rigour and fertility than the sociological theory based on Parsons's 'normative' abstraction.

Now let us take up Parsons's other line, that, considered as an account of all 'important' aspects of real life, the 'utilitarian' approach simply cannot say anything about the ends themselves, except that they are 'statistically random'. Or, more precisely, if an attempt is made to say more about the provenance of the ends, Parsons suggests, it must reduce them to either a function of the situation or to biological drives (1937, pages 64-5, 67-9, 82-4; cf. Rex, 1961, page 97). Considering how often Parsons repeats this (both in 1937 and in 1967, pages 3-34), it is notable how little he discusses the ideas about the provenance of ends which 'utilitarians' actually put forward. If anything, his argument seems to rest on a mere definitional *fiat*: any answer other than those he mentions is not really utilitarian.

Now, the psychological theory adhered to by most 'utilitarians' (such as Bentham and both Mills) was Hartley's 'associationism'. This is probably best described as a forerunner of modern so-called 'learning theory' (see, for example, Skinner, 1953) in that it explains the origins of most likes and dislikes by saying that anything which is frequently associated with something 'naturally' painful comes to be disliked itself, and vice versa. This conception of 'operant conditioning' may not have won universal acceptance, but it is obviously possible within it to provide an explanation (whether correct or not) of the way in which ends are acquired.

The nearest that Parsons gets to discussing the psychological views of a particular utilitarian is in the passage on

Hobbes previously quoted (1937, page 90) where he says that the 'passions' are 'discrete, randomly variant ends of action' and quotes Hobbes's statement that 'There is no common rule of good and evil to be taken from the nature of the objects themselves'. But this is a statement by Hobbes of what is now sometimes called 'value non-cognitivism' (see Oppenheim, 1968, and Nowell-Smith, 1954, Chapter 3), that is, the view that the goodness or badness of objects is not simply something inherent in them like their shape or weight, but depends on human interests and choices. If human beings were different, different things might be called good and bad. But to say that ends are the product of desire and sentiment and not of knowledge is not to say that they are 'random'. If this is the view Parsons takes, he is obviously in the grip of the kind of rationalistic fallacy that leads some people to want to say choices are 'arbitrary' if we cannot say they are true or false. And, incidentally, he would be upholding a position (the denial of 'value-non-cognition') which might well have been repudiated by his heroes.

3 PARSONS ON NORMS AND VALUES

Undoubtedly, the most serious charge against 'utilitarianism', which does not occur in the general statement of complaint quoted on pages 79–80, but does occur frequently elsewhere, is that it cannot solve the Hobbesian 'problem of order' because it cannot allow for the existence of values and norms, whereas the 'solution' in fact rests on the presence in all societies of a 'common value system'. There are, clearly, a number of assertions here. To begin with, is it true that 'utilitarianism' cannot allow for values and norms? Only, as far as I can see, if this is made true by definition.[8] Actual 'utilitarians' (even on Parsons's eccentric definition in terms of psychological premises) have found little difficulty in accommodating values and norms, nor is there any reason why they should not have done, for on associationist premises it is easy to see how children might be conditioned so that anti-social behaviour is

---

[8] The reader may well have felt suspicious of the wording of Parsons's statement of his case, quoted on page 77, that 'a *genuine* solution of [the 'Hobbesian problem'] has never been attained on a *strictly* utilitarian basis' (italics supplied).

associated with painful experiences, and 'values' of a social kind developed.[9]

If we look at those who, abstracting from the full complexities, take the wants of actors as given, we get the same answer: no problem. If an economist wishes to analyse a certain market taking the tastes for goods as given, he need not ask whether the demand schedule is the result of religious prohibitions, social approval, promptings of conscience, or any other 'normative' factor. So, too, Homans can introduce the social value of just distribution and the individual value of 'integrity' (roughly, doing what you think right) into his 'economic' analysis of social behaviour simply by making them additional bases for rewards and costs (Homans, 1961, pages 96–7 and 232–3).

Against this, however, we have to allow that (as we saw in Chapter II), although it is always possible formally to square norms with an 'economic' analysis by saying that violating the norm is costly, this may, where the norms are so stringent as to leave little latitude in compliance, leave nothing much for an 'economic' analysis of interactions between people to do. We finish up by saying, in effect, 'they do it because they believe they should', and all we can do then is go back to an account of how they came to believe that. Obviously, an alternative approach would be welcome here if it enabled us to say more. Unfortunately, the 'theory of action' does little more than enable us to say the same thing in different (and, if anything, less illuminating) words.

The two other assertions of Parsons that need to be examined are, first that 'utilitarians' cannot explain the existence of 'social order', and, second, that 'common value integration' can. The first need not detain us for long. In so far as 'normative' factors are required to explain 'social order', they can be (as we have just seen) invoked within a 'utilitarian' framework. It may be that actual 'utilitarians' have tended to play down such elements at the expense of material advantages, such as the avoidance of legal sanctions. But this brings us again to the empirical question of how much weight really *should* be given to 'normative' factors.

[9] See, for a clear exposition of this viewpoint, James Mill's *Essay on Education* (Mill, J., 1828). See also John Stuart Mill's discussion of the 'internal sanction' of morality (Mill, J. S., 1861, Chapter 3).

The second point is rather more complicated. It could mean that 'common value integration' is a necessary and sufficient condition of 'social order'. This would imply that, whatever other conditions obtain, so long as you have the first you will get the second. It would also imply that, whatever other conditions obtain, where you don't have the first you won't get the second. If, within the 'action frame of reference', 'there is no such thing as action except as effort to conform with norms', it is hard to see how we can avoid drawing the conclusion that 'common value integration' (provided the values are the right ones, of course) would be enough. But this merely pushes the question back one stage further, to the empirical adequacy of the framework: if we make those assumptions how far will we get? Parsons himself appears to believe that non-sanctioned norms would as a matter of fact be enough. I have already mentioned that he calls it a 'correct insight' of Locke that 'most societies would not dissolve into chaos on the breakdown of government' (see above, page 78), and perhaps the exceptions are conceived of as those not possessing an appropriate 'common value integration'.

If, however, we consider this implausible, as I have suggested, we might ignore the rigidities of the 'action frame of reference', and simply assess the weaker claim that 'common value integration' is a necessary (though not a sufficient) condition of 'social order', in other words that you do need it, but you need other things as well.[10] To be testable this would have to be stated so as to enable us to recognise a 'common value integration' when we saw one, and would also have to specify some *level* of 'integration' which was necessary. (It would also, of course, have to say how we recognise social order and, again, *how much* of it we are talking about.) An alternative, more

[10] There seems little doubt that Parsons holds at least this. See his recent statement: 'I start with a view that repudiates the idea that any political system that rests entirely on self-interest, force, or a combination of them, can be stable over any considerable period of time' (Parsons, 1967, pages 264–96). See also a recent remark which seems to go even further in devaluing force: 'Resources are inherently scarce relative to demands for their use; and benefits and obligations are differentially distributed to interest groups. To resolve these grounds of conflict two basic factors are needed: persuasion that the relevant subgoal is urgent for the collectivity as a whole and persuasion that shifts in the benefit-burden balance are fair' (Parsons, 1966, page 89).

plausible, formulation would be to say that within certain limits (which would have to be specified) one could substitute 'common value integration' for other things (such as coercion) and vice versa. To be testable, this would require a more elaborate quantification of 'integration' than that required for the simple 'on/off' formula; and it would also require a metric for the substitutable factors. Otherwise the theory would be reminiscent of Voltaire's remark that you can kill a flock of sheep with curses so long as you also give them enough arsenic at the same time.

4 VALUES AND SOCIAL ORDER

Let us take up this question whether 'common value integration' is a necessary condition for 'social order'. The answer cannot be discovered unless we know what is to count as a relevant amount of each. But, although some variant of this idea seems to have become almost a part of the 'conventional wisdom' among American political sociologists, little seems to have been done to provide operational measures of the crucial variables. Roughly speaking, 'social order' becomes 'stability' in the recent literature, and tends to be equated with the infrequency of unconstitutional changes of régime; but this is hardly the centre of Hobbesian 'social order', which is more concerned with the general issue of the control of violence and the fulfilment of expectations. 'Common value integration' appears as 'consensus' on certain values etc. The biggest problem here is what degree of agreement on what matters and at what level of generality is to count as consensus?

To prove a negative, however, requires only that we find a case where 'social order' exists without 'common value integration', and if we can find one that is sufficiently extreme, the finer points of definition need not matter. South Africa seems a plausible example of such a case. Although the society may be held together by more than pure repression, it seems hard to maintain that what keeps it going is 'common value integration'. (See Van den Berghe, 1963 and 1965.) Other quite persuasive contemporary examples might be drawn from any East European state, but I suspect that many past empires would provide examples at least as vivid.

The objection may, of course, be made that these are not

really cases of 'social order', that they are not 'stable over a considerable period of time' to quote Parsons. But how long is a 'considerable period'? Surely, the 'common value integration' thesis falls provided a social form lasts long enough to show it is not a mere flash in the pan. I do not see how it can be denied that these societies are 'stable' unless 'common value integration' is included in the definition of 'stability', in which case, of course, the whole thesis becomes trivial. The alternative would be to take some society which was unquestionably 'stable', and ask if it showed the postulated amount of 'common value integration'. This would involve much more work, but we might still find that Rex is correct in maintaining that no complex society contains the basis for this kind of consensus on values (Rex, 1961, page 114).

We can, however, reflect on the work discussed in the previous chapter. The writers we examined there were asking what are the normative conditions for 'stable democracy', where the relationship is conceived as one in which, other things being equal, a more favourable set of 'political orientations' among the citizens will make for a higher degree of 'stable democracy'. So far in the present chapter we have been speaking about 'social order' or 'stability' without reference to the kind of régime. This reflects the fact that Parsons is concerned with a 'frame of reference' suitable for the analysis of all societies: every society has to solve the same 'problems' in order to stay in business, and in every society the same 'exchanges' between 'boundary-maintaining' sub-systems must take place. Most of these observations are so metaphorical that it is difficult to know how to take them—the 'exchanges', for example, have such an abstract quality that it would be difficult to say whether they were occurring or not, while the idea of trying to reduce them to common units, so as to be able to say whether the exchanges were equal or not, is mind-boggling in the extreme. But since Parsons does not, in his expositions of the 'system', distinguish between different kinds of polity, the same processes (at the Parsonian level of abstraction) presumably take place in all. The other writers of our 'sociological' school do not take such a satellite's view of societies as does Parsons. They accept the Parsonian emphasis on values and norms, but instead of simply saying that every society must have suitable ones in order to be stable, they ask which a society must have if it is to be a stable *democracy*. This is, of course, a more limited question; but, as we saw in the previous chapter, that does not make it a simple one.

What conclusions can we draw from the detailed critique which was performed in Chapter III? Not, perhaps, very encouraging ones. All the pieces of work examined ran into three difficulties which, between them, cover a depressingly wide area. First, there were difficulties in defining the concepts: what is a 'democracy' or a 'stable democracy'? And what precisely are the values said to be conducive to it? Second, there were difficulties about the formulation of the hypotheses: if certain values are conducive to stable democracy, how much additional strength of the appropriate values must there be to compensate for a given size of deficiency in other respects, and vice versa? Finally, there were difficulties of evidence, and these were of two kinds. One involved the problem of establishing the existence of the relevant values in the population without simply redescribing their actual behaviour, which, in a democratic country, is presumably in some sense democratic by definition. The other was the problem that, even if the existence of the values could be independently established, this would still be a long way from giving convincing support to the hypothesis. For it would still remain to be shown that the causal connection ran from the values to the democratic set-up. Two obvious alternative explanations of the same empirical association would be (i) that the causal linkage goes in the other direction, in other words that democratic institutions produce democratic values, or (ii) that some common cause gives rise to both.

A question is inevitably posed by this brief account of the difficulties we found in our examination of the three theories linking democratic institutions to certain values. We must ask whether the whole attempt to explain phenomena in terms of values is mistaken, or whether, by taking more care and perhaps following different procedures, the difficulties encountered so far could be obviated. One encouraging pointer is the fact that the authors whose work we looked at met the various problems with differing degrees of success, for this suggests that there is scope for further development.

We can see this particularly clearly in relation to our first difficulty, about the definition of terms. Thus, the definitions of 'democracy' ranged from the extraordinary omission of any consideration of the matter by Almond and Verba, through Eckstein's elaborate, but confused and inconsistent, treatment of the subject, to Lipset's short definition, in terms of competitive elections, and clear (if slightly tendentious) list of countries. The discussion of the allegedly relevant values also varied in quality, with Almond and Verba making it fairly clear what their 'civic culture' consisted in, and Lipset this time at the bottom, failing to put into operational terms such distinctions as the élitism–equalitarianism one.

Our second difficulty, that the hypothesis was not put in sufficiently precise terms to be tested, applies more evenly to all three theories, but it still seems to me something that at least in principle could be improved. The development of indices of 'democratic institutions' and 'civic culture', for example, does not seem inherently impossible, since it seems to make perfect sense to speak of more or less of them in a country, and of much more or much less. This is not, however, to underestimate the task of actually doing the job satisfactorily.

The third difficulty, about evidence for any hypothesis of the kind we are considering, raises some general issues that are worth discussion, and I shall devote most of the remainder of the chapter to them. For, obviously, if it is impossible to imagine getting adequate evidence, the case against using 'values' to explain phenomena is made. I mentioned earlier that the difficulty about evidence is twofold: first, there is the problem of establishing the existence of the values independently of the behaviour they are used to explain, and, second, there is the problem of showing that an association between certain values and certain institutions comes about as a result of the right sort of causal link. I shall take up these points in turn.

5 VALUES AS EXPLANATIONS

The strongest form of the argument against the possibility of values as explanations is that by definition the evidence for a 'value' is simply a description of the behaviour it is then used to 'explain'. On this view explanations in terms of values 'are logically the same as the famous explanation of the effects of opium as being due to its "dormitive" qualities' (Moore, 1966, page 240). The passage continues in a way suggesting that Moore really has in mind another objection, which will be discussed at the end of this chapter. But could the thesis be maintained as stated? The argument in support would, I think, run as follows: to say someone has certain values is to say that he will behave in various ways, so you cannot explain his behaviour in terms of his values. Possessing a value is thus, on such a view, a dispositional property; and as such it would fall under Ryle's discussion of character traits and why they cannot be causes of action (Ryle, 1949). To say a man got angry because he is an irascible man is like saying a piece of glass broke because it is brittle, which in turn is like the opium example. Similarly, to say that someone defers to members of the aristocracy because he has ascriptive values is simply to invoke the generalisation that he does things like that as an explanation of his doing that sort of thing in a particular case.

But there is an answer to this. It can be replied that having a value is not just a *tendency* to do things of a certain kind. It means also believing that it is *right* to do these things. Saying opium has the *virtus dormitiva* is saying no more than that it has a tendency to put people to sleep. But saying someone has values that make him deferential is not merely saying that he tends to behave in a deferential fashion. Rather, it is giving one kind of explanation rather than another. For example, it conflicts with the explanation that he behaves deferentially solely out of a fear of sanctions for lack of forelock-touching.

There is, however, a weaker form that the objection may take. It might be allowed that the distinction between values and behaviour can be made conceptually, but it might still be maintained that it is practically unavoidable to fall back on behaviour as evidence. Thus, we arrive once again, but this time by a more indirect route, at a charge of tautology. This point is made by Judith Blake and Kingsley Davis in an article on 'Norms, Values and Sanctions' (Blake, 1964, page 104): '. . . the difficulty of proving the existence of the norm is great. As a consequence there is a tendency to take regularities in behaviour as the evidence of the norm. When this is done, to explain the behaviour in terms of the norm is a redundancy. Seen in this light, statements such as the following are also redundant: "Knowledge of a culture makes it possible to predict a good many of the actions of any person who shares that culture." Why not simply say: "Knowledge of behaviour in a society makes it possible to predict behaviour in that society"?' I think this criticism can be levelled against Lipset with some justification. The evidence for the values which he imputes to people in different countries is not about the things children are taught to value, the explanations and justifications of behaviour that are actually offered, the terms in which rebukes are administered, and so on but is, simply, the behaviour to be explained.

It should, however, be pointed out that there is nothing logically wrong in inferring values from behaviour, as the famous opening sentence of Hare's *The Language of Morals* illustrates: 'If we were to ask of a person "What are his moral principles?" the way in which we could be most sure of a true answer would be by studying what he *did*' (Hare, 1952, page 1). The only trouble is that a single action may be premised on any number of possible reasons, and the quickest (though not *necessarily* the most accurate) way of finding out is to ask the actor. For example, a working class man may vote for a Conservative candidate for any number of reasons, and it would be quite wrong to assume that we can use this as evidence by itself of a 'deferential' vote cast on 'ascriptive' value-premises. On the other hand, if we had enough information about the way he chose to act in other situations we might be willing to say that he was a 'deferential' voter; and we might even be prepared still to say this if he denied it. For example, he might say that he was moved by the (apparently achievement-oriented) criterion of educational qualifications, but that the Conservative front bench had greater educational qualifications than the Labour front bench. (This is a quite genuine example of a not uncommon survey response.) If so, one might, on the basis of other information about him, say that although 'education' sounds an achievement-oriented notion, his ascriptive outlook had led him to use as a criterion of 'good education' things such as attendance at a public school and the possession of an 'educated' accent.

G

Whether values are inferred from behaviour which is in accordance with them, whether they emerge from teaching and reacting to behaviour, or whether they are discovered by direct enquiry, they are not *simply* the restatement of tendencies to act in certain ways. People may do things for other reasons than the pursuit of their values, provided of course that 'values' can be distinguished as a sub-class of 'goals', and I think they can. Thus, I should be inclined to say that there is no insuperable difficulty in establishing the existence of values, even if recourse is made quite extensively to observations of behaviour; and that explanations couched in terms of values are not thereby automatically rendered tautological. But our discussion does suggest that the job of establishing the existence of certain values among a population is a formidable one, and certainly cannot be done in the anecdotal fashion beloved of writers such as Lipset and Eckstein.

6 THE PROBLEM OF CAUSAL INFERENCE

The other difficulty of evidence is simply that of ever showing convincingly that certain values are the cause of certain phenomena. The most straightforward case is where there are two factors operative, one involving values and the other not, and it is claimed that the former is of paramount importance. A neat example may be drawn from Max Weber (1965, page 249), who sets himself the following question: 'How does one explain the fact that no pious Jew succeeded in establishing an industry employing pious Jewish workers of the ghetto (as so many pious Puritan entrepreneurs had done with devout Christian workers and artisans) at times when numerous proletarians were present in the ghettoes, princely patents and privileges for the establishment of any sort of industry were available for a substantial remuneration, and areas of industrial activity uncontrolled by guild monopoly were open?' Weber divides the answers into two sorts. First there were 'external' difficulties: difficulties in organising labour and difficulties in obtaining sufficient security against expropriation to make investment in capital goods worthwhile. Second, and apparently considered by Weber as more important, was the cultural difficulty that, whereas dealings with non-Jews were considered a matter of ethical indifference, dealings with co-religionists were a matter of merit, and this inhibited adopting a 'businesslike' approach to them.

How could one hope to settle this question? There is no chance of a clinching demonstration, but evidence of various kinds would be relevant. Thus, if it could be made plausible that the 'external' difficulties would not have been sufficient by themselves to prevent production, the case for giving weight to the 'cultural' difficulty would be increased; conversely, if the 'external' difficulties were enough, the answer must be either inconclusive or (if there is other evidence) it must be that the 'cultural' factor was of less importance. Alternatively, one can resort to indirect evidence from other situations, comparable in some respect or another: thus, it might be pointed out that Jews successfully have engaged in industry employing other Jews both in the New York garment industry and in Israel; conversely, other examples of business failure in societies where there are broad obligations to others might be found. Clearly, supporting material might well be gathered on both sides, but this is true of most things. The important point is that rational discussion of such a question, with canons of evidence, is a possibility.

Another difficulty which bedevils most attempts to employ values in explanation, and has in fact cropped up a number of times already, is the problem of circularity. The characteristic 'sociological' view of the way values are formed reduces this difficulty to a minimum, but it is necessary to ask whether this view is itself acceptable. Parsons has written that 'among the learned elements of personality in certain respects the stablest and most enduring are the major value-orientation patterns and there is much evidence that these are "laid down" in childhood and are not on a large scale subject to drastic alteration during adult life' (Parsons, 1951, page 208). In line with this, Almond and Verba work on the assumption that people have mental sets towards, say, authority relationships, which are formed during childhood socialisation. Hence their attempt to link respondents' recollections of the way family decisions were taken with attitudes to government. Answers to questions such as the one about the chance of changing a government policy are not regarded as rational estimates of the true state of affairs, so much as projections of the underlying disposition towards all authority. (Notice in this connection that 'citizen competence' is defined purely in terms of such an attitude—it has nothing to do with actually being competent at anything.) The theory which embodies this kind of assumption can be set out schematically as follows:

SOCIALISATION ——▶ BASIC ATTITUDES

INSTITUTIONS

DEMOCRATIC STABILITY

Attitudes are thus fed into the political system from another part of the social system, and, in conjunction with the actual institutions (we need not ask at the moment where *they* come from), either produce or do not produce democratic stability. But it seems very hard to accept such a simple model. As we observed in Chapter III, there is surely a case for thinking that the reality of the régime may have some effect on attitudes towards régimes of that type.[11, 12] One way of representing this schematically would be as follows:

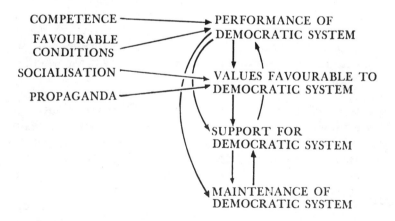

COMPETENCE ——▶ PERFORMANCE OF DEMOCRATIC SYSTEM

FAVOURABLE CONDITIONS

SOCIALISATION ——▶ VALUES FAVOURABLE TO DEMOCRATIC SYSTEM

PROPAGANDA

SUPPORT FOR DEMOCRATIC SYSTEM

MAINTENANCE OF DEMOCRATIC SYSTEM

---

[11] As in the inconclusive debate in the nineteen-fifties about whether there had been a change in American values (see Lipset, 1964, and Kluckhohn, 1958), a lot of time can be wasted in shadow-boxing over the question whether something is sufficiently fundamental to count as a 'value'. Obviously, Parsons's apparently empirical assertion about the

It is noteworthy what a relatively minor part values play in this scheme as determinants of system maintenance. But they are still there; and in a circular relationship. For system performance has an effect on values. System performance also has an effect on the level of support, both directly and through its effect on values. At the same time, however, the level of support affects the performance of the system. This sort of postulated circularity seems only too plausible, for surely one would expect support both to affect and be affected by the performance of the régime. It is in fact the basic political virtuous circle or, where it goes wrong, vicious circle. But the very fact that we can recognise its working suggests that we need not write off any circular process like this as completely beyond the reach of empirical check.

There is, however, a great distance between an intuitive feeling that many things affect many others and a serious attempt to estimate *how much* part a given factor (say, values) plays in the processes. 'If each of the hypothetical changes were to occur discretely, with a long enough interval between each change for the observer to note the temporal sequences involved, then the various contributions of each factor could be sorted out. But in reality most such changes occur either almost simultaneously or continuously rather than discretely. To make matters worse, in many non-experimental situations the observations are taken at a single point in time or at relatively infrequent intervals' (Blalock, 1968, page 163). Blalock notes that, where the theory is set out in words rather than in mathematical form, 'the theorist may dismiss the matter as merely a problem for empirical research' instead of recognising it for the methodological crux that it is. Perhaps the

---

childhood origin and later immutability of values could be made true by definition if everything else is ruled out as not fundamental enough. But then one has to ask how important values in *this* sense really are in the determination of adult behaviour.

[12] This presupposes that the system is itself (regarded as) democratic. A general version would be:

PERFORMANCE OF EXISTING SYSTEM

VALUES FAVOURABLE TO EXISTING SYSTEM

SUPPORT FOR EXISTING SYSTEM

MAINTENANCE OF EXISTING SYSTEM

only consolation is to be drawn from the reflection that there is still an enormous distance to go before we arrive even at the alternative which Blalock dismisses as 'a qualitative listing of the various supposed effects of each variable, with perhaps a rough guess of the weight each should receive'.

7 HOW IMPORTANT ARE VALUES?

There is one other objection to the use of values as explanations which is so important and fundamental that it must be examined before the chapter is closed. This objection is not concerned with the definition of the terms, the statement of the hypotheses or the question of evidence. It undercuts all of them by saying: suppose you have established a causal connection, so what? Values are at best the last link in the chain of causation before behaviour itself. They are not independent variables. A good explanation may incorporate values as intervening variables but then the values themselves must be explained. Thus the passage in Moore from which I quoted just the reference to the *virtus dormitiva* runs in full as follows: 'The failure of the Japanese merchant class to develop a critical intellectual standpoint comparable to that produced in the West cannot, in my opinion, be explained through psychological factors or some peculiar efficacy of the Japanese value system. Such explanations are logically the same as the famous explanation of the effects of opium as being due to its "dormitive" properties. They beg the fundamental question: *why* did this particular outlook prevail when and where it did?' (Moore, 1966, page 240).

As this quotation makes clear, Moore is willing to allow that one can talk intelligibly of a 'value system'. But he emphasises that value systems don't just happen: they are caused. 'To maintain and transmit a value system, human beings are punched, bullied, sent to jail, thrown into concentration camps, cajoled, bribed, made into heroes, encouraged to read newspapers, stood up against a wall and shot, and sometimes even taught sociology. To speak of cultural inertia is to overlook the concrete interests and privileges that are served by indoctrination, education, and the entire complicated process of transmitting culture from one generation to the next' (Moore, 1966, page 486). More explicitly, value-systems are maintained because it pays people in some way to ensure that they are: 'In a general way we know that human attitudes and beliefs fail to persist unless the situations and sanctions that reproduce them continue to persist, or, more crassly, unless people get something out of them' (Moore, 1966, page 335). Thus, to complete the first quotation, 'the answer to the question is historical: the conditions under which the Japanese merchant class grew up from the seventeenth century onwards. The isolation of the country, the symbiotic relationship between the warrior and the merchant, and the long political dominance of the warrior would seem to constitute the essential elements in any explanation of the merchants' limited horizon' (Moore, 1966, pages 240–1).

It seems to me quite easy to agree that 'values' or 'culture' should always be regarded as being themselves capable, at least in principle, of explanation. But this does not mean that they are therefore bogus explanations. If I arrive late for an appointment because I missed my train, this is an explanation even though one could add that I missed my train because I overslept, overslept because I stayed up late the previous night, stayed up late . . . and so on as far back as time and patience permit. However, Moore's claim is the much stronger one that the same kind of explanation can always be offered for any instance of 'values' or 'culture', namely that it was in the interests of whoever inculcated them to do so. This is as if the only occasion on which I ever missed trains was when I overslept. If one were trying to set out the causes of my being late for appointments, it would be reasonable to say that one cause of my being late was oversleeping (which resulted among other things in missing trains). It would be redundant to include missing trains as a separate cause, because it never occurred except when oversleeping was an antecedent condition. Similarly, if Moore were correct, one might simply say that one explanation of the way people behave is that 'values' or 'culture' are inculcated according to the interests of those doing the inculcating: there is no need to treat them as separate variables because they never occur in any other form.

But Moore is surely wrong about this. Certainly 'inertia' is no good as an explanation of cultural continuity—it is merely a redescription of the phenomenon. Sometimes, however, the explanation may be something humdrum like the tendency of parents to bring up children with the same outlook as themselves, or, in some fundamental ways, to reproduce their own childhood. Moore might argue that this tendency will be overridden where there is a strong enough interest in doing so, on somebody's part; but there are too many exceptions for even this to be taken as a general truth. If we consider the parents themselves we might remark, first, that parents do not always even try to imbue their children with values favourable to their own interests (e.g. the absolute duty of contributing to one's parents' upkeep), and that in any case socialisation is by no means an entirely deliberate or conscious affair. As for other agencies, such as schools, there seem to be limits to what, in most societies, they can achieve without support from parents, and in any case such institutions often achieve some autonomy from pressures by the powerful. I conclude then, that 'values' and 'culture' are worth separate treatment as causal factors in any attempt to explain what people do. This is so even though it always makes sense to ask how these values came to take the form they do, and even though the answer will often involve a reference to the interests of those in a position to exert influence on them.

CHAPTER V

The Economic Theory of Democracy

1 THE DOWNSIAN MODEL INTRODUCED

In the preceding three chapters, examples have been given of the economic and the sociological approaches at work on topics relevant to studying the politics of democratic government. We have dealt so far with political participation and the conditions for the maintenance of a democratic political system. In this chapter and the following two, we shall be concerned with a single large theme: the analysis of party competition for votes in elections. The present chapter will be devoted to an exposition of the 'economic' theory of party competition put forward by Downs. The other two chapters will examine the empirical evidence relevant to the theory and compare it with the kind of analysis of voting given by Talcott Parsons and by other members as the 'sociological' school.

The general conception of democracy with which Downs begins is that it is a mechanism whereby political parties, which are engaged in what Schumpeter called a 'competitive struggle for the people's vote' (1950, page 269), are obliged to take account of the preferences of the electors for one policy rather than another or one kind of outcome rather than another. There is no need to assume that the political parties (the units of his analysis) are motivated by a direct desire to give the voters what policies they want to have. Rather the parties are led to do this as a means to furthering their primary aim, which is to maximise votes. The parallel with Adam Smith is quite close at this point: just as the baker provides us with bread not out of the goodness of his heart but in return for payment, so the politician supplies the

policies we want not to make us happy but to get our votes.[1]
And, in both cases, a 'hidden hand' disposes things so that
competition among the entrepreneurs prevents exploitation
of the consumers. The gap in the analogy is, of course, the
difference between the private goods sold by businessmen and
the public goods of state policies which politicians trade in,
and we have already seen in Chapter II how important that
difference can be.

Downs's book is complex, but for the purposes of the present discussion we may concentrate on two models: first, the
general two-party model and, second, the two-party model
with all the voters being capable of being ranked along a
single dimension or (the usual example) left-right spectrum.
We shall also look briefly at the multi-party variant of this
model. The idea underlying the general case is that the two
parties put together packages of policies with which they try
to attract voters. This model is developed only in the context
of an assumption that the parties have perfect information
about the preferences of the voters and the voters have perfect
information about the actual results of government party
policies and the hypothetical effect of opposition party alternative proposals.

Given this exceedingly strong assumption, Downs derives
a number of interesting results, notably that, if the government always has to commit itself on each issue before the
opposition does, it may well find it impossible to avoid being
beaten at the next election. For the government party must
always take the position favoured by a majority of the voters,
otherwise the opposition can always win by matching it (i.e.
taking the same side) on every issue except one on which the
government party favours a minority. On this one issue, the
opposition backs a majority instead and thus, obviously, wins
the election. But the government party, although it will certainly lose if it deviates from a policy of supporting the
majority, cannot necessarily stave off defeat by doing so, for
the opposition party may be able to win by following the

[1] 'Politically speaking, the man is still in the nursery who has not
absorbed, so as never to forget, the saying attributed to one of the most
successful politicians who ever lived: "What businessmen do not understand is that exactly as they are dealing in oil so I am dealing in votes" '
(Schumpeter, 1950, page 285).

minority position on two or more issues and putting together a coalition of minorities. Of course, this requires special conditions: (i) the members of the minorities must not be the same people each time: there can be some overlap but they must at least add up to a majority of the electorate altogether. And (ii), on the issues where the opposition backs the minority line, a majority of the voters must feel benefited on balance even though (necessarily, by condition (i)) some will be supporters of the majority position on some of the issues. This means that they must feel more strongly about the issues on which they are in the minority than on those where they are in the majority (Downs, 1957, pages 54–60).[2]

Although this kind of exercise has a certain intrinsic interest, it has little relevance to any real electoral system, as Downs himself acknowledges. Most of his book, therefore, allows for the phenomenon of imperfect and costly information. This affects the electorate directly, and affects the parties both directly (they do not have perfect knowledge about the electorate) and indirectly (they must take account in planning their strategies of the fact that the electors will be more or less ill-informed).

Downs argues that the logic of information costs is precisely the same as that of voting costs (or, rather, he develops the argument first for information costs and then extends it to voting costs). If the intention of a 'rational' elector must be to use his vote so as to influence governmental outputs, he must presumably have some idea as to the effects of one party winning rather than the other, and of the way in which these effects relate to his own interests and value-preferences. But the worth of information in enabling one to cast a better-directed vote must be discounted by the worth of the vote itself—in other words, the party differential times the probability that this single vote will alter the election result materially. Judged on these criteria, the value of political information will be vanishingly small. If it is not worth casting a vote how much less is it worth incurring the much greater costs of working out which way to cast it?

[2] The crucial asymmetry here is, of course, between 'going first' and 'going second' in the game of making policy-commitments (not between government and opposition as such). There are other kinds of situation in which it pays to go first (Schelling, 1960, pages 121–3).

Individuals may use various methods of reducing information costs, Downs suggests. They may enjoy getting a certain amount, and beyond that they may in effect delegate information-processing to others, whose values they think correspond to their own, and simply take over these people's opinions. But the parties also respond to information costs among the electors, by standing not just on bundles of policies but creating and maintaining 'ideologies'. These embody some sort of general socio-economic stance from which the party's particular policies are alleged to be deduced. It is rational for the parties to do this because it is rational for at least some of the voters to vote in terms of them. Thus, these people vote not on specific policies but on the 'images' (as they have sometimes been called) of the parties. This does not entail that the voter under no circumstances compares the 'image' with reality, but it does suggest that (since the whole object of working by 'images' is to save time) he will coast along most of the time monitoring the parties' stands on issues only sporadically, and giving the matter detailed attention (if at all) only when a large discrepancy seems to have opened up.

None of this analysis presupposes that the 'ideologies' of the parties can be placed on a continuum along which all the voters can be situated. This is a special assumption, which Downs makes in order to get some more definite results; but if it turned out to be ill-founded one would have to go back to the general model and try again. The point is perhaps worth emphasising because many people's only acquaintance with Downs may well be through the references to him found in the work of the 'Michigan school' of electoral analysis (Campbell, 1966, pages 161–79, 212–42 and Converse, 1965), who invariably write as if Downs had no theory except that of the ideological spectrum. It should be said, however, that Downs himself seems rather to assume that it is in the nature of 'ideologies' always to permit electors and parties in any given system to be placed on a continuum.

The assumption of a one-dimensional spectrum or continuum on which everyone can be located is, obviously, a very strong one, and provides the basis for some interesting results. If every eligible elector votes for the party nearer his own position on the spectrum, and the parties have perfect information about the electors, the two parties (which, we are already assuming, are trying to win elections) locate themselves right next to one another in such a way that each gets half the votes. If, for example, ninety-nine electors can be ranked along a 'left-right' continuum, numbered from 1 on the extreme left to 99 on the extreme right, the election will be won by the party which is closest to the position on the spectrum of elector number 50. Suppose party A takes up a position that coincides with that of elector 49: party B can win by taking a position coinciding with that of elector 50. For then elector 49 and all those to the left of him will vote for A, while elector 50 and all those to the right of him will vote for party B. B will therefore win by one vote. Conversely, if A takes up a position at 51, B can again trump it by taking up the position at 50. And if A deviates further from the centre, B can win by bigger majorities. For example, if A goes to 30, B can go to 31 and pick up the votes of 31 and all those to his right, thus winning by 69–30. (See Figure 1.)

FIGURE 1

PARTY POSITIONS

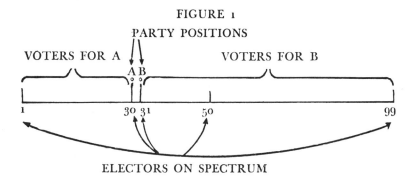

ELECTORS ON SPECTRUM

We can see, therefore, how, under the conditions postulated, parties will be forced to the centre—the centre, that is, of the electors, not necessarily of the spectrum itself.[3]

---

[3] This distinction presupposes that we are prepared to give a sense to the notion that electors can be put at different distances from one another in (say) leftness and rightness, rather than our merely being able to say one is more to the left than another. Most of Downs's treatment does require this assumption, though he at no point explains how the concept of distance (as against rank) could be operationalised.

We might indeed ask what there is to stop the two parties exactly coinciding at the position of elector number 50, and there may indeed be nothing. Thus, in the article in which the basic logic of spatial competition was worked out (Hotelling, 1929), the model was set up of a street with houses distributed with uniform density along its length. Each family buys at the nearest shop. If there are two shops, where will they locate if both are trying to maximise sales? Hotelling's answer is: next door to one another, half way along the street.[4] Smithies (1941) suggested adding transport costs, supposed to have the effect of making the amount spent an inverse function of distance from the nearest shop, and showed that this would give the shops a reason for moving from the centre, stronger the more marked were the effects of transport costs. Downs does not apply this directly to party competition by proposing that the probability of casting a vote might be inversely related to one's distance from the nearest party; but he does try to suggest ways in which differential abstention might force the parties away from the centre. We shall examine these ideas critically below when we consider the consequences of relaxing the assumption that everyone votes. Downs also argues that uncertainty gives rise to differentiation, and we shall also consider this when we look at the consequences of dropping certainty.

Short of relaxing these assumptions, there is still a way of introducing an incentive for the parties to keep a certain distance between them. It requires an amendment to one of Downs's fundamental premises, but this premise is open to improvement anyway. Downs, as was mentioned earlier, assumes that a party's aim is to maximise votes at the next election, and his analysis is at certain points based on this as against possible variants. But in introducing the assumption about party motivation he speaks more often of parties wishing to be elected or re-elected to form a government, and this is a slightly different point, for the two aims might conflict. Suppose that a party has two strategies open to it: one guarantees it 51% of the vote but is unlikely to produce more, the other will very probably give 70% but just might result

[4] Obviously, examples involving literal spatial relations do not permit the solution of identical position, but in another illustration taken by Hotelling, the sweetness of cider, identity would be technically possible.

in getting 49%. Obviously the 'expected value' (amount times probability) in votes of the second strategy is much higher than that of the first, but a party solely interested in winning elections would choose the first. On balance it seems more plausible to assume that a party would choose the first strategy.

There is also the restriction of the time-horizon to the next election which Downs implicitly accepts. As we shall see below, he allows for 'future-oriented' voters, who vote with long-run views of modifying the party-system, but why not allow for the same thing in parties? Adding these two things together we would say that parties are motivated by the desire to win as many elections as possible in the future (no doubt discounting success in the more distant elections at some appropriate rate). This would make the parties less given to speculative raids than a vote-maximising assumption might lead us to expect, and it would generally give a push towards cautiousness. A particular motive that we might attribute to parties (as a means to winning elections in the future and perhaps also as a separate end) is a strong desire to avoid the total electoral destruction of the party. This is again, of course, a deterrent to risk-taking and it provides the parties with a reason for not getting too close to one another.

An analysis of risk-taking in spatial competition has been undertaken by Boulding (1963), who points out that Hotelling's model turns on the assumption that the shops are competing solely on location. But if we allow for, say, price competition as well, a situation where the two shops are next to one another is pretty unstable. For suppose that people decide where to shop on a combination of nearness and price. Then, if the difference in nearness for any given customer is negligible, one of the competing shops will be able to get all the custom (and thus ruin the other) provided it can maintain its prices just a shade below those of its rival (Boulding, 1963, pages 75–6). Although Boulding does not discuss the relevance of this to political parties, it surely has some.[5] For the closer the parties become ideologically, the more people's votes are liable to turn on something other than ideology. But these other factors may well not have the same spread as ideological positions have. Rather, most

[5] For a 'viability' analysis of markets, which provides some interesting parallels, see Shubik, 1959.

electors may well think the same way on them, thus producing a much higher risk of one party's being virtually wiped out.

Downs suggests that voters would be rational to vote on performance if there is nothing to choose in issue-positions, and I think it is highly plausible to argue that the great volatility of the British electorate in the last six or so years, compared to the rest of the post-war period, is related to the increased tendency of the Labour and Conservative parties to drop their traditional appeals and concentrate on the question which can better achieve certain common goals, especially that of attaining economic growth and full employment without balance of payments crises. However, Downs admits also that, if otherwise indifferent, voters would be behaving with 'individual rationality' by voting 'for the party whose leader has the most charming personality' (page 275) though the results would be 'socially irrational'. Such voting does surely take place where parties are not ideologically distinct, and, again, there may be wide agreement on which party's candidate has the more charming personality, thus again introducing great volatility in elections. The best example of this is General Eisenhower's ability to win handsomely by means of massive defections on the part of Democrats. (See Campbell, 1960.)

However, the very existence of these examples might suggest that the risks cannot be a strong enough disincentive to prevent parties from approaching close to one another ideologically. This limitation can be explained by noticing a way in which party competition (at least in a two-party system) is quite different from competition between firms in a market. We suppose that for firms the equivalent of winning elections is making profits. The crucial difference is that, although a big turnover may be a means to profits, there is no particular market share which is necessary. But, for political parties in a two-party system, the only 'market share' that counts is enough to win the election. Thus, a firm in a duopolistic situation might be happy enough (in terms of *its* criterion, profitability) with a steady 40% of the market. (Indeed, the biggest firms tend not to have the biggest returns on capital, at least in Britain). But a political party—in terms of *its* criterion, winning elections—cannot possibly be satisfied with a steady 40% of the vote. Boulding, in his market example, points out that a newcomer to a line of business with one existing shop in the town might reasonably avoid siting himself near the already-existing rival because it is quite sensible to settle for less than half the market rather than engage in a possibly fatal trade war.[6] But a political party in a two-party system could hardly be content with such a modest aim. Whatever the risks, if the other party has gained possession of the 'middle ground' it must challenge it there and then try to find some extra item to beat the other party with.[7]

The market analogy would seem to be much closer in a multi-party system, where a party which can maintain a certain share of the vote (even if it is much less than half) can still take part in government and have a real effect on the course of policy and legislation. But the Hotelling solution does not apply to more than two shops anyway: if there are three shops, they will not all get next to one another because the middle one would get no custom at all. So the problem of finding an explanation for diversity does not arise in the same form.

It is, of course, an intriguing implication of this that (subject to what we have just said) the more effectively the parties operate the closer together they will get;[8] yet the closer together the parties, the less the 'party differential', until, where the parties' positions are identical, it falls to zero. As we have already seen, though, if the value of voting is

[6] The advantage of the existing shop, in scaring off competition, lies (a typical Schelling-type paradox) in the losses it would incur by moving.

[7] Thus, the Republicans in 1952, out of the Presidency for 20 years, accepted the broad outlines of the New Deal (a 'me-too' policy ideologically) and trumped the Democrats with the immensely popular Eisenhower plus Senator Joe McCarthy's exploitation of the domestic Communism scare, which was not purely a position on the ideological spectrum but to some degree a self-contained issue.

[8] Strictly speaking, as we have just seen, it requires only one party to act in an efficient vote-maximising way to get them very close together. But if one takes a position far from the median voter, the other does not have to take a position immediately adjacent to it in order to be sure of winning. If we assume (contrary to Downs but more realistically) that parties are more concerned to maximise their chance of winning elections than with maximising votes, then if party A is at 30, party B will be safer at 40 than 31. (This, of course, involves introducing some uncertainty into the model.)

computed as party differential discounted by the probability that one's vote will alter the result, voting would rarely if ever be a rational thing to do on 'economic' grounds. But would the lack of a real choice produce alienation from the system and thus also undermine the 'citizen duty' motive? This would presumably depend on what the *rationale* of the system was supposed to be. If actively exercising a choice between sharply contrasted alternatives is considered to be an end in itself, then the sort of finely-calculated entrepreneurial politics we are envisaging would obviously fail to satisfy the citizens.

If, however, we go back to the principle put forward by the 'economic' theorists themselves—that a system is to be judged by the extent to which it satisfies the wants of the voters—there is nothing inherently unsatisfactory in both parties being in the same place. For so long as they both play to win, the place they finish up is that occupied by the median voter. Or, to put it more enthusiastically, whatever the result of the election, we can guarantee that as many voters will be on the left of the government as are on the right. And this seems on the face of it a democratic enough result.[9]

2 INFORMATION COSTS AND STRATEGIC ABSTENTION

Downs recognises that the assumptions of perfect information on both sides and of no abstentions are very strong, and suggests some results of weakening them. However, this increased realism is bought at a heavy price in loss of rigour. Part of the trouble is that Downs seems sometimes to introduce *ad hoc* premises in an attempt to be able to deduce from his model predictions that correspond to what is well known to be the case. But it is inevitable that there should be some discrepancies between Downs's conclusions and the 'real world', because of the oversimplification inherent in his initial

[9] It should be noted that Arrow's conditions for a collective decision can all be satisfied when the voters' preferences are 'single-peaked', and this will always be the case if they lie on a single continuum (Arrow, 1951). Moreover, Black (1958) has shown that, on the same condition of single-peakedness, the position of the median voter is always the one that would win out if an exhaustive series of votes among all possible alternatives were taken. (See generally Murakami, 1968.)

premises, which are never revised, that parties are unified teams seeking solely to maximise votes (or win elections), and that electors, if they vote at all, are motivated purely by a wish to affect government policy. To remove discrepancies arising from these high-level assumptions by introducing special lower-order assumptions may, obviously, simply mean making the model incorrect in place of being incomplete—hardly an advance. Thus, Downs says at one point (page 100) 'It might at first seem that all the parties in our model will have very similar ideologies . . . why would they espouse strikingly different ideologies, as do parties in the real world?' One answer would appear to be that parties are sometimes run or at least influenced by people who are interested in promoting a certain ideology. But this is, of course, a point which takes us outside the model.

Downs himself argues that the differentiation of party ideologies arises from lack of information on the part of the strategists of the political parties. 'Uncertainty about effectiveness [of ideological positions] is thus necessary if ideological diversity is to persist' (page 101). This may often be so, but is it an adequate answer? An interesting case in point is the Goldwater phenomenon: how could Goldwater have got chosen as the Republican nominee in 1964? One answer (Converse, 1965) is that a lot of Republicans believed, incorrectly, that there was a large bloc of right-wing electors who usually stayed at home in presidential elections out of disgust at the tepid choices available and who would be roused by a Goldwater candidacy. But an alternative explanation (Baum, 1965) is that many of the activists who had captured the seats at the National Convention did not expect Goldwater to win, but preferred to lose with him than possibly (only possibly) win with a more 'moderate' candidate.

In his next chapter, Downs seemingly accepts himself the kind of myth attributed by Converse to the Goldwater fans. Having introduced the idea of an ideological continuum, he writes: 'the possibility that parties will be kept from converging ideologically in a two-party system depends upon the refusal of extremist voters to support either party if both become alike—not identical, but merely similar' (page 118). Downs apparently forgets that his previous explanation of ideological diversity among parties ought to cover, as a special (and simple) case, two-party systems with ideological continua. For he here ignores the parties' lack of information about the electorate, and argues in effect that they would take up different positions even if they knew the electorate's dispositions perfectly. But this new suggestion has a number of faults. It does not fit the facts; it is not coherent as an argument about rational behaviour; and in any case it would not necessarily generate the differences in party positions that are to be explained.

First, it is not true, at least in Britain and the U.S.A. (two prominent members of the fairly small class of two-party systems with some sort of ideological continuum), that the more 'extreme' members of the electorate vote with less frequency than those nearer the 'centre'. On the contrary, the pattern seems to be that 'extremism' tends to be associated with a relatively intense interest in politics and this in turn is associated with a propensity to vote.[10]

Second, let us consider the arguments by means of which Downs derives the conclusion that it is rational for extremists to abstain when the parties are close together ideologically. These arguments are not very coherent or persuasive. In a world of certainty (one in which the voters had perfect information) Downs suggests that 'future-oriented' extremists might abstain at one election so as to induce the party nearer them to move further towards their position by the next election. But this suggestion invites three comments. To begin with, if the point of abstaining is to increase the likelihood that the party nearer one will be defeated, would it not be even more effective to vote for the other party? Such a notion may appear paradoxical, but it really is neither more nor less self-defeating than abstaining. In both cases one deliberately reduces the short-run chances of the party nearer to oneself ideologically in the hope that this loss of support will encourage it to modify its position. Of course, this would be no use if the party one was trying to influence was un-

[10] See Converse, 1965. It might be replied that in these countries the parties are far enough apart to prevent the effect from being discovered. But at least some of the time they *are* close on any reasonable criteria. And in any case there should, if the theory is valid, always be some effect in the predicted direction, whereas the difference in voting strength goes in the other direction.

aware of what one was doing and why, but this too applies equally to abstention and voting for the other side. A second point to note is that the extremist's strategy, on this interpretation of his motives, is not particularly directed against a party which is close to the other party. It is directed against a party which is nearer to him than is the other party but which is still far away from his own position. And it is neither a necessary nor a sufficient condition for this that the parties be close together.[11] Finally there is a point which Downs admits but fails to deal with: someone who was motivated purely by an attempt to modify the result of an election (and this applies equally to modifying future elections) would almost certainly not vote anyway. Downs refers us, when mentioning this difficulty, to his later chapter on rational abstention. But this chapter (which we examined in Chapter II) is of no help in the present context, since it simply argues (even then, unsuccessfully) that people would vote to maintain the system rather than to modify policy.

Downs has another argument to establish the rationality of abstention by extremists. This one is based on an assumption of imperfect information, and asserts that extremists may be expected to find it especially difficult to perceive a difference between the parties if these parties are in fact close together. As a result, the extremists will be less likely to vote than the moderates. This line of reasoning *may* be correct, but as it stands it is simply an empirical assertion for which no evidence is offered. It does not follow deductively from anything else in Downs's theory. Moreover, this argument again relates voting or not voting to the size of the party differential, which we have seen cannot be taken seriously on purely calculative assumptions.

Suppose, however, that we waive these objections both of fact and logic. We still have to say that there is only a shaky

[11] Thus, Downs would have done better here to have kept a somewhat closer analogy with the Smithies 'transport cost' conception. Under this condition, purchases fall off the further away the nearest shop is—how close this shop is to some other shop is obviously irrelevant. However, though this would make Downs's argument consistent, this is not to say it is plausible, nor that the analogy from a market does in fact work. The distance from the nearest party is not remotely similar in implications to the distance from the nearest shop. Downs seems to recognise this but still wants to take over Smithies's results.

connection at best between the sort of individual behaviour referred to by Downs and the impact on party differences that he wishes to attribute to this behaviour. Take the idea that a threat by 'future oriented' extremists to abstain would induce the party nearer them to move closer towards their extreme position. A careful analysis shows that this is much less plausible than it looks at first sight. For, even under the most favourable conditions, it needs concerted action by a sizeable group of 'extremists', who must be united in making suitably small demands for change as a prerequisite of their returning to the fold. This sort of coordinated action by a group of (in a large national electorate) some millions seems difficult to imagine. In any case it is relevant only when conditions are favourable, and that means there must be extremists on *both* sides trying to use these tactics. Otherwise the threat of abstention, so far from shifting the party in one's own direction will in fact be counter-productive. Suppose that a bloc of those electors on the left threaten to abstain unless the party which is infinitesimally to the left of the median (the point which splits the electorate in half) moves to, say, the forty-ninth centile.[12] Unless the right-wing extremists have issued an ultimatum too, this is an invitation to electoral suicide. For, obviously, if everyone does vote, a party cannot win at the forty-ninth centile so long as the other party stays at the half-way mark or (even more effective) moves up to just to the right of the forty-ninth centile. On the contrary, the only thing to do would be to move to a point midway in the electorate *excluding* the 'extremists'. Thus, if 10% of the left-wing voters threatened to abstain, the equilibrium position of the parties would be at the 55th centile![13]

[12] Notice that this would require an extraordinary ability to guarantee that the members of the bloc would all abstain unless this were done and to vote if it were not. Thus, at a minimum, some organisation would have to exist to say whether or not the condition had been met.

[13] This assumes the parties can move anywhere on the ideological spectrum. If one assumes (as Downs does) that they cannot change places, the more left of the parties cannot move to the right of the median position which both parties are at initially. But this simply means it must lose whether it stays where it is or moves leftwards. If it stays where it is, the left-wing defection puts it in a minority; if it moves leftward, it loses because of the transfer of votes to the other party from some or all of those between its new position and the median. (Half if the other

Where both sets of extremists make threats to abstain unless their demands are met, there is no equilibrium position if the parties can move past one another on the ideological spectrum: the result will be a perpetual leap-frogging. If the parties cannot cross over, a determinate solution is obtainable for any particular combination of group sizes and minimum demands. In general, the result is that the parties will move apart to comply with the demands of 'their' extremists, provided the extremists' demands for a move from the centre are not too great in relation to the size of their bloc. But this is not a stable solution if we allow for the motivations of the blocs. For it will always be the case that the party whose bloc makes the less extreme demands will win the election (since everybody will vote and that party will necessarily be the one nearer the median voter). Thus, each bloc has an incentive to make the less extreme demands, since it will hardly be any use to it if the party which wins the election is on the *other* side of the 50% mark. This must presumably give rise to a Dutch auction between the extremist blocs, each demanding less than the other, until eventually equilibrium is reached—back with both parties in the middle!

Downs's alternative argument is pitched in terms of the effect of a low party differential on voting by 'extremists'. But even if Downs's postulate about the relationship is accepted, this might still not have the result of motivating the parties to draw apart. For the argument we have to consider is that where the parties are close together the extremists on *both* sides cease to vote. Thus, if party A moves to the left while party B stays in the middle, it does not follow that the left-wing extremists will turn out to vote for A and the right-wing extremists continue to abstain. Rather, on Downs's premises what will happen is that both sets of extremists will start voting. And even if there are as many left-wing as right-wing extremists who are brought into the election, A will lose because it is away from the median position of the electorate as a whole. Thus, B will get an extra bonus of the votes

party stays where it is, all if it moves up to an adjacent position.) Thus, we have to conclude that the party might move, but to a permanent minority position, unless we go outside the model and say that in the long-run the centre of gravity of the electorate will always move to a position between the parties.

of those *between* A and B who are nearer B than A. We must conclude, then, that *unless* there is a much larger bloc of non-voting extremists on one side than the other, and extremists can be got to vote by a small shift away from the centre, it will not pay either party to move. Moreover, even this holds only if the other party remains where it was, in the centre. Suppose it is astute enough to follow the other party, leaving the party differential as small as it was before. The extremists will then return to non-voting and the party that took the initiative in moving will lose because it is now to one side of the centre of those who do vote.

To illustrate this rather complex discussion, let us return for a moment to the example of 99 electors spread evenly along an ideological continuum. (This implies that all the voters have the same perception of a move along the continuum from one voter to the next as an 'equal distance' at any point on the line.) Now suppose that two sets of extremists numbered (left to right, as before) 1–20 and 90–99 abstain from voting whenever the distance between the parties is less than that sufficient to separate three voters from one another. An equilibrium with neither set of extremists casting a vote would lie at 55, since if each party were slightly to one side or the other of this point on the spectrum, the two parties would split equally the votes of electors 21–89. (See Figure 2.)

FIGURE 2

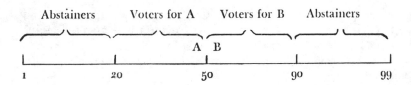

Now imagine that party A decides to move to the left, planning to open up a gap of more than three places between itself and B, thus bringing in all the extremist electors. By moving to 50, it might calculate, it will win by taking over half the votes in the full electorate. (To be exact, A would expect to take 1–52 leaving B 53–99). This presupposes that B remains at 55. Yet there is no reason why it should. If B moves along after A almost to 50, this will once more close the gap between the parties to below the critical distance hence once again removing the extremists from the effective electorate. Thus, only voters 21 to 89 will cast a vote, and B will win handsomely, picking up the votes of those from 51 to 89 inclusive, instead of only those from 56 to 89 inclusive (with 55 on both occasions tossing a coin to decide). This position is set out in Figure 3.

FIGURE 3

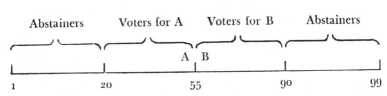

Of course, if the parties can move past one another on the spectrum, this too cannot be an equilibrium position, since it would pay A to leapfrog over B to 55, and B to follow. Thus, with unrestricted mobility, the final outcome is precisely the same as that shown in Figure 2; while, with leapfrogging impossible, the party that tries to disturb the status quo becomes a permanent loser. (See Garvey, 1966.)

Downs's attempts to allow abstention and imperfect information cannot so far be accounted successful, but before leaving the subject we should look at another application which Downs makes of the notion that information is costly and not, for the most people, worth acquiring. At least, it is largely presented as such an application, but much of its plausibility turns on a different point which has nothing to do with imperfect information. Downs here runs together two points, making them appear the same one. The first is that, given the electors' imperfect information, it will obviously pay a party, if it can get away with it, to channel different information about its policies to different sections of the electorate. This, of course, depends on being able to segregate the messages so that one intended for one set of recipients does not also get to a quite different set. The mass media of communication no doubt make this more difficult than it used to be, when a politician could adapt his speech to the group he was addressing.[14] And there are obvious limitations in a two-party system on the amount of confusion the government party can spread about its policy on some matter where it has actually done something, at least with Downs's model of monolithic parties. (With parties such as American Congressional parties there is much more room for equivocation, and the same goes for coalition governments in a multi-party system.)

The other point, which does not depend at all on imperfect information, is that, instead of regarding a party's position on the continuum as a single point, we might postulate that a party's position on any *issue* can be represented by a point somewhere on the continuum, but that a party need not occupy exactly the same position on each issue. Thus, the positions taken by a party might between them cover quite a lot of the spectrum. Instead of envisaging each party as occupying a point on the continuum, we should then have to conceive it as extending over a certain range. It would, of course, be possible to average the issue positions and express the result as a point, but Downs makes the important observation that different people may weight the items differently. Thus, to take a contemporary example, one person may regard nationalisation and similar kinds of economic issue as the most important element in an index of 'leftness', another may take attitudes on racialism as the most significant, a third attitudes to the legalisation of abortion, homosexuality, etc. Even if each person's position on one kind of question could be read off from his position on another (and this condition, unlikely to be fulfilled in practice, is necessary for there to be a single dimension at all) different people might still disagree on the location of the parties, *or, by the same token, of one another*. Downs does not notice this last point, which shows how close the notion of a continuum is to breaking down here, even though the conditions are still quite strong.

As Downs argues, it will pay a party to adopt positions in

[14] A vestigial survival of the practice a few years ago produced the perfect heckle: Harold Wilson, 'Why do I emphasise the importance of the Royal Navy?' A Voice, 'Because you're in Chatham.'

different parts of the spectrum when different people feel strongly about different policies, so as to be near the centre of opinion of those who feel strongly on each of several issues. But it must be noted that this does not mean the parties are being ambiguous. On each position it is known where they stand, and each voter can (if he thinks it worth the trouble) work out the relative attractiveness of the parties to him, allowing for his own views on the relative importance of different issue-areas. This point is worth emphasising because Downs somehow mixes up the two points of different messages for different audiences (if you can get away with it) and different positions on different policies, as if together they added up to the proposition that rational parties will be as ambiguous as possible to everybody about where they stand on issues. Downs's discussion is highly confused, but he seems to assume that if a party equivocates on an issue it will get the votes of people who would have deserted it had they known the truth, without losing any support that it might otherwise have garnered. From this he concludes that there is an in-evitable drive to vagueness. Parties will in fact compete with one another in a sort of vagueness stakes.

As we saw in Chapter II, Downs was faced with this prob-lem of self-interest being anti-social in his analysis of the decision to vote. There, he brought in the *deus ex machina* of a desire to save the system, which he hoped would suffice to motivate the electorate to act so as to avert a collapse. In the same way, here he suggests that the only thing preventing total vagueness of policies is the recognition by the politicians that this might lead to the collapse of the system through non-voting. He describes as a 'fundamental tension in the model' the clash between the voters' interest in knowing what they are choosing between and the politicians' interest in befogging the issues. But this dilemma is, I suggest, a bogus one. The proposition about the electoral advantages of vague-ness does not follow from either of the others which are, within appropriate limits, valid. Nor does it seem indepen-dently very plausible when stated in general terms. In a battle between two parties, one of which is explicit and the other totally vague, the explicit party will surely get the votes of all those who are closer to it than (calculated on some *a priori* basis of probability) the other party seems likely to finish up at. It will also attract the votes of those who might hope the other party would be nearer their own position but are overwhelmingly concerned that certain policies *not* be enacted, and thus find it rational to choose the devil they know. Finally, there may be other votes from those who simply prefer explicitness to vagueness. No doubt a certain degree of vagueness may help, because of the tendency people have to hear what they want to hear if you give them a chance; so this can in a way be regarded as a mechanism whereby you leave the electors do for you the job of receiving selective information. But this is surely limited in scope. It hardly entails that total vagueness is best of all.[15]

3 MULTI-PARTY SYSTEMS

So far we have concentrated on two-party systems. There are two reasons for this. One is that Downs himself works out the basic theory of party behaviour under conditions of certainty almost exclusively in terms of a two-party system. The other is that, even where he introduces multi-party systems, under conditions of uncertainty, he works out the theory (which, as we have just seen, involves the assumption of an ideological continuum) in terms of a two-party system first.

Unfortunately, the treatment of multi-party systems is not at all successful. If we take the simplest version of the 'con-

[15] This discussion has some interest in that the proposition about an inherent tendency to total vagueness is used by Riker as an argument against Downs's assumption that parties seek to maximise votes and in favour of Riker's assumption that they seek to win with the minimum number of votes consistent with that aim (Riker, 1962, pages 98–100). It is not worth spending much time on this book, but, briefly, the fallacies in Riker's argument are as follows: (i) there is nothing *inconsistent* in Downs's conclusion—if it were correct it would merely be unfortunate; (ii) the 'total vagueness' conclusion is not, as we have seen, entailed by Downs's premise that parties seek to maximise votes; (iii) conversely, if its premises are granted, the conclusion is equally consistent with the assumption that parties seek merely to win elections or even to win them by the minimum amount, for under fully competitive pressure parties will have to do their darnedest just to win. There is nothing different that they would do to win by a large majority unless the other party is being inefficient, in which case there is some choice; and (iv) although there is a lot to be said for the assumption that parties seek to win *elections* rather than maximise votes, there is nothing to be said for Riker's proposed modification, which is based on the false assumption that it necessarily costs more to win by a bigger majority.

tinuum' model, with every elector voting for the nearest party, we find that it does not have an equilibrium position for more than two parties. By an equilibrium position is meant here one where, if all the underlying conditions (such as the distribution of electors along the continuum) remain unchanged, none of the parties has any incentive to change its position. Thus, in the two-party case, we can say that a situation where the two parties are in adjacent positions at the median point (the point on the continuum where they bisect the electorate) is a situation of equilibrium. Movement away from the position by either party can only bring a net loss of votes.

But once we go above two parties, this interlocking of interests no longer obtains. If the parties in a system are never able to leapfrog over one another, so as to change their relative positions on the ideological spectrum, then there cannot in fact be more than two parties for long. The hapless party lying between the other two on the spectrum is squeezed out. For the others move up against it on each side so that there is no elector to whom it is nearest and so it simply gets no votes. Thus, there would be a continuous process by which, although there were never more than two parties actually getting votes, parties were constantly being created and annihilated.[16]

Downs, it should be said, always assumes that parties cannot pass one another on the ideological spectrum. But he does not give any reason for this. It does not follow from anything else in his analysis nor does it seem a universal empirical truth that parties cannot cross over in this way. More seriously still, many of Downs's results in fact depend on dropping the assumption that parties cannot change places. This can be seen clearly in relation to two-party systems, which is why most of the discussion in this chapter has been carried out without invoking the restriction. Thus, the demonstration of the crucial result that two parties will always converge on

[16] Of course, exact coincidence of position would be quite indeterminate with three or more parties as it would be with two. But a new party could locate itself to one side of two existing coincident parties. It would then draw just under half the votes even if the two established parties were exactly in the middle of the spectrum. They would be left with the remaining half of the votes between them. This would obviously be a highly unstable situation.

the centre of the ideological spectrum (or, more precisely, the centre of the electorate on the spectrum) itself depends on the possibility of leapfrogging. Suppose that one party, (A), starts off somewhere other than in the position half-way along the spectrum (reckoned in numbers of electors). If another party, (B), now arises, its best move is to get next to A, on the side nearer the half-way mark. Once there, it obviously has no incentive to move since it always wins, and, by the anti-leapfrogging stipulation it can permanently block movement towards the centre by A. The only way in which the parties could get to the centre, as predicted by Downs, would be if the parties could move past one another. A would then move past B, and it could establish itself a little nearer the centre than B. B would retaliate by moving past A, and so they would continue, moving one step (or *minimum sensibile*) at a time, until the centre was reached.

In the light of this, it is worth noticing briefly what would happen with the introduction of more than two parties if leapfrogging were not ruled out. The answer is that the parties would be in perpetual movement. Suppose, for example, that we started with two parties adjacent to one another. Now let us imagine that a third party moves in next to one of the existing parties, with the result that that party is boxed in and receives no votes. Obviously, the party in this predicament, which we have now allowed the possibility of moving past other parties, will relocate itself just outside one of the other parties, thus putting it in exactly the same squeeze. This could continue indefinitely, as a sort of Mad Hatter's tea party, unless the parties grew tired of it and settled (by tacit or explicit agreement) for some kind of market-sharing arrangement by spacing themselves out along the continuum. But the theory cannot say how they would do this.

There is another way of arriving at this sort of result, which would work even in the absence of leapfrogging. We have to bring back the assumption that when parties are close on the ideological continuum, a voter may not necessarily choose the closest but may go on performance, personality, etc. If, as we have also assumed, parties are averse to the risks this involves, they would have an incentive to move apart. With three parties one would then get one party in the middle and one either side some way away—how far away being determined by the strength of these flanking parties' aversion to risk. This is perhaps not a bad first shot at depicting the post-war British system.

As in the two-party case, though, the most direct way of giving the parties an incentive to stay apart is to introduce the idea that people abstain from voting if the nearest party is too far away. This is the method that Downs uses exclusively.[17] However, he introduces it as something of a throwaway, without making it clear how essential it is and without exploring its full implications. Thus he first states, without mentioning differential abstention, that, provided parties are not allowed to leapfrog, 'coupled with our device of variable distribution (i.e. different distributions of electors along the continuum), this attribute of the model nearly always ensures stable equilibrium' (Downs, 1957, page 123). As we have seen, this is simply not so. Downs then gives an example of an electorate uniformly spread along a continuum running from 0–100, and argues that if the number of parties is limited to four (this is simply to be taken as given) they will space themselves in such a way that each gets the votes of 25% of the electorate, as shown in the diagram, adding,

0	12·5	25	37·5	50	62·5	75	87·5	100
	A		B		C		D	

in brackets, 'assuming extremists abstain if A and D move towards the centre'. But this assumption is, in fact, entirely responsible for the result, and requires just the sort of organised bloc threat that we examined in the two-party case. Moreover, if the threat were to be strong enough to prevent A from gaining by moving in next to B (which would normally be the thing to do, yielding 37·5% of the vote instead of 25%) *all* those below 12·5 and a few more too would have to threaten not to vote unless A stayed at 12·5! But, in any case, why 12·5? No particular reason—it might just as well be any other number, except that 12·5 happens to produce the stated result. More likely, however, no effective threat could be mounted, in which case A and D would move up against B and C, while they in turn would in the short

[17] He seems to recognise here, incidentally, as he did not in the two-party case, that abstaining when the nearest party is too far away has nothing to do with abstaining when all the parties are too close together.

run gain from moving inwards, though in the long run they would then be eliminated.

Even if the two outer parties were held—arbitrarily, as we have seen—at 12·5 and 87·5, we may add that the equidistant position of the others is no less arbitrary. Downs says that B and C will take up these positions because they cannot make a net gain by moving to either side, since they would lose exactly as many votes to one neighbouring party as they would gain from the other. This is perfectly true, but we could equally correctly say that B and C cannot make a net loss by moving either, for exactly the same reasons. The positions Downs ascribes to B and C are in equilibrium. Not stable equilibrium, though, like a ball-bearing in an egg-cup, but (depending on the direction of the movement away) either neutral equilibrium, like a mat on a table, or unstable equilibrium, like a pencil standing on end.[18] Thus, any position for B between 12·5 and 62·5 would give it 25% of the vote, given the positions of A, C and D; while any position for C between 37·5 and 87·5 would do the same for it. Such moves might or might not have further repercussions, as other parties adjusted to the new situation, and the eventual result might even be the destruction of two of the parties. Thus the position is either neutral (no further change, but no tendency to return) or unstable (cumulative changes set in train) depending on the direction of the push.[19]

We must, I think, admit that Downs's theory of the positioning of parties in a multi-party system is not successful. Hardly surprisingly, his attempt to relax the assumption that the number of parties is given and to deduce the number of parties from the distribution is no better.[20] Downs suggests

[18] The ball-bearing returns to the bottom of the egg-cup if (within certain limits) dislodged. The mat, if pushed, stays where you push it. The pencil, given a small initial push, undergoes without additional outside interference further changes of position; it was originally in equilibrium because with a push it would have stayed where it was.

[19] Specifically, given the rest of the assumptions, if B or C moves outward, there is no incentive for anyone else to move, but if, say, B moves inward, the threat from the 'extremists' may no longer be strong enough to prevent A from moving in behind it.

[20] Downs does say that part of the explanation of the number of parties lies in the electoral system, but his discussion of this is confused, and in any case this sort of idea is a commonplace of political science which is not derivable from the model. The confusion lies in failure to distinguish adequately between election for a single national office,

that if the voters are concentrated in the middle of the spectrum, there will be 'room' for only two parties, that if there is a bimodal distribution there will be two parties, and so on (though he does not positively assert that the number of parties will equal the number of modes or clusters of voters). This is not, as it stands, at all persuasive. On the simplest model, we can say that, if there are two parties, it will pay them to be near the centre of the overall distribution, whatever its shape; and it will then always be possible for two other parties to enclose the first two, taking all their votes.

The only way of getting an equilibrium with a number of parties centred on different modes is to allow for (i) the wish to play safe and keep a certain amount rather than risking losing all, (ii) the 'stickiness' of changes in position which inhibits rapid realignments, (iii) the advantages in publicity of a party already in existence over a new party close to it ideologically, and (iv) the old abstention argument, extended from 'extremists' to enthusiasts for doctrinal purity at all points along the spectrum. There is a good deal of economic analysis which is germane to these topics (see, again, Shubik, 1959, for suggestive parallels) and it would be interesting to see if an economic theory of party formation could be worked out, starting from the premise that the political entrepreneur, in deciding whether to make his way up in an existing party or get in on the ground floor of a new one, has to take account of factors rather analogous to those facing an ambitious economic entrepreneur trying to decide what are the prospects for a new firm in some market. All that we can say at present is that Downs has not himself shown in any rigorous way how the distribution of the electorate and the number of parties might be related.

A more successful aspect of Downs's treatment of multiparty systems is his discussion of the problem of deciding how

---

such as the U.S. or French Presidency, and plurality elections in constituencies for representatives. National plurality systems have a strong effect towards creating two main contenders, even though a majority is required to win in the U.S. system (not a plurality as Downs seems to believe) while the French system includes a run-off election between the highest two candidates on the first round. A constituency plurality system has more of an effect in ensuring that there are only two contenders in any given constituency, but it does not rule out regional parties, such as the Irish party before partition, or regionally based parties in Canada.

I

to vote in such a system. Suppose, for example, that one were voting in the Fourth French Republic. The party to vote for, if one is attempting to modify government policy, is not necessarily the party one most prefers but the one an increment to whose strength would be most likely to bring about a coalition of a kind one would like to see. Under certain circumstances an increase in the strength of one's favourite party might lead it to enter a coalition which one likes less than one it would have gone into if it were weaker, to keep out of one it would otherwise have entered, and so on. But this requires both that one knows what coalitions would be formed for any given distribution of party strengths in the legislature, and that one knows how everyone else will vote. But, if the first is empirically impossible, the second is logically impossible for all the electorate simultaneously. The solution that people will most likely adopt, Downs suggests, is to vote for the party they prefer and leave it to get on with forming coalitions. Downs describes this as 'irrational', because it is not voting with a view to modifying government policy. But such a conclusion surely rests on an indefensible narrowing of the concept of rationality. It is one thing to say that voting purely by ethnic identification, or according to the pleasantness of the candidate's personality, or to please one's wife, is irrational. For these do not help make the system match the policy outputs of government to the policy wants of the electors—though heaven knows there are difficulties enough there.[21] But it is another thing to deny that voting for the party whose policies you prefer is irrational, for this *is* in general to increase the probability that the policies you prefer will be put into effect. The problem which Downs makes so much of would not exist if party supporters agreed on all policies and priorities with their leaders, since the decisions

[21] The general conception of rationality with which we have been operating is simply that rational behaviour is behaviour well adapted to achieving the ends of the actor, subject to the knowledge which (given his ends) it was, or would have been, worth acquiring. Downs is clearly working with a subset of this set of rational actions, namely those which are adapted to securing the government policies the agent wants. Downs admits that different grounds for voting may be 'individually rational' and recognises that he is deliberately introducing a limitation which is based on a conception of what the process is *for*. It is not at all clear, however, that one can speak, as Downs does, of 'rational abstention' in this context.

the leaders took would always be ones the followers would endorse. But where the problem does occur it does not seem any more serious than dozens of other difficulties in representative government.[22]

The dilemma which Downs presents is a false one: he argues that in a two-party system it is possible to know what government you are voting for, but difficult to know what the parties would do because of the premium on their being vague about their aims, whereas, in a multi-party system, the parties are more precise but it is more difficult to tell what one is doing by voting for one. As we have seen, however, there is little justification for the view that it would pay the parties in a two-party system to be vague, except to the extent that they could count on voters hearing what they wanted to hear, which might not entail a great deal of vagueness. Conversely, if Downs's argument that almost total vagueness pays is valid for the two-party case I do not see any reason for its being less true in the multi-party case, nor does Downs give one. As for the point about the difficulty of knowing what the results of voting for a given party would be, we have already noted that this is somewhat less tragic than Downs suggests. Even so, there are problems posed for a voter with coalition governments (though not all multi-party systems have coalition governments) in apportioning the responsibility for policies he likes or dislikes and thus deciding which member of the coalition to vote for. And, if he decides that he wishes to vote against the government, more information is again required in order to decide which non-government party to vote for than is needed if one can simply vote for 'the Opposition'. How seriously we take such problems must depend in large part on our estimate of the sophistication of electorates about such matters, and it is to empirical questions of this kind that we now turn.

[22] A more severe problem for voters in multi-party systems (one which Downs excludes from consideration by assuming proportional representation) arises where the electoral system gives the voter as many votes as there are seats to fill from the constituency without any possibility of transferring them at the counting stage or taking part in a second round of voting. This really does require trying to guess how others will vote, and is theoretically insoluble. In practice, published poll forecasts seem in Britain to be used rather intelligently by voters, so that, for example, Labour and Liberal voters often seem to switch to whichever candidate is best placed.

CHAPTER VI

Testing Theories of Democracy (1)

1 ISSUES AND VOTING DECISIONS: U.S. DATA

A critique of one of Parsons's more abstruse articles included the suggestion that he might beneficially make more use of 'semi-economic' models (Coleman, 1963). In his reply, Parsons went on the offensive, and wrote that 'An important, though neglected [*sic*], example of where minimising the "semi-" leads to very serious distortions is the book of Anthony Downs, *An Economic Theory of Democracy*. This is an attempt to treat power and influence systems as an example of economic process which simply fails to work' (Parsons, 1963, page 91). The main task of this chapter and the next is to ask how far Parsons's attack (which he nowhere amplifies) is well founded, and how our 'sociologists', including Parsons himself, acquit themselves when dealing with the same range of phenomena.

The most fundamental feature of the 'economic' model proposed by Downs is that the results of elections are determined by the policy-positions taken up by parties and by the actual or expected competence of their administrative performance in office; and this fact in turn determines the behaviour of the competing political parties. The 'positions' of the parties, as we have seen, need not be regarded as a set of discrete 'stands', but may be thought of as mediated (at least for some voters) through 'ideologies'. These ideologies can change over time under the impact of a whole sequence of changed policies, but they are not highly sensitive or volatile. Voting which is not related (at least at one remove, via ideology) to the positions of the parties is, Downs says, irrational from the point of view of the system. This means, as we have seen, that voting on such a basis is necessary for the system to achieve the postulated end of matching government policies to electors' preferences.

The most fundamental question to ask is: how far does the assumption built into Downs's model, that elections are determined by policies, correspond to reality? It is very difficult to say what is to count as conclusive evidence. There seems to be no doubt that the amount of information and articulated opinion to be found among many members of mass electorates is very low indeed. This theme has been most fully and elegantly developed by Converse (1964). He analyses the data collected by the Survey Research Centre as a result of interviewing the same American sample three times, with an interval of about two years between each interview. Among other things, the respondents were asked to give their opinions on a number of 'issues', phrased in such a way that one could either 'agree' or 'disagree'. Typical items were: 'The government should leave things like electric power and housing for private businessmen to handle', and 'If Negroes are not getting fair treatment in jobs and housing, the government should see to it that they do' (Converse, 1964, page 257). Converse writes that 'faced with the typical item of this kind, only about thirteen people out of twenty manage to locate themselves even on the same *side* of the controversy in successive interrogations, when ten out of twenty could have done so by chance alone' (page 239).

It might perhaps be argued, desperately, that this simply reflects the fact that people 'change their minds' with great frequency on these issues, but it is much more likely that many do not have a 'mind' on them at all; in other words, that they do not think about them at all except when being interviewed, and then respond virtually at random. Support for this can be derived from two features of the data. First, the variation in responses was greatest for the items which were furthest removed from personal experience and where it was most difficult to see the personal implications of the issue: foreign policy questions and the one about private versus public initiative in electricity and housing. The greatest stability occurred on questions about Negroes (school desegregation and the anti-discrimination question quoted), followed by one on government responsibility for maintaining full employment. This pattern supports the view that changes in response are more a matter of what Converse calls low 'centrality' of the issue than anything normally describable as a 'change of mind'.

A second feature of the data which lends further support to this interpretation is the pattern of changes over the three waves of interviews. 'Quite generally, we can predict t_3 position of individuals fully as well from a knowledge of their t_1 positions alone as we can from a knowledge of their t_2 positions alone' (Converse, 1964, page 242). That is to say, on any given issue there is a correlation of a certain size between the opinions offered in the first interview and those offered in the second, and there is a correlation of the same size between those offered in the second and the third interviews. But also, and curiously, there is a correlation of *the same size again* between the opinions of the first and third interviews.

Converse shows that this result could be brought about, in the case of the 'private enterprise' issue (which showed the greatest changes in response) if we supposed that the population were divided into two groups: 'a "hard core" of opinion . . . which is well crystallised and perfectly stable over time' and 'people who, for lack of information . . . offer meaningless opinions that vary randomly in direction during repeated trials over time' (pages 242, 243). The other issues show a less good fit to the model, and Converse suggests that one might suppose the discrepancy arises from the presence in the sample of a relatively small proportion of genuine opinion-changers moving between the first and second or between the second and third interviews from a stable position on one side of the issue to a stable position on the other. It would, of course, be possible to maintain that the other issues involved entirely different processes of 'opinion'-formation, but Converse argues plausibly that 'the existence of one issue that does fit the black and white model perfectly provides at least an intuitive argument that those that depart from it in modest degrees do not require a totally different class of model' (page 244).

What is the proportion of those with 'genuine' opinions in a mass public? Complications in estimating this arise because some of those who give the same answer three times will do so by chance (just as one trial in every four of spinning a coin three times gives either three heads or three tails) and because some changers will be 'genuine'. But just extracting all 'don't knows' and changers leaves 'issue publics' (that is, groups with 'genuine opinions' on a certain issue) ranging upwards from below 20% on the 'private enterprise' issue, to around 50%. This does not mean that over half the public have no 'genuine' opinion on anything. 'One man takes an interest in policies bearing on the Negro and is relatively indifferent to or ignorant about controversies in other areas. His neighbour may have few crystallised opinions on the race issue, but he may find the subject of foreign aid very important' (Converse, 1964, page 246).

Thus, the implications of Converse's results for a theory of democracy which relates voting to issues are not really clear. Obviously, many people are touched by only a few issues, and the rest of their responses are to be discounted; but, by the same token, these pseudo-attitudes can hardly be supposed to affect anyone's voting intentions. If, therefore, people's voting behaviour is affected by their *genuine* opinions, we could still hope to apply the general case of the Downsian model, according to which the competing parties offer a battery of policies some of which excite certain voters (either by attraction or repulsion) while leaving others cold, and the voters weight the issues however they choose. But do people 'vote their opinions' in this sense?

The simplest criterion is: given the strength and direction of opinion a voter has, is he voting for the 'right' party, either in terms of the positions of the parties as he perceives them or as an expert observer perceives them? On the whole, it seems fair to say that people do tend to finish up with the party that best corresponds to their own attitudes, at least as they perceive that party.[1]

The most extended study of this question, based on U.S. data from Gallup polls, is V. O. Key's book *The Responsible Electorate* (Key, 1966). Key compares the positions of voters on various 'issues' (at around the time of Presidential elections from 1940 to 1960) with their voting intention and their

[1] For example, some Southern whites in 1960 thought that the Republican party was the more pro-Negro, influenced perhaps by 'the flamboyant events at Little Rock, associated with Eisenhower, and hence the Republicans'. On the basis of this belief, they switched from Republican to Democrat (Campbell, 1966, page 233).

reported vote at the previous Presidential election. On the basis of this he suggests that in general those who changed their vote from one election to the next had reason to do so on 'issue' grounds. Those who voted for the same party both times also had reasonable grounds in their attitude to the 'issues' for doing what they did. Gallup data are not panel data but simply a series of different samples, so (apart from excluding the self-confessed 'don't knows') there is no way of confining the analysis to those respondents whose views on an issue were 'genuine'. Nor, even if an opinion is 'genuine', need the holder of it regard it as a very important issue to base a vote on. The most, therefore, that one could hope to find in the data is a tendency for positions on issues to match party choices. The clearest evidence produced by Key arises from a poll in 1960. Respondents were asked what they thought was the most important issue facing the country. They were then asked which party they thought could best cope with this problem. The tendency was marked for respondents to match their voting intentions with their answers to this question (Key, 1966, page 132).

But is the criterion of a simple matching between issue positions and vote intentions stringent enough? Does the vote intention perhaps come first, with the 'issues' being filled in by the respondent in the light of what he knows about the stands of the parties or candidates? Key himself is remarkably nonchalant about this possibility, acknowledging both *ad hoc* fudging up of answers for the interviewer (pages 45–6 and 60) and real changes in which 'some Republicans and some Democrats adjusted their views to make them conform with the positions of their party'. But he goes on: 'it is the parallelism of vote and policy view that is significant for our analysis, not its origin' (page 53). And elsewhere he spells this out by saying that 'however such opinions come into being, their supportive function in the political system should be the same' (page 46).

Now it is, of course, a significant consequence of a process in which opinions change to come into line with party choice that, if it works perfectly, there will always be at least half the voters approving of whatever the government does (though supporters of opposition parties will presumably always disapprove). But Key did not set out to argue that democracy is a stable form of government. He proposed to show that it is 'rational' in the Downsian sense, in other words that 'voters were moved by a rational calculation of the instrumental impact of their vote' (Key, 1966, page 47). 'The portrait of the American electorate that develops from the data is . . . one of an electorate moved by concern about central and relevant questions of public policy, of governmental performance, and of executive personality' (pages 7–8). Surely all this implies that voters must really have some views on these questions, with party choice being conceived as a means of furthering them. Issue positions cannot be a mere epiphenomenon of party identification. As Converse remarks, after noting that party preference is far more stable over time than any issue position (over ·7 correlation between responses two years apart to a question about party choice, as against correlations for issue positions running from below ·5 to below ·3), 'in theory of course the party usually has little rationale for its existence save as an instrument to further particular policy preferences of the sort that show less stability. . . . The policy is the end, and the party is the means, and ends are conceived to be more stable and central in belief systems than means' (Converse, 1964, pages 240–1).

All we have shown, however, is that the question which is the tail and which the dog cannot be ignored, and that in so far as the connections found by Key are a result of issue positions following party preference they do not support a truly 'instrumental' view of voting.[2] We have not, however, said that this is so, and the best conclusion seems to be that it is only a part of the total phenomenon. Consider, first, Converse's data just cited. It should be recalled that these are average correlations

---

[2] The same problem arises in economics. The original justification for a competitive market was that it provided customers (subject to their incomes, of course) with what they wanted. This presupposes that consumers have given tastes and firms compete to satisfy them. But if a firm could establish such a 'brand loyalty' that its customers would buy its product however inferior it were objectively to its rivals, would the same rationale apply? As critics of Galbraith (1952) have pointed out, it is not so easy to go on selling things by advertising, though one may induce people to try them. But the thesis is more difficult to break down in politics. For the cost to a voter of maintaining 'brand loyalty' to a party, even if it is the 'wrong' party for him, is negligible. And in any case the results of eating the pudding are much more open to dispute.

on issues. Thus for each issue the figure given includes those for whom it is very important and those for whom it has very low 'centrality'. If we assume (as is surely reasonable) that an issue with low centrality can have only negligible influence on a person's voting behaviour, the question becomes: for how many people does at least *one* issue have a constancy of response approaching that of voting preference itself? Converse does not give the answer to this, but he does say that for those (an unspecified proportion of the total sample) who showed from the interview schedule 'genuine self-starting interest' in a topic, consistency of response on the associated agree/disagree questions approached that for party support (Converse, 1964, pages 244–5). Surely here, at least, might be found people who would change their party if they perceived another as being closer on their hobby-horse issue.

The idea here proposed, that at least some of the direction of causation runs from attitude to party, is in fact that espoused by Key: 'Standpatters [those who vote the same way in successive elections], the evidence suggests, acquire their policy attitudes in at least two ways. Some persons more or less deliberately affiliate with the party whose policy emphases appear to parallel their own. Other persons, psychologically identified with a party, adopt those policy outlooks espoused by the more prominent spokesmen of their party' (Key, 1966, page 55, footnote 11). Moreover, switchers cannot simply have assimilated a party identification and then acquired attitudes to match. Of course, it might be suggested that people change parties as a result of some process not connected with policies and then change their attitudes as well, or that the same process is responsible for both changes simultaneously. But it seems impossible for the usually-proposed processes of group identification to explain the size and nature of the general run of changes from one election to another found in, say, Britain and the U.S.A., though the small turnover in other countries (Scandinavia, for example) would fit much better.

Moreover, where it *does* seem that switching is a pure result of group identification, no mania for consistency in attitudes obscures it. This reassures us that in the other cases where Key found a coincidence of attitude between the switchers and their new party, this was, at least partially, a result of the attitude's leading to the switch. The test case here is the U.S.

election of 1960, in which a group of people who had withstood the Eisenhower landslide in 1956 by voting for Stevenson nevertheless voted for Nixon. Overwhelmingly Protestant, and tending to live in the areas of strongest evangelical influence (the 'Bible belt'), these voters showed little enthusiasm for the Republican party on policy questions, many doubting its capacity to solve their own selected 'most important problem' (Key, 1966, pages 133–5).

Finally, to suppose that a good deal of the turnover between elections is accounted for by response to issues just seems to be the most parsimonious explanation of electoral change. A clear example is the American Presidential election of 1964, in which there were (or appeared to be) clear differences in policy between the candidates, with the Republican candidate forfeiting a substantial proportion of Republican votes in most of the country but picking up many Democratic votes in the South.[3] Indeed, Converse and two colleagues wrote that the 1964 election proceeded 'after the manner of a classic script' whose 'most fertile elaboration' is found in Downs's book: 'that is, the "outer" ideological wing of a party captures its nomination, leaving a vacuum toward the center of gravity of national opinion. This vacuum is gleefully filled by the opposing party without any loss of votes from its own side of the spectrum. The outcome, logically and inexorably, is a landslide at the polls' (Converse, 1965, page 321).

2 ISSUES AND VOTING DECISIONS: NON-U.S. DATA

This discussion has been carried out almost entirely in terms of U.S. data, mainly relating to Presidential elections. Published evidence on the stability of attitudes elsewhere is rare. It requires that the same people be interviewed twice for the minimum computations of correlations, and at least three times for most of the analyses carried out by Converse. Data for France, collected by Converse and Dupeux (Campbell, 1966, pages 269–91), enable correlation coefficients to be calculated for a number of issues put to a national sample in

---

[3] This is not a question of 'group identification'—Johnson was himself a Southerner. Goldwater was 'perceived by the southern whites as a defender of segregation, even to a point well beyond any that the Senator actually took' (Campbell, 1966, page 241).

1958, but the period between the interviews was only five weeks. Even so, the relationships were not very strong, and suggest much the same picture as the American data (Campbell, 1966, pages 286, 287).

The association between policy positions and partisan preference has been more fully studied, though nobody has really overcome the problem of confining the analysis to issues on which the person himself feels strongly. The Michigan data could in principle be used to do this, employing Converse's test for centrality, but as far as I know this has not been done. Giving equal weight to all the questions which are asked by the interviewer, it seems that British voters are in general in the appropriate party, though the liberal humanitarianism of most Labour M.P.s finds little reflection in the party's mass electorate, and nationalisation is not very popular. (See Benney, 1956, and Abrams, 1960.)

The multi-party systems of Norway and France also exhibit connections between policy and party which are fairly high if one reckons how much 'noise' is introduced by the large amount of random response to issue questions.[4] In both instances the test applied is the extent to which the supporters of a party come out on the same side over a given issue (Campbell, 1966, pages 245-91). Strictly speaking, of course, the supporters of a party might agree with one another and disagree with the official position of the party. Since the actual distributions of opinion are not given for France, we cannot be sure this is not occurring. In Norway, the differences between supporters seem to be in line with the differences between the party élites, except that half the supporters of the (Labour) government thought defence expenditures were too high, whereas supporters of other parties tended to be more enthusiastic about the defence budget (Campbell, 1966, pages 260, 263).

In both countries the distinctiveness of voters for different parties is much above that found in the U.S.A. On the question which Downs regards as paradigmatic of the 'ideological' spectrum—the size of the government budget—there are

---

[4] In other words, if for each respondent we could exclude the questions which have low centrality and (as we have suggested) can hardly affect his voting behaviour, there must in general be a strong connection between the remaining issues and party preferences.

much sharper differences between Norwegian partisans than American, though in both countries these are among the sharpest divisions (Campbell, 1966, pages 260–2). Thus, among 'strong' supporters of the Norwegian Labour party, 27% thought that taxes were too high, as against 74% of the 'strong' Conservatives, with the Liberals, Christians and Agrarians lying between. (For 'weak' supporters the contrast was 23% to 56%.) In the U.S.A., 34% of 'strong' Democrats, as against 13% of 'strong' Republicans, thought the government had not done enough to cut taxes ('weak' figures, 24% and 16%); and this seems more a partisan response to Eisenhower's Presidency at the time of the survey than a view on the appropriate proportion of the national income to be taken by the state. Converse computes an index of 'party-relatedness' on issues for France and the U.S.A. which gives the same picture. Even leaving out the American South, the highest indices found among 'identifiers' of the major parties on the issues selected are ·21 on federal aid to education and ·19 on the duty of the state to provide full employment, while on foreign affairs and civil rights none exceeded ·07. In France, most of the indices for identifiers exceeded ·2, but there are far fewer 'identifiers' in France. However, even non-identifiers, who simply expressed an intention of voting one way or another, were more distinct in France than were identifiers in the U.S.A. (Campbell, 1966, page 287).

This all contributes to a picture of considerable confusion in American politics, a picture which is confirmed by a study of Stokes and Miller (Campbell, 1966, pages 194–211) of midterm Congressional elections, which showed widespread ignorance about which party controlled Congress, and little inclination to make any connection between the party supported, the view taken of the previous Congress's performance, and the belief about which party controlled it. This no doubt largely reflects the fact that American politics *is* confusing. But our previous discussion is not invalidated, because the Presidential elections which Key studied unquestionably make more impact on the electorate. He himself remarked that 'the data for systematic study of voting for nonpresidential office, if they were available, would doubtless reveal the voter in roles both of bewilderment and wisdom' (Key, 1966, page 8, footnote 2). Apart from certain exceptional contests, Congressional elections seem to specialise in the former.[5]

3   THE PROBLEM OF DIMENSIONS

The most intriguing feature of the French and Norwegian data on the 'party-relatedness' of issues is the fact that in both countries some of the most party-related issues have been found to be religious in nature. In Norway, agreement with the proposition 'The government has done too little to promote Christian morals and Christian faith' ranged from 29% for Labour supporters to 89% for supporters of the Christian party, the other three falling between. One other issue spanned a range of 65%: agreement with the proposition 'The government has interfered too much in economic life' ran from 9% (Labour) to 74% (Conservative) (Campbell, 1966, page 260). In France, the two religious questions ('state support of religious schools' and 'current threat posed by clergy') had the highest indices of party-relatedness among party 'identifiers', followed by 'strikes by government employees', 'freedom of press' and 'private responsibility for housing'. Among those who did not identify with a party but had a clear voting intention, the party-relatedness of the religious issues held up, as did the group-directed question about government employees; but the 'ideological' question about housing dropped from ·22 to ·04 (Campbell, 1966, page 287).

The most obvious reflection is that one dimension is not enough to accommodate these issues: there is, at the least, a religious dimension and a 'left-right' dimension. Of course, differences in content do not *ipso facto* constitute different dimensions. If, for example, positions on religion correlated highly with positions on the 'left-right' spectrum, we could treat them as one dimension. But in Norway, as we can see by contrasting the tax and government intervention questions and the religious question, the dimensions are clearly

[5] The period in which the interviews for the Stokes and Miller study were carried out (the 1958 elections) was one where in spite of Eisenhower's large majority in 1956, the Democrats had a majority in the Congress. Perhaps less bewilderment would be found when both branches were in the hands of representatives of the same party.

separate. On the two economic questions, the Labour and Conservative supporters take the extremes, with Christian party supporters between them; whereas on the religious question the Labour and Christian supporters take the extremes, with the Conservative supporters between them. The two dimensions are not entirely unrelated (orthogonal), as is shown by the position of the Labour supporters at an extreme of each; but they are not by any means identical either. Similarly, the French M.R.P. was the most committed to a confessional position but moderate on the left-right issues, with the Communists taking the place of Norway's Labour party as the upholder of an 'extreme' position on both.

Multi-dimensionality in multi-party systems has been interestingly explored by Converse (1966), using the answers given when respondents are asked to give an order of preference among the political parties in their country. Clearly, if parties could be properly thought of as strung along one dimension, only certain combinations of preferences could occur consistently with the assumption that each voter had a location on this dimension and read off the distances of the parties from it. Using Finnish and French data, Converse shows that the replies do not fit a one-dimensional model of this kind, but that if the parties are plotted on more dimensions a better fit can be obtained.[6] Of course, these dimensions have to be

---

[6] Given *any* collection of distances between points, one can try to find a consistent representation of them. For an example where this is done more rigorously than in Converse's article, see the 'smallest space' analysis of 'distances' (measured in terms of mobility) between occupations in Blau, 1967, pages 69–75. Blau and Duncan explain the procedure helpfully as follows: ' Let us represent the 17 occupations [retail sales, farm labour, etc.] by 17 objects and the differences between them [the ease or difficulty of movement over a generation from one to another] by wires of varying length. Every occupation is tied by a wire of a specified length to each of the 16 others, so that 136 wires connect the 17 objects. The task the computer programme performs is analogous to placing the 17 objects into positions that make all the wires taut. If this can be done by stretching the objects along a straight line, a one-dimensional solution is found. If there is too much slack in the wires, spreading them out on a table might make them all taut, which would correspond to a two-dimensional solution. Excessive slack in two dimensions might require distributing the objects in a three-dimensional space to straighten out all the wires, and although the physical analogy breaks down at this point, introducing further dimensions may be necessary to make all wires taut' (Blau, 1967, pages 70–1). Thus, to give a very simple

interpreted, and we infer the attitude clusters from the way in which the parties arrange themselves. In both cases, a 'left-right' dimension is the best single one, in the sense that if the parties were fitted as well as they could be on to one dimension the resultant ordering would correspond to the usual 'left-right' one. The second dimension in the French instance is the religious one, while in Finland the 'agrarian' dimension and a special one for Swedish descendants both seem needed. Norway might well need an agrarian and a religious dimension in addition to the left-right one, and it seems on the face of it unlikely that any of the other multi-party systems of Western Europe could be fitted into less than two dimensions.

If this were the only modification required to Downs's one-dimensional model of 'ideological' distribution, it could be accommodated quite easily. An early article extended Hotelling's original analysis into two dimensions (Smithies, 1941); and Boulding (1963) conducts the bulk of his discussion in terms of two dimensions. Tullock (1967, pages 50–9) has also recently put forward a two-dimensional version of Downs. Instead of a line, voters are now conceived as distributed over a surface. The positions of the parties are points on this surface, and as before in the simplest case it is supposed that they attract all the voters nearest them, and that parties try to win elections, pursuing that end rationally. As in the one-dimensional case, if there are two parties they will be in stable equilibrium next to one another. And just as, with voters uniformly distributed along a line, the parties will come together in the middle of the line, so, with voters uniformly distributed over a circle, the parties will come together at the centre of the circle. (If we went up to three dimensions, and had a uniform distribution of voters within a sphere, the two parties would come together in the middle of that.) Without an even distribution of voters the solution is more difficult, but it is still clear that the parties would come together where they divide the votes between them equally.

As in the one-dimensional case, there does not seem to be

---

example, if A is two inches from B and B is two inches from C, there can be a one-dimensional solution for the three objects only if A is four inches from C.

in general a stable solution for more than two parties. Boulding suggests (1963, page 77), admittedly for a more complicated case, that if shops were setting up on a circular island, with the customers uniformly spread over its surface, they would locate near the centre in such a way as to get territories that divided the island into segments like the slices of a pie, until at some (unspecified) point new entrants would find it preferable to locate further out. But in fact it must always be the case that the best place for the third entrant is where he can take all the trade of the first or second entrants, thus getting half the total instead of the quarter he could hope for by a quasi-co-operative move aimed at getting a distinct slice.[7] The same cut-throat logic applies to further entrants, and also seems unaffected by additional dimensions along which the voters might be distributed. For the basic idea is simply that if the existing firms or parties are already maximising efficiently, the most profitable thing for a new entrant *must* be to capture virtually the entire market or voting support of one of the existing competitors, rather than carve things up so as to make room for one more.

The point is worth making because critics of Downs have sometimes said how artificial it is to treat a multi-party system, such as the French, as if the voters and parties were distributed along only one dimension; and then moved from this correct observation to the suggestion that the existence and workings of a multi-party system could be adequately explained by allowing for more than one dimension. We have tried to show, however, that extending the Downsian one-dimensional analysis to more dimensions does not in itself give reasons for expecting a number of parties nor for the parties to be anywhere except in the middle of the voters as they are distributed over the n-dimensional space. This is not to deny plausibility to the idea that there is a relation between the number of dimensions along which political division exists and the number of parties. It is, though, to assert that

---

[7] Concretely, suppose that A and B are next to each other just west and east of the centre. The best position for C is just west of A or just east of B, thus in effect replacing one of them. The 'pie-slice' move would be to go just north or south of the centre, getting all those customers between north-west and north-east, or south-west and south-east, of the centre.

the connection cannot be established by a simple extension
of Downs's one-dimensional model. The construction of an
n-dimensional model to account for the observed characteristics of multi-party systems still remains a challenge.

But, in any case, is an assumption of more than one dimension sufficiently nearer reality to provide an adequate basis
for a theory of party competition? This is difficult to answer
without a clearer view of the potentialities of such an analysis,
but it may be doubted whether it could satisfactorily model
an entire electorate, though it might well be suitable for the
informed and involved sections of a mass public. Converse,
in the article already mentioned (Converse, 1966), proposes,
to make sense of his Finnish and French data on 'party distances', an ingenious modification of the model in which
everyone in a country can be located somewhere in the same
space. This modification takes the form of postulating that
everyone can be located along the same axes, but the relative
lengths of the axes vary from one person to another. For example, someone for whom the left-right issue is highly salient
but who is not greatly concerned about the religious issue can
be regarded as having a long left-right axis and a short
religious one. What this means is that the 'distance' of a party
from his own position will be mainly affected by its location
on the left-right continuum. Thus, a party at the opposite
extreme to himself on the religious issue could still be fairly
close if it was compatible with his own views on the left-right
question, because the distance between the ends of the
religious axis would not be very great. Similarly, a person who
was mainly interested in the religious question would have a
long 'religious' axis and would thus finish up by ordering
parties in terms of distance from himself mainly on the basis
of their religious positions.

No 'economic' model of party competition has been produced to cover this kind of n-dimensional space, where the
relative length of the co-ordinate varies from person to
person. It gets us further away from ordinary physical space
—we would have to imagine that some consumers are
especially sensitive to how far north and south of their homes
a shop is, while others are particularly affected by a shop's
distance away in an east-west direction. The simplest model
would be one in which part of the population is exclusively

concerned with position on one axis and the rest is exclusively concerned with position on another axis. Interestingly enough, this model seems to work in much the same way as an ordinary two-dimensional one. Although intuitively one might expect a multi-party system to follow especially easily, the only stable situation seems to be two parties each splitting both sets of voters down the middle.

A little reflection should suggest that the fully-complicated version of the Converse n-dimensional model is in essence a special case of the general analysis of party competition which in Downs's book, is the only alternative to a one-dimensional distribution that is explored.[8] Of course, by ignoring the dimensional aspect one would be passing up information about the structure of attitudes, but at present there is no way of using it in a Downsian type of analysis, anyway. Moreover, how realistic is even this sophisticated type of dimensionality, when imputed to a mass electorate? Converse's 'party distances' are, he admits, based on aggregating the responses of all those who put a given party first: the actual responses themselves form almost every combination logically possible. Although Converse does not return to the point after introducing the model with individually variable axes, it hardly seems likely that all the sequences of individual party preferences could be fitted into the same two or even three dimensions, even if the lengths of the axes were allowed to vary so as to get the best fit in each case. Moreover, the French data analysed consist of the responses of those who (i) said they would vote for another party if their own were not available and (ii) gave a preference ranking for all the major (Fourth Republic) parties. Even leaving aside the first point, it is clear that these responses are typical only of a politically interested minority of the electorate. Many other electors apparently had difficulty in thinking of other parties than the one they supported.

We should also ask how far the possibility of putting *parties* on (say) two dimensions entails that *issues* can similarly be represented on two dimensions. This is crucial for a Downsian

[8] Downs's voters who are 'strong' or 'weak' on this or that complex issue might (though they need not) be so situated as a result (or, more precisely, a partial manifestation) of the relative lengths of two or more axes.

analysis in spatial terms, because the space in which the
parties are located is defined in terms of issue-dimensions. It
seems clear that there is no entailment, for a dimension of
party distances could be based on anything. Parties might, for
example, be identified with ethnic or occupational groups,
and these groups form a continuous chain of 'social distance'
from one another. Of course, one could say that ethnicity or
occupation is itself the issue here, but then what has happened to the meaning of the word 'issue'?

4 WHAT IS AN ISSUE?

Until now an 'issue' has been taken to be a matter of public
policy on which two (or more) courses might be taken. We
have already seen how, working mainly from American survey
data, Converse has shown how superficial many of the
'opinions' offered on 'issues' are. The main thrust of the
article (Campbell, 1966, pages 212–42) is, however, directed
to the less general point that most people do not have the
'contextual information' that would enable them to integrate
their opinions into a coherent expression of a certain outlook,
so that different people's attitudes cannot be fitted into a
common framework. I am less convinced than is Converse
that the customary élite idea of 'what goes with what' (anti-
discrimination with large domestic public expenditure and
with internationalism, for example) is simply a matter of contextual information—is not the fact that they are thought to
go together itself learned?—and in any case even among
élites (U.S. legislators, for example) there are separable
dimensions (Macrae, 1958; Truman, 1959). But the contrast
is still well taken, and it is reinforced by the familiar S.R.C.
findings on the small proportion of the sample who gave
'ideological' reasons for supporting one party rather than the
other, and the rather striking lack of familiarity with the
standard American terms for the ends of the 'ideological'
spectrum: 'liberal' and 'conservative'.[9] Policy considerations,
even outside an 'ideological' framework, are still put forward
only by a minority in explaining party preference, but the

[9] Campbell, 1960 Campbell, 1966. For similar findings on Britain
see Butler and Stokes (1969) in which remarkably low familiarity with
the terms 'left' and 'right' is shown.

invocation of a group interest is quite common, especially, it seems, among those who support the Democratic party.[10] Whether such 'group-interest' responses are to count as 'issues' matters for two reasons: first, if they do, they greatly expand the applicability of a general Downsian analysis, and, second, in so far as the groups form a continuum (e.g. a single dimension of stratification over all occupational groups) the spatial Downsian model can be applied here. The criterion for 'rational' voting within Downs's model is that the voting decision should be aimed at modifying (or preventing change in) government policies. Voting on a basis of group interest surely falls under this, though at one remove. Nor is the one remove necessarily irrational itself. Given the need to make a little information go a long way, it seems quite sensible to try to form an impression of the social groups favoured by each party in its policies. As for the other point, it does seem in many ways as if occupations form a status continuum in modern industrial societies (Blau, 1967), and it does not seem ridiculous to imagine saying that a party has moved its appeal upwards or downwards socially.

There is in the S.R.C. protocols another kind of reason to be found for supporting a party, which again raises both the 'issue' and the 'dimension' questions. This is the sort of response referred to by Campbell as the 'goodness/badness of the times'. This is the kind of thinking that associates the Democrats with war or Labour with economic crisis. If it were purely backward-looking it would not count as 'rational' voting in Downsian terms, but Downs himself points out correctly that the soundest way in which to choose with the future in mind is to look at the past. Hence, such voting seems in principle 'rational', though one might well have qualms about the crude conception of social causality underlying it.

Do such judgments admit of spatial representation? Stokes, in his article on spatial models (Campbell, 1966, pages 161–179), suggests that issues fall into two kinds, which he calls

[10] See Converse, 1966. In Britain, too, the Labour party gets a big 'good for the working class' response, or at least it did some years ago (Abrams, 1960). This probably reflects the tendency for the less educated to give group-interest responses rather than implying anything about the altruism of the middle class Republicans or Conservatives.

'valence' issues and 'position' issues. 'Position issues' are 'those that involve advocacy of government actions from a set of alternatives over which a distribution of voter preferences is defined', while 'valence issues' are 'those that merely involve the linking of the parties with some condition that is positively or negatively valued by the electorate' (Campbell, 1966, pages 170–1). As Stokes points out, if parties are to compete by taking different positions on 'dimensions', it is a necessary condition of this that the issues be 'position' rather than 'valence' issues.[11]

I do not, however, think this a very happy distinction. It makes a division into two classes of issue where all we really have is a continuum from issues on which an electorate is evenly divided to issues on which hardly anyone is in the minority. How many people have to be in favour of, say, a Russian occupation of Britain to make it a 'position' issue? Conversely, could one say that being opposed to unrestricted Commonwealth immigration is now a 'valence' issue in Britain, since the liberal side is held by so few? There is no point in giving an answer to these and similar questions because, as Downs has shown, if an electorate is lopsidedly divided on an issue, the tendency will be for the parties to take the majority side.[12] No special process supervenes when the minority falls to a certain size.

Is Stokes really doing more than to utter the tautology that if the parties take the same position on an issue then they

[11] He fails, however, to make it explicit that this is not a sufficient condition. There can be three or more policies in a given area such that no single ordering exists among a group with certain preferences (Arrow, 1951). Thus, in a Vietnam-type situation some may wish to 'win' at any cost, failing which they would prefer to withdraw completely, with continuation of the *status quo* least liked. If others would like withdrawal most, but would settle for the *status quo* in preference to 'winning', no way can be found of putting the three policies in a line which will fit both groups. It is not, of course, their having different preferences that causes the difficulty, but their having different *structures* of preference. (If one set of preferences ran A, B, C and the other ran C, B, A, we should have a common structure.)

[12] We are now, in effect, considering the degenerate case of a 'dimension' with only two points on it (Campbell, 1966, page 170). The word 'tendency' covers the situation in which the minority feels more strongly about the issue than the majority. In such circumstances it may pav a party to espouse the minority side.

cannot be competing by taking different positions on that issue? He is saying more, but to get to what it is we must clear the valence-position dichotomy out of the way. It implies that some issues by their nature make for identical positions being taken by the parties, while others do not. But whatever the distribution of opinion on an issue, the parties may take the same position on it, and Downs shows that it will often pay them to. The question is, what happens then? The valid part of Stokes's analysis is the suggestion that the voters may ask themselves which party is most likely to be effective in carrying out the general lines of the policy on which they agree, and that this sort of calculation does not lend itself to spatial representation. Whether such agreement is as common as Stokes suggests in his presentation of 'valence' issues is doubtful. Both parties may agree that a certain end (peace, or full employment) is desirable, but they may still place different priorities on these ends. We can measure this in terms of the other goods (flag-wagging, or stable prices, for example) that the parties are prepared to see given up to attain the ends in question. Or, again, the parties may differ openly on the means by which the end is to be pursued, and on this a voter might have direct views, not merely by judging the likely success of the methods but because of the nature or side-effects of the methods themselves. The relative *priority* given to a certain end could obviously be put on a line, and in some matters the choice of means might also be. Thus in these cases spatial representation could still be used.

Returning to the straight 'effectiveness' cases: where (as in 'goodness-or-badness-of-the-times' judgments) the judgment is simply that one party is best at keeping out of war, or avoiding slumps, it should be noted again that this is still 'rational' in Downsian terms, in that it is addressed to government policy. The point is worth emphasising because Stokes seriously misrepresents Downs at this point. He writes, 'To be sure, Downs makes allowance for valence-issues by granting that some voting is 'irrational', that is, nonideological in his spatial sense. He asserts, in fact that rational behaviour by the parties of a two-party system tends to encourage irrational behaviour by voters. As the parties converge to ideologically similar positions (assuming a unimodal distribution of voters) their relative position provides fewer grounds for choice, and the voters are driven to deciding between them on some irrational basis' (Campbell, 1966, page 173).

The first misconception embodied in this passage is that voting is rational, for Downs, only in so far as it distinguishes between parties on the basis of difference in position along an issue–continuum. As we have tried to make clear, the spatial model is only one of Downs's models—though a striking one—and the basic logic of voting and party competition is laid out before it is introduced. The second sentence in the passage is accurate, but the third, which purports to give the reasoning behind it, is based on a conflation of two separate points, discussed above, in Chapter V. It is not the identity of the parties on the issues that fosters 'irrationality', but the way in which (Downs claims) they deliberately equivocate, trying to be all things to all men. In fact, Downs explicitly argues that, if the parties are identical on the issues, the rational way to decide how to vote is to look at the performance of the party in office and try to estimate how relatively competent its rivals would be (Downs, 1957, pages 41–5).

CHAPTER VII

Testing Theories of Democracy (2)

1 THE AIMS OF POLITICAL PARTIES

In Chapter VI, we were asking how far the known characteristics of mass electorates fit the premises of Downs's theory.
It is difficult to summarise this labyrinthine discussion, but
we can conclude that the conception of voting as related to
the policy positions of parties stands up better than do the
more specific assumptions about the nature of policy dimensions that are needed to make any spatial model work. There
are also, however, assumptions in all Downs's work about the
behaviour of political parties, and we need to examine the
realism of these, too. On the analogy of the profit-maximising
firm, Downs makes two assumptions about parties: first, that
we can talk about 'the party', treating it as a team of single-
minded men with a common goal; and, second, that this goal
is invariably and solely to maximise votes at the next election.
The statement of this aim might well, as we have seen, be
amended by internal criticism to 'maximising the long-run
average of votes' or (especially in two-party systems) 'winning
as many elections as possible'. But for our present purpose
these can all be lumped together as variants of 'electoral
success' as an aim, and contrasted with other possibilities.
Thus, still keeping a monolithic 'party' as the unit of
analysis, we might ask whether the implementation of a certain programme or at least the furtherance of a certain direction of change (or non-change) should not be regarded as a
primary goal of some, if not all, parties. Instead of comparing
parties with the most general case of a firm, we should perhaps
pick, say, newspapers for an analogy. Some newspaper pro-
prietors (Lord Thomson being a notable current example)
maintain that they are in the business purely to make money.
Their papers still have editorials expressing opinions, but

these are presumably there simply to help sell the paper (or possibly because writing editorials is a perk which helps attract able editors, who in turn make more money for the proprietor). At the other extreme is a proprietor such as the late Lord Beaverbrook, who professed to run his papers purely as propaganda instruments. But since, in the long run, covering costs is a necessary condition of keeping up the propaganda, the circulation must be kept up. A large circulation is, of course, also directly relevant to the aim of maximising influence over opinion.

If we were to give up the assumption that the 'party' can be treated as a monolith, we should be opening up unlimited possibilities for further complication. Thus, even if party leaders regarded policies purely as a means to an end, the end might be the satisfaction of personal ambition rather than the success of the party. They would then care about the electoral success of the party only in so far as this was a necessary condition of their own personal success. Or we could well imagine that different party leaders had different ends—some mainly office, some the promotion of one line of policy, others the promotion of another conflicting line, and so on. We could also break down 'the party' into groups whose members tend to have different aims—front-benchers, back-benchers, and party activists in Britain, for example.

Although it seems clear that abstracting from the internal life of a party is risky, it is still possible that the official policy positions of parties can be the subject of an analysis which ignores the pushes and pulls by which they were arrived at. Let us, for the purposes of this chapter, follow Downs in regarding the parties as opaque, as 'black boxes' relating policies to environments. We return, then, to the question whether electoral success is a sufficiently common primary aim to make the assumption that it is a universal sole aim a workable basis for building a model of competitive politics. This is a difficult question to tackle, and one to which little systematic attention seems to have been given. It is hardly satisfactory to ask politicians, for there is a widespread value that politicians should not be motivated purely by the desire for office but by some desire to further the public weal. This fact gives rise to a variant of the Cretan paradox (the Cretan who said 'All Cretans are liars'). For a politician solely motivated by personal ambition would always deny it, at least in public. Nor, even if sincerity could be guaranteed, would it be easy to discount the capacity of politicians to believe their own humbug.

The only solution is to study the actual behaviour of parties and try to decide how far a party's behaviour corresponds with what we would have predicted on the assumption that its activities were directed to a goal of electoral success. But the path from observation to inference is a thorny one. A party cannot implement any policies unless it wins elections, and to win elections it may have to compromise its policies. Thus, even if a party attributed no value at all to winning, but was entirely concerned with getting a set of policies adopted, it would still be rational for it to give up all its policies but one, if this were the price of getting the chance to enact the remaining one, rather than letting the opposition win and do something different on this last issue. Conversely, a party concerned exclusively with winning elections would obviously have policies, and (as Downs suggests) it would not pay it to change them too sharply.

Thus, although it would be relatively straightforward to spot from its behaviour a party which, in season and out of season, proclaimed the same policies, it would not be so easy to distinguish a party which saw winning as a means to furthering policies from one which saw the pursuit of policies as a means of gaining office. Take, for example, the drastic change in the official Labour party line on Commonwealth (read, 'coloured') immigration, from Gaitskell's opposition to the Conservative Commonwealth Immigrants Act of 1962 to the humiliating submission to panic in 1968 which resulted in the legislation on Kenyan Asians with British passports. The most obvious construction to put on this is that it was motivated by the desire not to lose votes; but the problem is that, even if we accept that this was so, it is very far from conclusive evidence that Labour policy-makers are concerned only to win elections. It would be possible for someone wholly concerned with policy to argue that keeping a liberal policy would so decrease the probability of re-election as actually to reduce the total amount of socialist, radical or egalitarian content in national policy over the next, say, twenty years.

Even if this sounds hollow, the point is in general a valid one. It suggests that, except for what might be called 'witness' parties (who conceive it as a duty to bear witness to some belief), the assumption of electoral calculation can be expected to fit parties at least approximately. The most vivid demonstration of this comes from the two-party one-dimension case which, though too simple to have application itself, reveals the logic of competition most clearly. As we have seen, two parties intent solely on winning elections would in equilibrium station themselves next to one another at the position of the median voter on the ideological spectrum. But so would two parties one of which was concerned solely to get extremely 'left' policies implemented, and the other extremely 'right' policies. For, if they started equal distances from the centre, one could always beat the other (and thus move the policies implemented to its own side of the centre) by moving in a little way; but then the other could beat it in turn (and move the policy implemented to *its* side of the centre) by moving in a little further than its rival; and so on until they reached the middle.

A complication in this analysis lies in the fact that, if one party is concerned with policy and the other with winning, it will pay the policy-oriented party to adopt its own preferred position, no matter how extreme, and let the other party move up to a position somewhere between the centre and itself (immediately adjacent if it is literally a vote-maximising party), thus beating it, but on a platform nearer its own position than any it could hope to win on itself. However, this effect would be moderated by the danger to the electoral party of both existing parties being on the same side of the centre. For the imbalance might tempt political entrepreneurs to start another electoral party or take over the 'shell' of a minor policy-oriented party in the unrepresented area. This should emphasise a point of general significance. In the long run one must expect electoral parties (if organised with a modicum of efficiency) to displace non-electoral parties, because they are in business to succeed in those terms.

Everything so far depends, of course, on the plausibility of chains of reasoning, and, given the shakiness of the premises, it can properly be distrusted. But the question of party motivation has not been studied directly very much. Richard

Rose has studied the 1964 election campaign in Britain, explicitly mentioning as something to be tested Downs's assumption that 'the actions of all politicians [are] aimed solely at maximising votes' (Rose, 1967, page 23). But, although he draws the sweeping conclusion 'that the rational, vote-maximising politician . . . is a myth' (Rose, 1967, page 195), the allegedly mythical element seems to lie, on his own evidence, more in the rationality than the vote-maximising intentions. And even this finding is of uncertain significance, because Rose confined his attention to campaigning. Since, as he admits, propaganda probably has little effect on voting relatively to the experience of the effects of government policy, the crucial question still remains how the policies are decided rather than how the product is promoted, and to this Rose pays little attention. He does quote one Conservative politician bemoaning the fact that Cabinet ministers tend after a time to think more as members of a government than as members of a party facing an election. But this has to be squared with the well-timed booms which won (or helped to win) elections in 1955, 1959, and only failed in 1964 by the tiniest margin. The apparent paradox can probably be solved easily enough. Most of a minister's day is involved in decisions which are of little electoral moment, and electoral considerations fade into the background; but this is quite consistent with electoral advantage playing a large part in decisions where it is thought to be at stake. If we are interested in the genesis of a particular government policy, we may find that an analysis in terms of competitive electoral politics has very little help to give. This fact is important as a limitation of its explanatory power, but it does not mean the model will not work on issues where significant portions of the electorate have views that (whether sensible or not) are firmly and strongly held.

2 THE EFFECTS OF PARTY COMPETITION

We have now looked at the realism of the two basic assumptions underlying the Downsian model: that voters have definite policy preferences or positions along ideological continua on the basis of which they cast their votes, and that parties are not motivated solely by the desire to gain and hold office. But it is also worth looking separately at the realism of Downs's conclusions. For, although we cannot expect an exact fit between the deductions of a model and the facts, the less close the fit the less confidence we can have that the processes of the model approximate those of the real world.

Does party competition, then, have the effects Downs argues on the basis of his theory it should have? This needs a little care in interpretation before we look at 'the facts', for Downs does not attach supreme weight to actual close competition between parties but rather to the continuous possibility of a party's being challenged by another. According to him, the most important determinant of what happens is the distribution of the electorate on the ideological continuum. Thus, to press this beyond the point to which Downs extends his analysis, if there were only one party it would not pay it to take unpopular stands because this would encourage political entrepreneurs to enter the market with an excellent chance of winning. Where there are two parties of unequal size there is similarly good reason for the large party to behave competitively, since at some point the inertia of the electorate might be broken and a large switch to the other party occur. (Downs's analysis of voting can easily account for 'stickiness' in electoral decisions.) Of course, disfranchisement of sections of the population, or sanctions (legal or other) against the formation of parties must alter the situation entirely. But *de facto* non-voting or dominance by a party need not produce markedly different effects from universal voting or an equal division of electoral support among the parties.

Thus, the best test of the Downsian conclusions is to see if the course of legislation and administration changes in a direction more favourable to some group in the population when, after previously having been excluded from the franchise, it is granted the vote. Or, more generally, we should try to see if there is a connection between the distribution of benefits of government action and the extent of the franchise. A full-scale study of these questions would be eminently worth undertaking, great as the difficulties would obviously be. In its absence, all one can do is to express an opinion (on admittedly non-systematic evidence) that the possibility of voting plus the possibility of forming parties does seem to operate as some assurance that the opinions and interests of at least large groups in the population will be taken into account by the government to a greater degree than is usually found in the relations of governments and subjects where these conditions do not hold.

Unfortunately, the systematic work that has been done is related not to the possibility of voting or forming parties but to the actual degree of competition between parties in the different states of the U.S.A. ('Competition' is measured by the closeness of statewide races and the frequency with which parties take control from one another.) Taking governmental outputs as their dependent variables, several writers have shown that differences in output (such as per capita welfare expenditures) do show correlations with the level of party competition. But both of these are also correlated with the per capita income of the state, and this obviously raises the question what are the causal relationships (Lockard, 1959; Dawson, 1963 and 1968; and Dye, 1966).

Should we, however, expect actual competitiveness to be significant? I have suggested that potential competition should be more important. It is also not at all clear that we should predict a high per capita level of welfare expenditures in the U.S.A. as an effect of party competition. Downs argues that the tendency in democratic systems is for the government to redistribute income in a direction of greater equality, because the gainers from this are more numerous than the losers (Downs, 1957, page 198). But, with a 'diamond-shaped' income distribution as in the U.S.A. (the middle income bands more heavily populated than the top or the bottom), equality would probably not benefit markedly more potential voters than it hurt. And, in any case, it is doubtful whether an increase in welfare expenditures is redistributive in its net effects, given the regressive basis of much American state and local taxation.[1]

3 SOME SOCIOLOGICAL EXPLANATIONS

It is instructive to contrast Downs's conception of the workings of party competition with that of Parsons. Parsons has addressed himself to the question of party choice in his review

[1] This last point does not apply to one of Lockard's measures, namely the proportion of business and gift taxes in the total state revenue.

article on *Voting* (Berelson, 1954). This essay, which is entitled ' "Voting" and the Equilibrium of the American Political System' (Parsons, 1967, pages 223–63), rests partly on a very uncritical acceptance of the authors' interpretations of the significance of their findings, and partly on some assumptions introduced by Parsons, some from his general theory and others out of a hat.[2] Among the last category is the statement that 'the intellectual problems involved in a rational solution are not practicably soluble' (Parsons, 1967, page 235). By a 'rational solution' to the problem of deciding how to vote, Parsons means one in which the vote is treated as a means to the end of influencing the direction of government policy. It should be noticed that this is precisely the conception of rationality espoused by Downs. Voting rationally, for Downs, does not merely entail pursuing one's ends effectively (e.g. voting so as effectively to achieve the end of pleasing one's wife), but it restricts the class of ends to cover only states of affairs resulting from the total distribution or number of votes cast. In other words, voting for a certain party is a means to the end of increasing infinitesimally the probability that the government elected will pursue policies of a preferred kind, or at the least it is a means to the end of infinitesimally increasing the chances of the democratic system's surviving. It is true that Downs allows for the phenomenon of the 'opinion leader', but he explains this as a rational delegation of the task of data-processing to someone with ascertained similar values to oneself. Voting in accordance with the advice of an 'opinion leader' is thus still instrumental in intention. The end is still that of having an effect on what actually happens. All that is different in this case is that the calculation of the means is left to somebody else.

As we saw in the last chapter, it is difficult to get a clear answer to the question how far voters have policy-preferences which they try to further through their decision to vote one way rather than another. But we can with some confidence reject Parsons's argument for its being impossible. According to Parsons, 'to judge rationally in terms of the "welfare of the country" is an intellectual task of a very high level of

[2] For a critical discussion of the actual interpretation by Berelson of his findings and the significance for democratic theory that he attaches to them, see Berg, 1964.

complexity and difficulty. Since even the most competent technical experts in such matters, political and social scientists, are far from being agreed on the better direction in a given case, how can the average voter have a competent and well-grounded opinion?' (Parsons, 1967, page 235, footnote 11).

The breathtaking naïveté of these remarks provides a remarkable glimpse of the way in which consensual assumptions form part of the way in which Parsons actually sees the world.[3] First, Parsons assumes—without any supporting evidence— that the only end of public policy which anyone could desire to further by his vote is the promotion of the 'welfare of the country'. And, second, he apparently believes that the determination of the means to the 'welfare of the country' is a purely technical question, so that if the 'experts' disagree this must simply reflect the difficulty of sorting out the causal relationships. But there is no reason why we should follow Parsons on either point. Many people, probably most people, are more concerned with their own prospective welfare, or with that of some other group smaller than the whole society (family, neighbourhood, co-religionists, members of the same class) than with the 'general welfare'. It may not be a very difficult question (perhaps even most 'experts' would agree) which party would, if elected, benefit such a group the most, given its characteristic values and interests. And for those who do try to maximise the 'welfare of the country', the position need not be as hopeless as Parsons states it. When such an expression is used to denote a catch-all end, as in this instance, it means little more than that everybody is supposed to be considered. It leaves open the question what is to count as welfare, and how its ingredients are to be weighted, what is the proper principle of distribution between different people now, or between people now and people in the future. Thus the disagreement of the 'experts' has less significance than Parsons suggests, for disagreement is at least in part a product of different values.[4] One is reminded of Burke's definition of

[3] Parsonian Man thus has at least one exemplar—in Parsons himself!

[4] A rough guide might be that wherever nearly all 'left-wing' economists (sociologists, etc.) agree with one another and disagree with nearly all 'right-wing' economists, we have a *prima facie* case of value-related disagreement. But when the lines of cleavage in opinion cut across the

L

a party as a body of men united by a common view of the public interest. A group of 'experts' with such a common view might be able to agree most of the time on specific policy recommendations; and, in any case, it is only necessary for a voter to choose a party, so all that is required is the ability to discern which one has a view of the public interest more consonant with one's own than the views of its rivals.[5]

We must conclude that it is a mistake to try to argue about voting from the impossibility of rational (policy-oriented) choice. We can, however, look as well at Parsons's view of the way voting decisions are in fact determined. 'Since the intellectual problems involved in a rational solution are not practicably soluble, my thesis is that the mechanisms are typically non-rational. They involve stabilisation of political attitudes *in terms of association with other members of the principal solidary groups in which the voter is involved.* In terms of party affiliation this may be called "traditionalism".' (Parsons, 1967, page 235; italics in original.) Parsons maintains that the evidence from *Voting* is consistent with this idea, but this is not enough if we do not accept that the instrumental conception of voting was demolished by the argument from impossibility. For the features of voting behaviour which are consistent with the 'solidarity' thesis are equally consistent with the 'policy-orientation' thesis. Thus, Parsons observes that 'there is a marked tendency to agree in voting preferences with certain categories of others'. Primarily, this is true of the family, then 'friends, occupational associates, fellow members of ethnic and religious groups, and class associates—this last

---

usual boundaries, we are more likely to have a dispute in which the main source of disagreement is empirical uncertainty—though it may, of course, be a question that involves a dimension of value that is not usually relevant.

[5] Curiously enough, Parsons, in the same footnote, recognises that the choice is between a few alternatives only. But, instead of concluding that this should make it easier than if one had to cast a vote on each of a great number of policies, he argues that it makes it impossible to be rational, because other people with different 'specific ends' from one's own will finish up voting for the same candidate. This looks like a cousin to F. M. Cornford's description of 'the method of *Prevarication*' which, he says, 'is based on a very characteristic trait of the academic mind, which comes out in the common remark "I was in favour of the proposal until I heard Mr. ——'s argument in support of it" ' (Cornford, 1908, page 26).

the more so in proportion to the individual's class identification' (Parsons, 1967, page 239). This tendency is explained
by Parsons as a way of feeling 'comfortable' in the absence of
a rational basis for decision. 'I suggest that it is symbolically
appropriate that, in performing an "act of faith" which
establishes a relation of trust the consequences of which, however, cannot be directly controlled [i.e. voting—B.B.], a
person should feel most secure in associating himself with
persons who, by virtue of their real solidary relationship to
him, are the ones he feels most naturally can be trusted'
(Parsons, 1967, page 240).

An alternative to this 'instinct of the herd' interpretation
of the phenomenon would be to point out that those with
common positions in a society are likely to have common
interests and values. Parsons himself notes that members of
his groups have to a greater or lesser extent 'a common fate
in the face of whatever vicissitudes may come and go'. Surely
a common fate implies a common interest? The aside that
class is a more important determinant of voting behaviour
the stronger the sense of class consciousness bears this out perfectly, since class consciousness is precisely the belief that one's
interests are the same as those in a similar situation.[6]

An obvious difficulty with a theory of voting behaviour of
the kind put forward by Parsons is accounting for electoral
change. A certain amount can be done by appealing to demo-
graphic changes (differential birthrates and mortality-rates,
changes in the occupational structure, and so on) but not
enough. Parsons, following *Voting*, identifies the changers as
those who are 'cross-pressured', that is to say belong in two
or more 'solidary' groups with opposed voting norms. But,
although the 'cross-pressured' might provide a pool of voters
so evenly-balanced by the forces of social affiliation as to introduce an element of randomness into the results, this would

[6] One may indeed ask whether a class need be a 'solidary' group, in
the sense in which this conception fits into Parsons's general scheme
under which voting is related to the 'integrative system'. In Banbury,
for example, Margaret Stacey's study showed that the idea of being
'working class' functioned as a 'reference group' for many of those who
were not integrated into the local community and, it would appear, not
particularly integrated among themselves. But they still voted Labour,
whereas the 'locals' tended to vote Conservative. See Frankenberg, 1966,
page 165.

mean that the result of any election which turned on the votes of the 'cross-pressured' would be literally inexplicable, since it would have turned on random changes.[7] (And it is hard to see why these random movements should not, over a large number of electors, cancel out.) Nor can the theory explain permanent shifts in the proportions of the electorate supporting the different parties, such as the political realignment after 1932 which made the Democrats a permanent majority party in terms of voter registrations and (nearly all the time) Congressional seats. Nor can it account for sharp changes of a more temporary kind, such as the two Eisenhower victories in 1952 and 1956. Parsons in fact introduces here an *ad hoc* explanation in terms of the general's 'charismatic' qualities. In this sort of context (as against Weber's use of the term in the context of types of legitimate rule) talking about 'charisma' merely repeats what is to be explained, namely that Eisenhower was electorally popular. But, in any case, this sort of 'explanation' hardly seems to fit the Johnson–Goldwater election of 1964, which makes much more sense in terms of a Downsian analysis, with Goldwater out on the right of the centre of the ideological spectrum.[8]

This raises the question of the predictive force of Downs's

[7] The mechanism postulated by Berelson is apparently communication: you vote the way the majority of the people you speak to say that they intend to vote. But, as Luce has pointed out (Luce, 1959), the evidence they provide (a table relating present voting intention to opinions of person last spoken to) does not support their 'billiard-ball' model any more strongly than it supports the alternative view that you talk to those you expect to agree with your present views. An important technical point is that Berelson *et al.* discuss only vote-changing within the campaign period; but the significant definition in explaining electoral change is a change from one *election* to the next. This is important because those who change during the campaign are probably different from those who change before. (See Key, 1966.)

[8] More generally, if people vote with their solidary groups, the 'cross-pressured' coming down randomly, how can we explain the way in which in a series of elections social groups will split in different proportions? Even more striking is the way in which a similar pattern of cleavage may arise in two elections separated in time by a number of others, when the same issues recur as the most salient ones. See for example the analyses of voting in certain Midwestern states by Rogin, 1967, and the classification of American elections into types by Burnham, 1968. An interesting attempt to show what would have happened in the 1960 election if different issues had been salient is Pool, 1964.

theory as against Parsons's. Apparently the only claim by
Parsons to have deduced anything from his theory is in connection with the location of party support in the 'integrative
system', hence in solidary groups (Parsons, 1967, page 263).
And, even then, Parsons qualifies this by saying 'I have only
provided certain "theoretical boxes" into which these findings can be fitted and have tested the goodness of fit in a broad
way' (Parsons, 1967, page 259, footnote 48). I am not at all
clear how Parsons believes one tests goodness to fit into a box
(should it be a snug fit or one that leaves plenty of room?) but
it certainly sounds a lot less exacting than verifying a theory.
Very little seems to follow in turn from the notion of solidar-
istic voting. It can be predicted that there will be little turnover between elections, and that what there is will be mostly
random, but, as we have seen, this prediction has to be supplemented by *ad hoc* additions to fit the facts. Nothing seems to
follow about the behaviour of parties, since there seems no
room for anything they do to alter the results of elections from
what demography and chance together ordain. Severely as
we have found it necessary to criticise Downs's theory, it
can hardly be denied that it comes out well from this comparison.

I do not know of any other exponent of the 'sociological'
approach who has committed himself to a broad description
of the process of party choice in the way that Parsons has. But
it is worth taking note of some sociological discussions of
support for Senator Joe McCarthy in the nineteen-fifties. For
here we find the same devaluation of the manifest content of
issues, and the same tendency to explain behaviour as a non-
rational expression of the actor's social position. According
to this line of analysis, support for McCarthy was a manifestation of 'status panic'. Times of prosperity, the theory
runs, are times in which 'status politics' flourishes, whereas
times of economic depression and hardship lend themselves
to the politics of interest—'class politics'. The early nineteen-
fifties were a period of established prosperity, and were thus
ripe for the exploitation of status anxieties. McCarthy
appealed to those who had made the grade economically,
but felt that their standing in the community had not risen
commensurately. These would typically be members of
ethnic groups other than the dominant 'white Anglo-Saxon

'Protestants', who could enjoy vicarious status, so to speak, by hearing McCarthy attack the occupations ('striped-pants diplomatists') and the institutions (Harvard) associated with the high-status group. More generally, all upwardly-mobile people might be liable to status anxiety. (See Bell, 1962, for a collection of influential statements of this sort of view.)

The most obvious alternative to such an interpretation is to follow an 'economic' approach. This means asking what McCarthy actually stood for, and seeing whether those who voted for him or expressed support for him held views such that doing so represented a rational, issue-based, political decision. This is a view that has been put forward persuasively by Michael Paul Rogin (Rogin, 1967; see also Polsby, 1960). Supporters of McCarthy in public opinion polls were much more likely to be Republicans than Democrats (McCarthy was a Republican). And on both foreign and domestic issues McCarthy adherents tended to have right-wing attitudes (Rogin, 1967, pages 233–5). 'Most people supported McCarthy because he was identified in the public mind with the fight against communism' (Rogin, page 242). Working class support, expressed in public opinion polls, was an anti-communist reflex, Rogin suggests. It did not imply enthusiasm for his methods. These were much more likely to be salient for more educated people, who tended to respond negatively to questions about McCarthy. Roman Catholics also tended disproportionately to express support for McCarthy, but this again need not involve explanations such as those which invoke 'status anxieties'. McCarthy was himself a Roman Catholic, and the pattern of voting in 1960 showed that a Roman Catholic can pick up votes from his co-religionists simply *qua* Roman Catholic. Moreover, there are good reasons why Roman Catholics should be particularly sympathetic to anti-communism as an issue, for the Church was officially strongly anti-communist both on general ideological grounds and because of the hostility of the newly installed communist régimes in Eastern Europe to the traditional position of the Church (Rogin, 1967, page 246).

As Rogin observes, saying in a poll, when asked about McCarthy, that he is doing 'a good job' is a long way from actually being prepared to vote for him or for candidates supported by him, and most of the vaguely 'pro' responses were not associated with an expressed willingness to vote for McCarthy-backed candidates.[9] Wisconsin was the state which McCarthy represented in the Senate, and the pattern of his voting support has been carefully analysed on a county-by-county basis by Rogin. This shows that McCarthy ran ahead of the regular Republican ticket in the area of Wisconsin from which he came and was presumably most well-known— a common effect dubbed by V. O. Key Jr. 'friends-and-neighbours' voting. He was also supported disproportionately by Catholics in his own state; this may be explained, as we explained the vaguer national support among Catholics, partly in terms of McCarthy's own Catholicism and partly in terms of the Church's anti-communism. Finally, McCarthy was especially popular among the descendants of Polish and Czechoslovak immigrants. But this tallies well with the interpretation of support for McCarthy as reflecting genuine concern with the anti-communist issue, for 'these groups must have been aware of recent Communist seizures of power in their native countries' (Rogin, 1967, page 96).

Here, then, we have juxtaposed two rival accounts of the same phenomenon, support for Senator Joe McCarthy. Obviously the two accounts could both be true, one account applying to some supporters and the other to the remainder; or both might apply simultaneously to some people. But, in fact, the claims that have been made for the *predominant* importance of one factor or the other are clearly incompatible with one another. It seems to me that on the present evidence most weight should be given to overt political component, if only because we know that it relates to support for McCarthy whereas the coincidence of a favourable attitude to McCarthy and feelings of 'status anxiety' is a pure postulate of the 'sociological' theorists. No doubt, 'status anxiety' is rampant in any society in which social status is not wholly ascribed at birth. The question is whether those who did not support McCarthy suffered from it any less than those who did. (See Wolfinger, 1964, page 274.)

---

[9] 'In January 1954, when a majority of the total American population favoured McCarthy, only 21% said they would be more likely to vote for a candidate he sponsored, while 26% said they would be less likely to' (Rogin, 1967, page 244).

4 JUSTIFICATIONS OF DEMOCRACY

To conclude the chapter, let us compare briefly the values underlying the analyses of Downs and Parsons, and in so doing note a line of criticism which would, if accepted, deal a serious blow to both of them considered as justifications of democratic government, though not necessarily as descriptions of the way it actually works. The justification of democracy implicit in Downs is fairly straightforward: the system of competitive parties provides a practicable method for the aggregation of wants for different government policies among the members of a society. With his conception of the parties as each offering a package of policies to the electorate, Downs can provide a solution of sorts to both the 'Arrow problem' of collective intransitivity of preference (the 'paradox of voting') and the 'Dahl problem' of the so-called 'intense minority', the case where the members of the minority on an issue feel on the average more strongly about it than do the members of the majority.[10]

Arrow shows that if there are more than two voters and more than two mutually exclusive policies for them to put into rank-order, the preferences of the voters may be such as to make it impossible to reach a consistent 'social decision' by any procedure which satisfies certain prima facie 'democratic' conditions.[11] That part of Downs's analysis which is concerned with two-party competition avoids the problem by ensuring that on any issue there are only two alternatives. Where he admits more than two parties he likewise assumes away the problem by always supposing that the voters' preferences can be placed on a continuum. (It is known that with this sort of preference-structure the 'Arrow problem' cannot occur.)

The 'intense minority' problem is met somewhat more satisfactorily. It is clear that if all policies were decided in separate independent votes, whichever policy had a majority would always win, even if much of the time the majority was

[10] For the 'Arrow problem' see Arrow, 1951, and Murakami, 1957. For Dahl's discussion of the 'intense minority' problem, see Dahl, 1956.

[11] A 'consistent social decision' is one such that, if policy A is socially preferred to policy B and policy B is socially preferred to policy C, then policy A is socially preferred to policy C.

much more lukewarm than the minority. But the parties, in aggregating a number of stands on different issues into a single electoral package, have an incentive to take into account intensities of preference among the voters, since, as we saw in Chapter V, a 'coalition of minorities' strategy may be profitable.[12]

Parsons's conception of the working of democratic politics cannot be so readily identified with a view of its *raison d'être*. It seems safe enough to say that it does *not* involve any idea about the matching of government policies with the wishes of the voters to have one policy rather than another pursued. For, as we have seen, Parsons regards the determinants of voting as lying outside the issues on which elections are ostensibly fought, so the parties would seem to have no motive for taking the voters' attitudes to issues (if they have any) into account. Perhaps the only point Parsons wishes to hold to is that in an advanced industrial society, stability can be assured only within the framework of a political system which encourages as many people as possible to give it their voluntary support. Democratic politics is a way of sublimating violent conflict without invoking state coercion on the scale of most communist régimes.[13]

What both of these justifications share is a view of political participation as something to be judged according to the results it brings about. If there were some better way of engineering consensus in a complex society, it would follow from these value-premises that the alternative should be adopted in preference to a system of parties competing for votes. A contrary view, with which neither theory can really cope, is that political activity is itself a good, and that it is therefore by no means a matter of ethical indifference what is the means by which policy decisions binding on a society

[12] This requires, of course, that the voters should split along different lines on different issues. A group—say an ethnic, racial or religious minority—which is in the minority on every issue can take no comfort from Downs. For, whatever its intensity of feeling (or, if that sounds too capricious and subjective, whatever the amount it stands to lose) it can still summon up only a minority of votes.

[13] Lipset's notion of the 'democratic class struggle' seems to fit this (Lipset, 1963). Two statements along the lines indicated are Plamenatz, 1966, and Dahrendorf, 1968. For an attack on the view that democratic politics provides an antidote for violence, see Moore, 1968.

are reached.[14] Thus, Peter Bachrach has suggested that recent theories of the kind we have been considering treat men's interests as lying solely in the outcome of government policy, rather than allowing, as 'classical theorists' did, that 'interests also include the opportunity for development which accrues from participation in meaningful political decisions'. (Bachrach, 1967, page 95. See on this also Duncan and Lukes, 1963.)

It is easy enough to point out that John Stuart Mill or Rousseau attached importance to participation in political decision-making as an end in itself rather than regarding it merely as a means to some further end. What is much more difficult is, notoriously, to get beyond this and say how a modern state might be organised in such a way as to give everyone (or even a large proportion of the population) 'participation in meaningful political decisions', where this means not merely voting but actually taking part personally in the disposition of political issues. Bachrach admits, in the final chapter which he devotes to the question, that the problem of providing for general participation is insoluble if we confine the realm of politics to the state. If we are prepared to allow, however, for the fact that large business corporations are sufficiently important for their decisions to count as 'political', the problem reduces to the somewhat more tractable one of 'workers' control'. It would take us too far to go into the question of the feasibility of providing 'political' experience at work. Suppose, however, that we conclude (as I would be inclined to do) that much more could be done along these lines than is now done in, say, Britain. This still leaves the state to be run in the same way as before.[15] So we still return to the question of what are the appropriate criteria for the operation of a state, if the value of personal participation in decision-making as a means of self-development is treated as inapplicable. And the idea that policies should take into account the interests and aspirations of the citizens seems to me no contemptible one.

[14] See, for a very abstract development of the view, Arendt, 1958. A less hieratic, but still elusive, statement of it is Crick, 1962.

[15] This was, of course, the stumbling-block for the Guild Socialists, who tried, implausibly, to get round it by relabelling the state as a co-ordinating body for the industrial guilds.

CHAPTER VIII

Conclusion

1 CONCEPTIONS OF 'THEORY'

In this final chapter, we shall leave behind the close attention to detail of the preceding six chapters. Rising into rarer, more intoxicating, air, we shall conclude our survey from a greater distance, in the hope that some general features of comparison will emerge. We shall focus attention on two points. First, to what extent are the various components of an 'approach' necessarily tied together? Do we have two mutually exclusive packages, or is the connection between one item and another merely conventional, or is it something in between? And, second, what are the prospects for the future of the two approaches or (if we decide it is possible) for a combination of them?

In order to provide a basis for settling the first question, I shall start by enumerating the ways in which the paradigmatic 'economic' and 'sociological' theorists differ.

If we compare Downs, as a representative of the 'economic' school, with Parsons, as a representative of the 'sociological' school, we can see that, except for a common tendency to distance themselves from the 'facts', they are contrasted at every point. Downs operates with a psychological assumption of utility-maximising, whereas Parsons heavily emphasises normative constraints and asserts the impossibility of conceiving action in other than normatively-conditioned ways. Parsons offers in his main books successive refinements of a framework for analysing all social phenomena, whereas Downs concentrates on party competition in his first book and bureaucracy in his other, more recent, book (Downs, 1967). Underlying these differences are opposed ideas about the nature of a theory and the basic conceptual elements such as 'system' and 'equilibrium'. So far in this book we have kept clear of the 'higher methodology'—that bourne from which no traveller returns—but the object of this final chapter demands that some note should now be taken of it.

What is a theory? For the economists, a theory consists of a set of axioms from which deductions can be made. If the axioms correspond to the facts, the propositions deduced will be true; conversely, if the propositions deduced are false, there must be something wrong with the axioms. Downs, and Olson as well, insist that their theories give rise to assertions which are capable of being checked, thus disconfirming or supporting the theory.

For Parsons, a theory can be satisfactory even if no testable propositions can be deduced from it. 'A theoretical system in the present sense is a body of logically interdependent generalised concepts of empirical reference' (Parsons, 1954, page 212). A *theory* is, in Parsonian usage, the same thing as a *conceptual scheme*. This emerges clearly in the opening sentences of *The Social System*: 'The subject of this volume is the exposition and illustration of a conceptual scheme for the analysis of social systems in terms of the action frame of reference. It is intended as a theoretical work in the strict sense. Its direct concern will be neither with empirical generalisation as such nor with methodology . . .' (Parsons, 1951, page 3).

This is not, however, intended to imply that a theorist's conceptual proposals are immune from criticism on the basis of empirical study. There is a criterion for distinguishing a good set of concepts from a bad one: 'usefulness in empirical research' (Parsons, 1951, page 3). *The Structure of Social Action* depends entirely upon this criterion. For it would obviously be void of persuasive force to argue that there was a convergence of conceptual frameworks among a number of writers if the works of these writers were admitted to be worthless. The argument must be that Weber, Durkheim and Pareto said true and important things *and* that they would not have been able to do so had they not adopted the 'conceptual frameworks', whose common features Parsons claims to have set out in *The Structure of Social Action*.

Though Parsons employs a conception of 'theory' different from that in which mechanics or economics can be said to be theories, it should not be imagined that he slights the sort of theory from which deductions can be made. On the contrary, 'the ideal solution is the possession of a logically complete system of dynamic generalisations which can state all the elements of reciprocal interdependence between all the variables of the system. The ideal has, in the formal sense, been attained only in the systems of differential equations of analytical mechanics' (Parsons, 1954, page 216). Parsons adds that 'economics has directly followed the methodological model of analytical mechanics and has been able to do so because, uniquely among social disciplines, it can deal primarily with numerically quantitative continua as variables' (Parsons, 1954, page 224). He points out, however, that it is not possible actually to solve all the equations for any real-life economy, so most economic analysis proceeds on the basis of simplified illustrations.

These quotations should be enough to show that Parsons regards his own kind of theory simply as the best that can be done, given the complexity of social phenomena. Whether he thinks it is the best that could ever be done is less clear, and perhaps he is not sure himself. He is certainly not against making general statements of fact, and, in his 'applied' articles especially, he makes many himself, though he denies that isolated generalisations should be called 'theory'. In attacking as misguided the kinds of very broad generalisation about societal evolution and so on put forward by Comte, Spencer or Marx his point seems to be, not that what they were trying to do was intrinsically impossible, but that it was premature. It was an attempt 'to attain, at one stroke, a goal which can only be approached gradually by building the necessary factual foundations and analytical tools' (Parsons, 1954, page 219).[1]

Those we have identified as the followers of Parsons in the study of politics do not apparently share Parsons's view of the meaning of 'theory', since they tend to use it more broadly than he would do. Almond and Verba come closest in that the 'theoretical' part of their treatise consists of the development of a typology of kinds of political orientation. The vernacular use of 'theory' as in 'I've got a theory about that'—roughly

---

[1] It may be that Parsons now considers the foundations have been sufficiently well laid. See Parsons, 1966b, which seems to be engaged in much the same kind of broad generalisation about social evolution he had earlier criticised.

speaking, a speculative assertion—seems to account for the way Lipset and Eckstein employ it. (Thus Eckstein's 'Theory of Stable Democracy' is simply the unsubstantiated *proposition* that stable democracy depends on 'congruence'.) The main point to note is that the 'economic' notion of a theory, as an axiomatic set and its deductions, is absent from all examples of 'sociological' analysis.

2 CONCEPTIONS OF 'SYSTEM' AND 'EQUILIBRIUM'

'System' and 'equilibrium' are so closely related that they are best treated together. Economists talk fairly unselfconsciously about the 'economic system' and make a good deal of use of the concept of 'equilibrium'. By speaking of the economy as a 'system' all that is usually meant, I think, is that it can be regarded as a set of parts which are causally interrelated, not in the sense that a change in one changes all the others, but in the sense of forming a network in which everything is connected to something else and there do not exist proper subsets such that no member of the subset has a connection with any part outside it.

As far as equilibrium is concerned, the most important point to make is that it is a theoretical notion. That is to say, it is not something to be directly observed. Rather, it forms part of the deductive apparatus within a theory. An equilibrium position occurs when none of the actors has any reason (within the theory's assumptions about motivation) for wishing to change his behaviour.

'Equilibrium' does not mean the same as 'stable equilibrium'. In a stable equilibrium (as against an unstable or a neutral equilibrium) a disturbance of the original position leads to a return to that position. Thus, in the theory of games, a 'saddle point' (so called because of its appearance in a three-dimensional representation) is an equilibrium because no player has an incentive to depart from it; and it is a stable equilibrium because if one player does depart from it, he has an incentive to return to it, whereupon the others also have an incentive to return to it, even if it paid them to deviate in the interim. Similarly, in Downs's analysis of two-party competition, the position of the two parties in adjacent positions on the ideological spectrum is an equilibrium position because neither has an incentive to move, i.e. neither can hope to increase its support by so doing. Given unrestricted mobility, we can add that adjacent positions in the middle constitute a stable equilibrium situation. For if one party did move away from the middle, it would have an incentive to move back again.[2]

If we ask what Parsons means by 'system' and 'equilibrium' we cannot avoid becoming involved, however cursorily, in the issue of 'functionalism'. Cutting ruthlessly through the tangle, we may identify two interesting ways in which Parsons can be regarded as a functionalist.[3] First, it might be asserted that Parsons indulges in teleological explanation: that is, he sometimes explains the existence of something by pointing to its effects in bringing about or maintaining some other phenomenon, such as the maintenance of the variables of a certain system within certain boundaries. I believe Parsons does do this, and that to do so is always invalid. But I mention it here only to get it out of the way and to distinguish it from the second kind of 'functionalism', which may have grievous faults but is not, like the first, to be dismissed as simply invalid.

This second way in which Parsons may be regarded as a functionalist is relevant to the present discussion because it involves a special assumption about the sort of system that is a social system and the sort of equilibrium to be found in it. According to this, a social system is a homeostatic system and equilibrium is to be understood not merely as equilibrium in general, not even as stable equilibrium, but as an even more rigorous kind of self-adjustment. A system is called 'homeo-

[2] If we follow Downs in introducing a restriction on movement such that the parties can never move past one another on the spectrum, all we can say is that any position with two parties adjacent to one another is one of *neutral* equilibrium. For, if one moves, from whatever point on the spectrum, in the only direction it can (given the presence of the other party next to it on one side or the other) the other party will have an incentive to follow it, and neither will then have an incentive to move again. (The one that made the first move will, of course, have lost by it and may be supposed to *wish* it could return to the *status quo ante*, but this is ruled out by the prohibition on passing.)

[3] There are also uninteresting ways in which, on some definitions of 'function', *everyone* can be regarded as a functionalist.

static' if it contains mechanisms capable of changing its performance so as to keep a certain variable or certain variables within some limits. (See Nagel, 1956.) The usually cited examples are a thermostatically controlled central heating system (with respect to the temperature of air in the house) and the human body (with respect to, among other things, blood temperature).

A homeostatic equilibrium differs from a stable equilibrium in that a stable equilibrium does not entail a move back to the *status quo ante* if the system is disturbed by a change in the exogenous variables. Thus, on Downs's theory, we can identify the mid-point of a given ideological spectrum as a position of stable equilibrium for both parties because it would not pay either to move away and if one did it would have an incentive to move back. But if the distribution of the electorate on the spectrum changed (a change in an exogenous variable) the old position of the parties would no longer be an equilibrium and we would expect them to move to a new one at the new mid-point. But, in a homeostatic system, the equilibrium position is supposed to be maintained in the face of changes in the environment.

Parsons has never given any explicit reasons for thinking that social systems are most usefully treated as homeostatic systems. He argues that, since social phenomena are not amenable to the kind of treatment found in mechanics, the alternative must be a 'functional' type of analysis. In this, 'factors and processes' are regarded as 'important' in so far as they have a 'function' for the 'structure'—'that system of determinate patterns which empirical observation shows, within certain limits, "tend to be maintained" or on a somewhat more dynamic version "tend to develop" according to an empirically constant pattern (e.g. the pattern of growth of a young organism)' (Parsons, 1954, page 217).

But it is a long way from observing that certain things stay roughly the same over time to being justified in assuming the presence of a homeostatic system. We can draw weight curves for babies and say, on the basis of experience, that if a baby loses weight due to an illness it will tend to catch up again when it recovers to the point where it would have been in the absence of the illness. We could never say that on the basis of studying just one baby, but social systems are much more dissimilar than babies. Suppose that we observe a constant level or steady trend in some social variable in a society: this cannot by itself be accepted as evidence for the existence of a homeostatic process. A price might be constant because there is no change in the supply and demand schedules for the good, or because there are changes in both which happen to cancel out. It would be quite fallacious to deduce from the fact of stability that there is any mechanism which would compensate for changes in the system (an increase in the cost of producing the good, or a greater taste for it) in such a way as to bring the price back to the same level.[4]

Connoisseurs of confusion may relish the following passage, (from Lipset, 1964, pages 7–8): 'Sometimes, if one utilises a stable equilibrium model, one emphasises the self-regulating and restorative mechanisms. For the purposes of this book, I have tried to think of a dynamic (that is, moving or unstable) equilibrium model, which posits that a complex society is under constant pressure to adjust its institutions to its central value system, in order to alleviate strains created by changes in social relations . . .' Lipset first disavows homeostatic equilibrium, while calling it stable equilibrium; then conflates the entirely different notions of dynamic, moving and stable equilibrium; and finally espouses homeostatic equilibrium in the fallaciously teleological form ('in order to'). The truth is, I think, that homeostatic conditions are fairly rare in social life—where they occur it is usually, as it is with physical systems, because someone has designed them —and their analysis is in no sense easier than that of non-homeostatic systems.

The contrast between a 'functionalist' approach and that of, say, Downs is easy enough to see. If you assume that you are dealing with a homeostatic system, you start by trying to identify the end-states which the system tends to maintain, and then you look for the mechanisms whose 'function' it is to do the maintaining.[5] Now recall the way in which Downs

[4] This is quite consistent with the existence of a stable equilibrium, since stable equilibrium requires only that, if the price for some reason departs from the equilibrium level while the factors affecting the equilibrium remain the same, it will tend to return to that level.

[5] As mentioned earlier, believing that the mechanism is *explained* by its 'function' is an optional error, which may or may not be adopted at this point.

M

and Olson proceed. Rather than positing an end-state and then asking how it is brought about and maintained in spite of changes in the 'environment', they set up a system of general assumptions and then ask how things can be expected to work out under various 'initial conditions'. These can be regarded as exogenously determined, or given by the 'environment' of the system. Examples are the opinions of the voters in Downs's theory and the selective rewards or sanctions potentially available to an organisation in Olson's.

For Parsons, as we saw in Chapter IV, the end-state to be explained is the maintenance of 'social order'. This has subsequently been described as 'system integration', and it would appear that it can best be recognised as a state of affairs in which the expectations of each actor about the behaviour of others are by and large borne out. (See Parsons, 1951, pages 36–9, and 1954, page 231.) The main mechanism is the system of values and norms, which are instilled in the individual by socialisation in the family, and maintained in the society at large by special agencies, notably religion.

Here, as in other matters, the political writers whom we have picked out as heirs of Parsons have tended to extract the more directly applicable parts of Parsons, without worrying too much about the complex structure in which these parts are embedded. Thus, all the writers we looked at took the maintenance of an end-state as a point of reference, and in each case it was 'stable democracy'. This is obviously a much more concrete, institutionally specific, end-state than that chosen by Parsons; but the emphasis on 'stability' shows clearly enough the kinship with Parsonian 'social order' or 'system integration'. And, of course, the method by which the end-state is to be maintained is, for Parsons's followers as for Parsons himself, the inculcation of appropriate values through socialisation and through the use of suitable rituals or symbols[6]. Thus, Verba has written, *à propos* of the reactions to the assassination of John F. Kennedy: 'He [the President] is the symbolic referent for the learning of political commitment; children first become aware of political matters through an awareness of and diffuse attachment to the President. As

---

[6] For a bizarre, though seriously intended, example of the latter, see Shils, 1953. A recent article, drawing together statements of the theme from contemporary political sociologists, is Lipsitz, 1968.

Durkheim pointed out, complex social collectivities . . . are not easily the direct objects of emotional attachment or commitment. Rather some common symbol . . . is required . . . This central symbolic role in a modern secular society is preempted by the political symbols that stand on the highest level for the society—in the American case by the presidency above all' (Verba, 1965, page 353).

3 UNDERLYING VALUES

What is the relation of these two academic schools, the 'economic' and the 'sociological', with the nineteenth-century ideologies of utilitarianism on one hand and romanticism/ historicism/reaction on the other? This is not the place to discuss the general issue of the feasibility or desirability of 'value-free social science'. But I think it will be useful to point out now that when one speaks of an 'ideology' one is not referring solely (or perhaps even mainly) to a set of prescriptions about the way to behave but also to a general way of conceiving man and society. It is in this sense rather than the first sense in which we can say that the economic and sociological approaches to politics still trail shreds of ideology.

Let us begin, though, by trying to detach the 'values' from the preconceptions in which they are rooted. The most overt difference between Bentham and Coleridge is, after all, that Bentham was a utilitarian and Coleridge was an anti-utilitarian. For the utilitarians, the criterion of a good society was that it should maximise happiness, where, as Bentham plainly indicated, the best way of finding out what gave a man happiness was to see what he decided to do when offered a choice. Coleridge, and those who thought like him, conceived of the good life not as one in which the maximum amount of want-satisfaction took place but as one in which character was developed in desirable directions and potentialities realised. (An obvious problem arises when these two criteria conflict.) A good society would thus be one which facilitated the attainment of these objects.

Commitments to general evaluative positions are, of course, much more muted than this among contemporary political theorists of either the 'economic' or the 'sociological' school.

But it does not require great detective powers to discover a continuing link. To illustrate this it is only necessary to refer again to alternative justifications of democratic politics. Downs shows clearly that he regards the justification of democracy as lying in the capacity of party competition to force governments to take account of the wishes of the citizens. Though he supposes that most citizens attach value to the maintenance of a democratic system, they do so purely because they expect to get more wants satisfied under such a system than under any likely alternative. This is, of course, a line of argument put forward in some detail, though less formally, by Bentham in, for example, the *Constitutional Code* (Bentham, 1843, Vol. 9) and James Mill in his *Essay on Government* (Mill, J., 1828).

The 'sociological' writers are less explicit, but they are non-utilitarians in that they endow democratic institutions with a value apparently not derived from criteria of want-satisfaction. There is, of course, a difficulty in dealing with the evaluative positions of writers who posit an end-state; one may assume too easily that the end-state is supposed by the writer to be desirable. Nevertheless, a reader is left in little doubt by Almond and Verba, Eckstein, or Lipset, that 'stable democracy' is something to which value is attached. Want-satisfaction is valuable in so far as it contributes to 'stable democracy', and not vice versa.

Parsons is relatively detached about the value to be attributed to his end-state. It is sometimes suggested (and much more often denied!) that functionalism is 'conservative' in its implications because of its concentration on the conditions of stability. But Parsons's own policy-oriented writings suggest that it is possible to decide first whether a given social system is one that one wishes to preserve. Thus, in his essay on McCarthyism (Parsons, 1960, pages 226–47) he adopts an explicitly conservative stance, calling for a rally of 'business and non-business elements' in defence of the status quo. 'Broadly, I think, a political élite in the two main aspects of "politicians" whose specialties consist in the management of public opinion, and of "administrators" in both civil and military services, must be greatly strengthened. . . . But . . . there must also be close alliance with other, predominantly "cultural" elements, notably perhaps in the universities, but also in the churches' (Parsons, 1960, page 247). This is pretty scary stuff, but it is a reflection of Parsons's own views rather than a consequence of his functionalism as one can see by comparing it with his paper on the right way to treat Germany after the Second World War. (Parsons, 1954, pages 238–74; paper originally published in 1945.) This emphasises the advantages of division within Germany for the facilitation of social change and argues that stability should be prevented from coming about too quickly, since early stability could occur only if power fell into the hands of those who had held it before.

4 IMPLICIT ASSUMPTIONS

In the sense of ideology in which it is concerned with a general outlook on man and society, Parsons is undeniably ideological. George Orwell once said that there are some people who *always* assume that the Bishop has a mistress. There are others who will go to some lengths to continue believing that the Bishop simply believes pastoral care is a twenty-four hour duty. Parsons is surely numbered among them. Thus, for example, he believes American doctors are not interested in maximising their incomes (Parsons, 1954, pages 62–4) and *defines* power as a resource used 'in the interest of collective goals' (Parsons, 1960, page 181). To some extent, this can be regarded as a peculiarity of Parsons, but an emphasis on 'values', which is of course common to the 'sociological' school, does seem to have implications which reflect a rosy glow on the features of societies at which radicals might look askance. Thus, the most important inequalities are seen as those of status, but these differences simply correspond to the different extents to which different people fulfil the *common* criteria of social honour. And, of course, if there are severe material inequalities without revolts, this is again to be ascribed more to the acceptance of common values than to coercion or lack of organisation.

Still at this level of general conceptions about man and society, we must point to perhaps the most important: the way in which the economic approach requires certain psychological assumptions in order to make it work. These 'liberal' assumptions have been attacked from the right and the left: de Maistre and Marx join hands here. Underlying the work of Downs and Olson is the assumption that men rationally pursue ends, and that the ends and means can be disentangled sufficiently for us to be able to say that a man does something so as to produce such-and-such a state of affairs which he wants. Especially clearly in Olson (though implicitly in much of Downs) we have the further assumption that an end is some future state of the actor himself. Plamenatz, in his attack on the utilitarians, has made much of the objections to this way of looking at people: 'Man is not just an animal who, unlike the others, is provident and calculating. . . . He . . . wants to be one kind of person rather than another and to live one kind of life rather than another . . . How men see themselves . . . is intimately connected with their mental images of the community; they are not mere competitors, however benevolent, in a market for the supply of personal wants; they are members of society, and their hopes and feelings, both for themselves and others, would not be what they are apart from their group loyalties. They see themselves as having rights and duties, as moral beings, because they have some conception of a social world with parts for themselves and others to play in it.' (Plamenatz, 1958, pages 173–5. See also Plamenatz, 1968.)

This passage suggests not merely that the 'economic' approach is based on an ideology, for that is true of the 'sociological' approach too, but that it is based on assumptions so false as to make it worthless. Any discussion of this must in effect be an overall evalution of the economic approach, so it seems best to compare the advantages and disadvantages of the two approaches at this point in the chapter. The crux lies in the question of abstraction: at what point does the price of unrealism paid for simplicity and deductive power become too high? As we have seen, Parsons claims that outside the area of economics (defined in the traditional terms of the 'measuring rod of money'), the price becomes too high. But whether or not this is so cannot be settled by any kind of *a priori* argument. It is a great convenience to have money as a metric, but there are other possible measures in social science, including votes. At the least the theories of Downs and Olson suggest that the extension of the methodology of the physical sciences beyond economics is not an absurd undertaking. Both theories can be faulted for failure at various points to correspond to the facts. But the most hopeful feature of theories that really try to explain phenomena is that they have a built-in pressure toward, and possibility of, correction, whereas nothing forces one to change a conceptual scheme such as that of Parsons. Moreover, even if dissatisfaction with the results of using the scheme does eventually lead to the conviction that changes are needed, it is still left as an open question where in the scheme the changes should come.

Plamenatz's criticisms of the 'economic' approach also centre on the issue of abstraction, though less obviously than those of Parsons. For the question is, or should be, not whether the assumptions underlying the use of the economic approach are invariably and totally 'true', but whether they are, under some circumstances, true enough for the purpose of constructing a workable political theory. It could be argued with some force that, while classical utilitarian principles would be rather thin as a sole basis for personal conduct, utilitarian considerations are entirely adequate for arguing about the reform of laws and institutions. Somewhat analogously, it may be suggested that economic modes of analysis apply sufficiently well to be used in some situations, though not in others. The difficulty is, of course, to provide a general description of the kinds of situation in which the economic approach is suitable. Unfortunately, I am unable to find any way of specifying the area except in an unhelpful and circular form, namely that the area is one in which the features of human life and human society stressed by Plamenatz are of relatively little importance.[7] This answer

[7] The whole of economics, which depends heavily on the premises attacked by Plamenatz, would have to be convicted *en bloc*, for anything that he says to the contrary. Since at least some usable analysis can be based on such premises, this shows it is not impossible to find areas in which the factors mentioned by Plamenatz can be discounted without disaster. Parsons seems to have moved a little on this point. In his early essay on 'The Motivation of Economic Activities' (1954, pages 50–68; essay originally published 1940) he stresses that 'economic motivation' is the result of 'certain features of the structure of social systems of action' (page 53) and seems to suggest that this vitiates any economic analysis based on simple 'maximisation' postulates. But, as we have seen, Parsons elsewhere apparently admits that economics does work as a self-contained body of theory, although (as he quite correctly says) these postulates might themselves be a subject for further analysis.

means in effect that the question has to be for the present left open. We can, however, provide illustrations of circumstances in which the 'economic' assumptions are, or are not, appropriate.

Return for a moment to the problem raised in the second chapter: participation in action to secure a collective benefit. As we saw, there are cases where a theory which regards activity as a cost which must be offset by extrinsic benefits (or relief from extrinsic sanctions) does not work very well. One reaction to this would be to say that the theory is based on psychologically, even metaphysically, false premises, and should simply be abandoned. Thus, according to C. B. Macpherson, the liberal idea of democracy, like the liberal idea of the economy, is based on an assumption which is a travesty of the human condition', namely that every expenditure of energy is painful. 'The notion that activity itself is pleasurable, is a utility, has sunk almost without trace under this utilitarian vision of life' (Macpherson, 1966, page 38).

But need we bring in the human condition? It depends what we want to do. If the argument is about what sorts of society are possible, given a certain level of technology or whatever, it is obviously important to establish that the 'economic' assumptions are not universally and immutably true. Whereas, if we are interested in explaining or predicting collective action in actual situations, the only question is how much mileage we can get from a set of simple assumptions. And the answer, in the present instance, we have found to be, roughly, that the theory falls down when it is applied to people for whom participation is not a cost, and these, at any rate in our sort of society, are predominantly middle class people. Otherwise the 'economic' postulate does have some explanatory force, over the long haul—in the short run it is possible for participation to be elicited by dramatic and exciting events.

It would, however, be a mistake to regard the issue between the economic and sociological approaches as one of abstraction as such. The point made by Parsons was that outside the usual sphere of economics it is not possible to find simple enough social phenomena to allow the construction of theories with premises from which conclusions may be deduced. This seems too sweeping, but it does not mean that

Parsons's non-explanatory theories, or conceptual frameworks, are not abstract. Indeed, much of his recent work requires us to entertain the idea of 'exchanges' between entities so abstract that the imagination fails to respond. More significant for the present purpose is the fact that the emphasis on the place of 'values' in social life embodies as partial a view of man as that objected to in the economic approach.

What one might call Parsons's 'official' position is, as we saw in Chapter IV, that he is simply putting forward a 'frame of reference' in which human action is *defined* as following norms. But even this commits him to something in that he also holds that a good conceptual framework is one which promotes fruitful work, and presumably such a conceptual framework will be fruitful only if action *is* largely in accord with norms. In fact, he has recently been quite explicit on this point. In his book *Societies*, the concentration on cultural factors is most of the time spoken of as a 'point of reference' rather than as embodying a causal theory. But towards the end, he says: 'I believe that, within the social system, the normative elements are more important than the "material interests" of constitutive units. The longer the time perspective, and the broader the system involved, the greater is the *relative* importance of higher, rather than lower, factors in the control hierarchy, regardless of whether it is pattern maintenance or pattern change that requires explanation' (Parsons, 1966b, page 113). Lipset goes further and describes Parsons as 'perhaps the foremost contemporary exponent of the importance of value systems as causal factors', though the supporting quotation from Parsons that he gives is in fact an exposition of the 'official' doctrine that values are merely a 'main point of reference' (Lipset, 1964, page 3).

As we have seen, the members of the 'sociological' school do use 'values' as 'explanatory variables'. But there are grave difficulties in carrying out their programme, as we saw in Chapter IV. Even if circularity is avoided in setting up the hypothesis and determining what is to count as evidence, there are enormous difficulties of causal imputation which no study has so far squarely faced. (Of course, there are great problems involved in any attempt to attribute causation among complex large-scale social phenomena, but 'values' do

seem to present special problems.) Suppose that these problems are solved and that hypotheses relating values causally
to institutions *are* tested properly. The next point is that they
may not be found to stand up. Values often seem more
plausibly regarded as consequences than causes of other social
phenomena.

We cannot come to any simple conclusion about the relative merits of our two approaches, because they are so little
of the time competing in the same league. The economic
approach can permit the production of theories which yield
genuine predictions when their assumptions are satisfied.[8]
But the general psychological assumptions are often not satisfied and there does not seem to be any non-trivial way of
setting out in general terms the conditions under which they
are satisfied. Moreover, many problems do not lend themselves to the economic approach, because of the difficulty of
finding a simple and tractable representation of the situation.
There are only very limited aspects of politics to which an
economic analysis has been applied, and, though one would
not wish to say other applications are impossible, it has to be
recognised that most situations are too complex to provide
the premises for theories in which determinate solutions can
be derived. The sociological approach, on the other hand, can
be used to tackle big problems, but does not in practice seem
to provide much of a purchase on them.

5 RELATIONSHIP OF THE TWO APPROACHES

This is the cue to reopen the question whether the two
approaches are really packages, which have to be bought
entire or not at all, or whether the elements might be recom-
bined. If the second alternative is right, could one imagine
reconstituting a package embodying the best of both? We
have already seen that the two approaches are solidly
grounded in the historical opposition of two ideologies. But
this does not settle our question. A tendency for the same
clusters of phenomena to recur in different societies can be
'explained' either functionally or in terms of diffusion from
a common origin. Similarly, we could say either that the com-

[8] In Coleman's terms, it allows the formulation of 'sometimes true'
theories (Coleman, 1964, pages 516–19).

ponents of our two approaches had a strong internal relationship, or that their cohesion is a product of history more than of logic.

The answer to be argued for here is that there is no logical impossibility in recombining the elements of the two packages, but that some recombinations may not be very fruitful. To begin with, then, there does not appear to be any connection of a stringently exclusive logical kind among most of the members of our clusters of ideas. Of course, one could not be simultaneously primarily concerned with conditions of stability and *not* primarily concerned, nor could one simultaneously assume total rationality and *not* assume total rationality. But there would be nothing logically inconsistent in combining, say, methodological individualism and non-rationality, rationality with a concern for the conditions of stability, or an emphasis on norms with a theory in which goals are rationally pursued subject to constraints. And, even where the items are mutually exclusive by definition, this does not entail that one could not combine them in a weaker form: there is nothing inconsistent in having a concern that is not an exclusive or even primary concern for conditions of stability, or making the assumption that behaviour is partly rational and partly irrational.

But some recombinations are more likely to be successful than others. At one extreme, there seems to be no particular reason why a concern for stability should be combined with a belief that societies have built-in stabilising tendencies, or why either should be combined in a pre-ordained way with other elements in the packages. For example, one might take the achievement of stability as problematic and then ask by what means it could be achieved, given rational goal-seekers. In fact, the simple economic treatments of stabilising demand or procuring a certain rate of economic growth are rather like this. An obvious political example is Hobbes's own solution to the 'Hobbesian problem' of order. Conversely, one might take all the 'sociological' assumptions about the importance of norms and values but neither assume a homeostatic system nor ask what are the conditions under which a system achieves certain end-states.

The connections between the assumptions made and the kind of theoretical enterprise pursued are less flexible. As we saw in Chapter II, we may find, if we try to complicate the psychological assumptions of the 'economic' approach to take account of norms, that we have destroyed the possibility of deducing interesting conclusions from our premises. We would then find that everything could be explained, but only trivially. Thus, it may turn out that Parsons was correct in saying that deductive theories are not possible, given premises of the kind he espouses. On the other hand, there is no reason why 'economic' assumptions have to be used only in contexts which permit the development of a deductive theory.

An example to the contrary is Barrington Moore's *Social Origins of Dictatorship and Democracy* (Moore, 1966). In this, Moore takes on problems on the largest scale, especially the question which we pursued in the company of the 'sociological' writers: under what conditions do countries become democratic? But, as we saw in Chapter IV, he is a trenchant critic of explanations in terms of values, and treats patterns of socialisation as being themselves matters to be explained. His own account is pitched in terms of such things as the strategic calculations of the landowning and manufacturing classes in the early years of a country's industrialisation. This is not the place to enter on a critique of Moore's stimulating book. All that I need assert for the present purpose is that it is not less distinguished than the 'sociological' treatments of the same question which I discussed in Chapter III, and thus serves to suggest the possibility of taking on large-scale cross-national comparisons without placing 'cultural' factors in the foreground.

6 A PROSPECT

What should be the main lines of future development? If I have in any way succeeded in what I set out to do in writing this book, the reader should by now feel that he has in his own hands the material with which to make judgments of this kind. But I shall not regard that as absolving me from offering an answer. The most striking fact, to me at least, is how primitive is the stage things are still in. By this I mean partly that the theoretical literature of both 'economic' and 'sociological' approaches is surprisingly sparse, in spite of the number of new books on politics that appear each year. The books of Downs and Olson, plus a handful of articles, really do exhaust the field of worthwhile attempts to get from general premises to substantive political conclusions. And, though the 'sociological' school is less clearly defined, the references in each author to the others suggest that the studies analysed in Chapter III do comprise a fairly complete set.

When I say that this is an underdeveloped area I am not primarily referring to the fact that books are thin on the ground, but to the distance still to go to the goal of verified theories and general propositions. It is not just (or mainly) a question of getting together some facts and lining them up against the theories. In most cases, there is a prior need for work to put the theories into a form in which data can be brought to bear. As we saw in Chapters III and IV, this is especially clearly the case with the 'sociological' theories, where there are still grave difficulties remaining in the concepts themselves, such as 'democracy', and where there is a lack of precision in the statement of the hypotheses. But it is also surprisingly difficult to test the correctness of Downs's theory, as we have seen in Chapters VI and VII; and there is more work to be done in establishing precisely what are the conclusions to be drawn from his premises, showing where additional, different or more precise premises are needed to get results, and so on. Olson's theory is perhaps the only one of which we can say that the main objection to its presentation is that the evidence is too anecdotal, and shows only that some examples do fit. But even here the main task is more theoretical work, since, as we saw in Chapter II, it is not really difficult to find counter-examples to Olson's theory. The problem is to amend the theory to take account of them without becoming vacuous.

'More of the same, but better' may seem a pretty banal prescription, but I would hope that, taken in the light of the earlier detailed discussions, it does suggest possible directions of development. More speculative is the prospect for further attempts to stir the contents of the two packages together. The spirit of compromise is out of place here. There is no *intrinsic* advantage in mixing up opposed ideas, and the result can easily be a muddle. Yet it is hard to imagine that political scientists will continue indefinitely, like French politicians, to fight out the battle between the Enlightenment and the Reaction. We shall know that the prehistory of the discipline is past when we are no longer haunted by the ghosts of dead ideologues—unless, of course, their places are taken by live ones.

Bibliography

The bibliography begins by giving guidance for further reading in four areas. First, there is a discussion of recent works on the 'state of the discipline', the 'methodology of the social sciences', etc. Next, some suggestions are made about reading in the empirical literature of voting studies—a literature which, obviously, underlies some portions of the text. Sections 3 and 4 give a selection of writings manifesting the 'economic' and the 'sociological' approaches respectively.

These notes are followed by an alphabetical list of books and articles cited. The date given is, in general, the date of first publication of the book or article in question.[1] Page references in the text, however, are given to the most accessible source of each book and article: this means paperback reprints of books wherever possible and, in the case of articles, any easily obtainable reader or collection which contains the article referred to. Wherever page references are based on any version of a book or article other than the original one, this is stated immediately after the details of its original date, place and publisher, and full details are given of the version to which page number references are given.

1 POLITICS AS AN ACADEMIC SUBJECT

The most influential of the post-war discussions of the 'state of the discipline' is *The Political System* (Easton, 1953). The

[1] There are three exceptions. Where an article first appearing in a periodical is subsequently republished as part of a collection of essays by the author, no mention is made of the original. Also, where reference is made to a later edition (not merely reprint) of a book, the date given is of the first appearance of the edition cited. (Wherever an edition other than the first is referred to, the fact is stated in the bibliography.) Parsons's *Essays in Sociological Theory* illustrate both points: the essays in it are identified under the date 1954, which is when the *revised* edition was first published. Finally, translations and books first published before 1800 are dated by the first appearance of the edition used.

later chapters of this work adumbrate the 'systems theory' which Easton has developed since, but the earlier part of the book is a history and critique of political science in the U.S.A. from its institutionalisation in separate departments around the turn of the century. The main thrust of its attack is on the atheoretical nature of most of the work hitherto done. What do you do when the libraries are full of 'case studies' which are not designed to support or attack any hypothesis? Simply let them gather dust on the shelves while you press on with more? Easton's answer is to call for the creation of 'empirical theory' under which the 'cases' might be subsumed, and to which they should be designed to contribute. A brief statement along the same lines and from the same period is Macridis, 1955.

There are other critics of the discipline who regard the attempt to 'go scientific' as an intellectual and perhaps a moral (or even theological) error. The trouble with these critics is that they find it easy enough to pick holes in the work of particular writers (especially since they tend to choose highly vulnerable ones) but are much less convincing when arguing that this is inherent in what these writers are attempting. The best example of the *genre* is probably a collection written by disciples of Leo Strauss with a blistering round-up by the master himself (Storing, 1962). Other examples are Crick, 1959, Germino, 1967 and Stretton, 1969.

Two general surveys of the state of contemporary political theory, written from a generally sympathetic, though sceptical, standpoint, are Mackenzie, 1967, and Meehan, 1967. Mackenzie's book is a masterpiece of compression. It covers an enormous range of recent work, introducing each author with a pat on the back, dismissing him with a dig in the ribs, and usually succeeding in making some pertinent remarks in between. Moreover, in a world of overpriced American heavyweights, it is excellent value for money. Meehan is more ambitious, but the general methodological discussion of the opening and closing chapters (1, 2, 6, 7) is not in my view very successfully carried off. The three central chapters, on functionalism, psychological explanations and formalism (game theory and information theory) are useful, however. A somewhat different kind of survey of the field, and much more fun, is Somit, 1964. This is based on a questionnaire mailed to a systematic sample of members of the American Political Science Association in 1963, and tells us who and what the respondents thought to be the best political scientists, areas of specialisation, journals, departments, and what they believed to be the most potent factors making for professional advancement (volume of publication came top, teaching ability last, and quality of publication in the middle, flanked by 'having the right connections' and 'luck or chance').

A third variety of literature worth attention is the 'approaches' literature. The usual set-up is that a number of articles are commissioned, the authors of which are expected to plug some 'approach' with which they are identified. Sometimes the author will adduce examples of results produced by following his 'approach', but more often the tone is exhortatory. An early and influential example is Young, 1958. Two more recent ones are Easton, 1966, and (fuller and better) Charlesworth, 1967. Slightly different, but very valuable, is Polsby, 1963, a large 'reader' which contains some good and methodological pieces and also good samples of various 'approaches' at work. Another of the same kind, containing an interesting introductory essay by Eckstein, is Apter, 1963.

A final category should be added for those who wish to follow the argument towards the philosophical end of the spectrum. In this area come books which keep in the foreground general issues about the possibility of doing this or that. The argument tends to be conducted at an *a priori* level; actual pieces of work figure, if at all, merely as illustrations. Two books dealing at this level specifically with the study of politics are Van Dyke, 1960, and Meehan, 1965; the former is better though neither is of more than routine interest. It might be better to turn to books which discuss at the same sort of level the social sciences generally. Two provocative little books are Winch, 1958, and Homans, 1967: one the work of a highly convoluted intellect, the other of a *terrible simplificateur*. Two 'balanced', and dull, treatments are Brown, 1963, and Gibson, 1960. An excellent 'reader', with a broader subject-matter than the title suggests, is Gardiner, 1959. Another, which is certainly the best all-round collection, is Brodbeck, 1968. Nagel, 1961, can be warmly recommended as a discussion of problems in many areas of science, with excellent chapters on the social sciences.

2. EMPIRICAL STUDIES OF POLITICAL PARTICIPATION AND ELECTORAL CHOICE

There are two surveys of empirical findings on the determinants of participation. These are Lane, 1959, and Milbrath, 1965. More precisely, these are studies of the *correlates* of participation in the U.S.A.; for they scarcely have enough theoretical basis to make causal language appropriate and make little use of non-American data. Both begin by presenting a psychological (stimulus-response) model, but neither gives it more than a few perfunctory mentions later on. Of the two, Milbrath is the less ambitious, and the more useful for anyone who wants a workmanlike summary of research findings.

Six American community studies may be recommended for more concrete study of the contexts and consequences of participation: Dahl, 1961 (New Haven), Banfield, 1961 (Chicago), Eldersveld, 1964 (Detroit), Agger, 1964, Presthus, 1964, and Vidich, 1958 (smaller towns). Dahl's analysis of the *homo politicus*, the sort of person who (often due to some accident) gets drawn into politics and then derives intrinsic satisfaction from political activity, is valuable in suggesting how a population can become differentiated into political entrepreneurs and others.

Books based on survey data usually deal with both voting as against non-voting and voting for one candidate rather than another. Three American studies will be found informative: Berelson, 1954, Campbell, 1960, and Key, 1966. See also the collection of papers written by Campbell and his associates (Campbell, 1966). Two other useful collections containing good examples of recent work are Crotty, 1966, and Dreyer, 1966. The last also includes useful bibliographical notes to each section.

3 THE ECONOMIC APPROACH

The best introduction to the economic approach might be not through a conventional textbook of economics but through reading an exposition of the theory of games. The standard work is Luce, 1957, but this is quite difficult in parts. A more easily assimilable exposition, limited to the simpler parts of

N

the theory, is Williams, 1964. Neither of these books contains more than a passing reference to politics. An attempt to use the theory of *n*-person zero-sum games in the analysis of political coalitions has been made by Riker, 1962. In my view his model is in general inapplicable, because there is not in general a fixed amount of value to be shared out among the winners in politics. But there are some cases, such as the competition for high office, where zero-sum conditions do approximately hold. Leiserson, 1968, has tested theories of coalition formation, including Riker's, in just such a situation, namely the competition for cabinet posts among factions of the dominant Japanese Liberal-Democratic Party. A useful general discussion of coalition theory is Leiserson, forthcoming. Game theory, as well as other forms of economic analysis, are used in Buchanan, 1962, which is criticised in Barry, 1965, pages 237–285. The theory of bargaining includes game-theoretic and other 'economic' approaches. Schelling, 1960, originates in game theory; the main application is to the theory of nuclear deterrence. Two articles by Harsanyi (1956 and 1963) are well worth consulting, though they remain at a pretty abstract level.

A useful way of following developments in the 'economic' theory of politics is to read the issues of a continuing series of publications from the Thomas Jefferson Center for Political Economy, Charlottesville, Virginia, U.S.A. The first two volumes were called *Papers in Non-Market Decision Making*, and appeared in 1967. Subsequent volumes (1968–) are called *Public Choice*. They are edited by Gordon Tullock. Another source of some relevant articles is the *Journal of Conflict Resolution* (Ann Arbor, Michigan, U.S.A.).

4 THE SOCIOLOGICAL APPROACH

There are a number of accounts of Parsons's theories. Still useful is the collection edited by Max Black (Black, 1961), which concludes with a reply to his critics by Parsons. A book-length exposition of Parsons, from the standpoint of politics, is Mitchell, 1967: not very penetrating, but adequate. The relevant sections in Mackenzie, 1967, and Meehan, 1967, may also be consulted with profit. If one had to pick one book of Parsons as a sample, the best choice might be *The Social*

System (Parsons, 1951). Parsons has also provided a number of shorter accounts of his system at different times. The most useful is probably 'The Political Aspect of Structure and Process' (Parsons, 1966a). A longer one is the introductory essay in *Theories of Society* (Parsons, 1961). The main specifically political essays are all collected in *Sociological Theory and Modern Society* (Parsons, 1967), except the one on McCarthyism ('Social Strains in America'), which is in *The Radical Right* (Bell, 1955). Two textbooks which follow the Parsonian line pretty faithfully are Johnson, 1961, and Mitchell, 1962, Johnson covering sociology in general, Mitchell 'the American polity'. Mitchell, 1967, has a bibliography of Parsons, also one of works alleged to have been influenced by him, which is useful though the inclusion of some items is highly questionable.

Two general round-ups on 'systems', the first more confined to our 'sociological' approach than the second, are Wiseman, 1966, and Young, 1968. Neither can be recommended. *The General Systems Yearbook* contains relevant articles. A useful collection of papers on 'functionalism' is Demerath, 1967. The discussion of functionalism in general and Parsons in particular in the Introduction to George Homans's collected papers (Homans, 1962) is very readable but cuts much deeper than a casual perusal might suggest.

POSTSCRIPT 1978

To update this bibliographic essay I should like to begin by commending Paul Diesing's *Patterns of Discovery in the Social Sciences* (Chicago: Aldine-Atherton, 1971). This book, by a philosopher of the social sciences, tries to make sense of what social scientists actually do, rather than simply lamenting that what they do doesn't look like physics. I should also like to suggest, as a critical but sympathetic review of 'economic' theorizing by sociologists, Anthony Heath, *Rational Choice and Social Exchange* (Cambridge: Cambridge University Press, 1976).

The concept of rationality has been subjected to some intensive examination in recent years, and useful discussions of the way in which it functions in social science can be found in S. I. Benn and G. W. Mortimore (eds.), *Rationality and the*

Social Sciences (London: Routledge and Kegan Paul, 1976), and in Martin Hollis and Edward Nell, *Rational Economic Man* (Cambridge: Cambridge University Press, 1975). Hollis's more recent book, *Models of Man* (Cambridge: Cambridge University Press, 1977), also bears on some of the issues raised here. Ronald Rogowski, *Rational Legitimacy* (Princeton: Princeton University Press, 1974), is an application of 'rational choice' theory, and the Introduction provides a general discussion of the approach and contrasts it with alternatives.

Voting studies have, of course, continued; the two most elaborate since *The American Voter* are David Butler and Donald Stokes, *Political Change in Britain: Forces Shaping Electoral Choice* (London: Macmillan, 1969; 2nd ed., 1974), and Norman H. Nie, Sidney Verba and John R. Petrocick, *The Changing American Voter* (Cambridge, Mass.: Harvard University Press, 1977). The most interesting thing from the present point of view, however, is that there has recently been a greatly increased willingness among those engaging in voting research to conceive of voting as a purposive activity rather than the outcome of psychological 'forces'. See Arthur S. Goldberg, 'Social Determinism and Rationality as Bases of Party Identification', *The American Political Science Review*, 63 (1969), 7–25; Michael Margolis, 'From Confusion to Confusion: Issues and the American Voter (1956–72)', *The American Political Science Review*, 71 (1977), 31–43; Norman Frohlich et al., 'A Test of Downsian Voter Rationality: 1964 Presidential Voting', *The American Political Science Review*, 72 (1978), 178–97; and *The American Political Science Review*, 70 (1976), 753–849, on the Survey Research Center analysis of the 1972 election, especially 'Comment: What Have You Done for Me Lately? Toward An Investment Theory of Voting' by Samuel Popkin et al., 779–805.

The idea that parties and candidates manoeuvre in policy space to gain votes has been subjected to imaginative and sophisticated empirical study (taking Britain as the site) by David Robertson in *A Theory of Party Competition* (London: Wiley, 1976). See also I. Budge and D. Farlie (eds.), *Party Competition and Beyond* (London: Wiley, 1976).

Finally, a book that takes off from the characterization of the 'economic' approach set out here, carrying it in new directions, is Samuel Popkin, *The Rational Peasant* (Berkeley and Los Angeles: University of California Press, 1978).

ABRAMS, M.; ROSE, R.; HINDEN, R. (eds.) (1960). *Must Labour Lose?* Harmondsworth, Penguin Books.

AGGER, R. E.; GOLDRICH, D.; SWANSON, B. E. (1964). *The Rulers and the Ruled: Political Power and Impotence in American Communities.* New York; John Wiley & Sons.

ALMOND, G. A.; VERBA, S. (1963). *The Civic Culture: Political Attitudes and Democracy in Five Nations.* Princeton, N.J.: Princeton University Press.

ALMOND, G. A.; POWELL, G. B., JR. (1966). *Comparative Politics: A Developmental Approach.* Boston: Little, Brown and Company.

APTER, D. E. (ed.) (1964). *Ideology and Discontent.* New York: The Free Press.

APTER, D. E.; ECKSTEIN, H. (eds.) (1963). *Comparative Politics.* New York: The Free Press.

ARENDT, H. (1958). *The Human Condition.* Chicago: University of Chicago Press.

ARENSBERG, C.; KIMBALL, S. T. (1940). *Family and Community in Ireland.* Cambridge, Mass.: Harvard University Press.

ARROW, K. (1951). *Social Choice and Individual Values.* New York: John Wiley & Sons.

BACHRACH, P. (1967). *The Theory of Democratic Elitism.* Boston: Little, Brown and Company.

BANFIELD, E. C. (1958). *The Moral Basis of a Backward Society.* Glencoe, Ill.: The Free Press.

BANFIELD, E. C. (1961). *Political Influence.* New York: The Free Press. Page references to Free Press paperback edition.

BARRY, B. (1965). *Political Argument.* London: Routledge and Kegan Paul.

BARRY, B. (1968). 'Warrender and his Critics'. *Philosophy*, 48, 117–137.

BAUM, W. C. (1965). 'On Electoral Myth and Reality'. *American Political Science Review*, 59, 693.

BAUMOL, W. J. (1952). *Welfare Economics and the Theory of the State.* Cambridge, Mass.: Harvard University Press.

BELL, D. (ed.) (1955). *The New American Right.* New York: Criterion Books. Republished in 'an expanded and up-dated version' as *The Radical Right* (New York: Doubleday Anchor Books, 1963).

BELL, D. (1960). *The End of Ideology.* Glencoe, Ill.: The Free Press. (Reprinted in paperback.)

BENNEY, M.; GRAY, A. P.; PEAR, R. H. (1956). *How People Vote.* London: Routledge and Kegan Paul.

BENTHAM, J. (1843). *The Works of Jeremy Bentham, Now First Collected Under the Superintendence of His Executor, John Bowring.* In 11 vols. Edinburgh: William Tait.

BERELSON, B.; LAZARSFELD, P.; MCPHEE, W. N. (1954). *Voting: A Study of Opinion Forming in a Presidential Campaign.* Chicago: University of Chicago Press.

BERG, E. (1964). *Democracy and the Majority Principle.* Scandinavian University Press.

BLACK, D. (1958). *The Theory of Committees and Elections.* Cambridge: Cambridge University Press.

BLACK, M. (ed.) (1961). *The Social Theories of Talcott Parsons: A Critical Examination.* Englewood Cliffs, N.J.: Prentice-Hall.

BLAKE, J.; DAVIS, K. (1964): 'Norms, Values and Sanctions' in FARIS, R. E. L. (ed.), *Handbook of Modern Sociology* (Chicago: Rand McNally and Company). Reprinted in WRONG (1967), 97–107.

BLALOCK, H. M., JR. (1964). *Causal Inferences in Non-Experimental Research*. Chapel Hill, N.C.: University of North Carolina Press.

BLALOCK, H. M., JR.; BLALOCK, A. B. (eds.) (1968). *Methodology in Social Research*. New York: McGraw-Hill Book Company.

BLAU, P. M.; DUNCAN, O. D. (1967). *The American Occupational Structure*. New York: John Wiley & Sons.

BLONDEL, J. (1963). *Voters, Parties and Leaders*. Harmondsworth: Penguin Books.

BOULDING, K. E. (1962). *Conflict and Defense: A General Theory*. New York: Harper & Brothers. Page references to Harper Torchbook paperback edition.

BRAMSON, L. (1961). *The Political Context of Sociology*. Princeton, N.J.: Princeton University Press.

BRODBECK, M. (ed.) (1968). *Readings in the Philosophy of the Social Sciences*. New York: The Macmillan Company.

BROWN, R. (1963). *Explanation in Social Science*. London: Routledge and Kegan Paul.

BUCHANAN, J. M.; TULLOCK, G. (1962). *The Calculus of Consent*. Ann Arbor: The University of Michigan Press. (Reprinted in Ann Arbor paperback edition.)

BURNHAM, W. D. (1968). 'American Voting Behavior in the 1964 Election'. *Midwest Journal of Political Science*, 12, 1–40.

BUTLER, D. E.; KING, A. (1965). *The British General Election of 1964*. London: The Macmillan Company.

BUTLER, D. E.; STOKES, D. E. (1969). *Electoral Change in Britain*. London: The Macmillan Company.

CAMPBELL, A. (1962). 'The Passive Citizen'. *Acta Sociologica*, 6, 9–12. Page references are to the reprint in CROTTY (1966), 400–412.

CAMPBELL, A.; CONVERSE, P. E.; MILLER, W. E.; STOKES, D. E. (1960). *The American Voter*. New York: John Wiley & Sons.

CAMPBELL, A.; CONVERSE, P. E.; MILLER, W. E.; STOKES, D. E. (1960). *Elections and the Political Order*. New York: John Wiley & Sons.

CARTWRIGHT, D.; HARARY, F. (1956). 'Structural Balance: A Generalization of Heider's Theory'. *Psychological Review*, 63, 277–293.

CHAMBERS, W. N.; BURNHAM, W. D. (eds.) 1968). *The American Party Systems: Stages of Political Development*. London: Oxford University Press.

CHARLESWORTH, J. C. (ed.) (1967). *Contemporary Political Analysis*. New York: The Free Press.

CLARK, P. B.; WILSON, J. Q. (1961). 'Incentive Systems: A Theory of Organization'. *Administrative Science Quarterly*, 6, 129–166.

COLEMAN, J. S. (1963). 'Comment on "On the Concept of Influence"'. *Public Opinion Quarterly*, 27, 63–81.

COLEMAN, J. S. (1964). *Introduction to Mathematical Sociology*. New York: The Free Press.

COLEMAN, J. S. (1966). 'Individual Interests and Collective Action'. *Papers on Non-Market Decision-Making*, 1, 49–62.

CONVERSE, P. E. (1964). 'The Nature of Belief Systems in Mass Publics', in APTER (1964), 206–261.

CONVERSE, P. E. (1966). 'The Problem of Party Distances in Models of Voting Change', in JENNINGS, M. K.; ZEIGLER, L. H. (eds.), *The Electoral Process* (Englewood Cliffs, N.J.: Prentice-Hall), 175–207.

CONVERSE, P. E.; CLAUSEN, A. R.; MILLER, W. E. (1965). 'Electoral Myth and Reality: the 1964 Election'. *American Political Science Review*, 59, 321–336. Page references are to reprint in CROTTY (1966), 349–379. Also reprinted in DREYER (1966), 23–34.

CORNFORD, F. M. (1908). *Microcosmographia Academica: Being a Guide for the Young Academic Politician*. London: Bowes and Bowes. Page references are to 6th edition, 1964.

CRICK, B. (1959). *The American Science of Politics*. London: Routledge and Kegan Paul.

CRICK, B. (1962). *In Defence of Politics*. London: Weidenfeld & Nicolson. (Reprint by Penguin Books.)

CRICK, B. (1964). *The Reform of Parliament*. London: Weidenfeld & Nicolson.

CROTTY, W. J.; FREEMAN, D. M.; GATLIN, D. S. (eds.) (1966). *Political Parties and Political Behavior*. Boston: Allyn and Bacon.

DAHL, R. A. (1956). *A Preface to Democratic Theory*. Chicago: University of Chicago Press.

DAHL, R. A. (1961). *Who Governs? Democracy and Power in an American City*. New Haven, Conn.: Yale University Press.

DAHL, R. A.; LINDBLOM, C. E. (1953). *Politics, Economics and Welfare*. New York: Harper & Brothers.

DAHRENDORF, R. (1958). 'Out of Utopia: Toward a Reorientation of Sociological Analysis'. *American Journal of Sociology*, 64, 115–127. Reprinted in DEMERATH (1967), 465–480; and in DAHRENDORF, *Essays in the Theory of Society*. London: Routledge and Kegan Paul. (1968).

DAHRENDORF, R. (1959). *Class and Class Conflict in Industrial Society*. Stanford, Calif.: Stanford University Press.

DAHRENDORF, R. (1967). *Conflict After Class: New Perspectives on the Theory of Social and Political Conflict*. London: Longmans. 3rd Noel Buxton Lecture at the University of Essex.

DAHRENDORF, R. (1968). *Society and Democracy in Germany*. London: Weidenfeld & Nicolson.

DAWSON, R. E. (1968). 'Social Development, Party Competition and Policy', in CHAMBERS (1968), 203–237.

DAWSON, R. E.; ROBINSON, J. A. (1963). 'Interparty Competition, Economic Variables, and Welfare Policies in the American States'. *Journal of Politics*, 25, 265–289.

DEMERATH, N. J. III; PETERSON, R. A. (eds.) (1967). *System Change and Conflict: A Reader on Contemporary Sociological Theory and the Debate over Functionalism*. New York: The Free Press.

DEUTSCH, K. W. (1963). *The Nerves of Government*. New York: The Free Press. (Paperback edition with new introduction.)

DEVEREUX, E. C. JR. (1961). 'Parsons' Sociological Theory', in BLACK, M. (1961), 1–63.

DOWNS, A. (1957). *An Economic Theory of Democracy*. New York: Harper & Brothers. (Paperback edition with same pagination.)

DOWNS, A. (1967). *Inside Bureaucracy*. Boston: Little, Brown and Co.

DREYER, E. C.; ROSENBAUM, W. A. (eds.) (1966). *Political Opinion and Electoral Behavior: Essays and Studies*. Belmont, Calif.: Wadsworth Publishing Company.

DUNCAN, G.; LUKES, S. (1963). 'The New Democracy'. *Political Studies*, 11, 156–177. Reprinted in MCCOY, C. A.; PLAYFORD, J. (eds.) *Apolitical Politics: a Critique of Behavioralism*. New York: Thomas Y. Crowell Company, 1967, 160–184.

DYE, T. R. (1966). *Politics, Economics, and the Public: Policy Outcomes in the American States*. Chicago: Rand McNally & Company.

EASTON, D. (1953). *The Political System: An Enquiry into the State of Political Science*. New York: Alfred A. Knopf.

EASTON, D. (1965). *A Systems Analysis of Political Life.* New York: John Wiley & Sons.

EASTON, D. (ed.) (1966). *Varieties of Political Theory.* Englewood Cliffs, N.J.: Prentice-Hall.

ECKSTEIN, H. (1966). *Division and Cohesion in Democracy: A Study of Norway.* Princeton, N.J.: Princeton University Press.

ELDERSVELD, S. J. (1964). *Political Parties: A Behavioral Analysis.* Chicago: Rand McNally & Company.

ETZIONI, A. (1961). *A Comparative Analysis of Complex Organizations.* Glencoe, Ill.: The Free Press.

EYSENCK, H. J. (1954). *The Psychology of Politics.* London: Routledge and Kegan Paul.

FRANKENBERG, R. (1966). *Communities in Britain.* Harmondsworth: Penguin Books.

FRIEDMAN, M. (1953). *Essays in Positive Economics.* Chicago: University of Chicago Press.

FRIEDMAN, M. (1962). *Capitalism and Freedom.* Chicago: University of Chicago Press.

GALBRAITH, J. K. (1952). *The Affluent Society.* Boston: Houghton Mifflin.

GARDINER, P. (ed.) (1959). *Theories of History.* London: Allen and Unwin.

GARVEY, G. (1966). 'The Theory of Party Equilibrium'. *American Political Science Review,* 60, 29–38.

GERMINO, D. (1967). *Beyond Ideology: The Revival of Political Theory.* New York: Harper & Row.

GIBSON, Q. (1960). *The Logic of Social Enquiry.* London: Routledge and Kegan Paul.

GOLDSMITH, M. M. (1966). *Hobbes's Science of Politics.* New York: Columbia University Press.

GOLDTHORPE, J. H.; LOCKWOOD, D.; BECHHOFER, F.; PLATT, J. (1968). *The Affluent Worker: Industrial Attitudes and Behaviour.* Cambridge Studies in Sociology, 1. Cambridge: Cambridge University Press.

GROSS, F. (1958). *The Seizure of Political Power in a Century of Revolutions.* New York: The Philosophical Library.

HALÉVY, E. (1928). *The Growth of Philosophical Radicalism.* London: Faber & Faber. Page references to Beacon Press paperback edition.

HARE, R. M. (1952). *The Language of Morals.* Oxford: The Clarendon Press.

HARRINGTON, J. (1955). *The Political Writings of James Harrington: Representative Selections.* Ed. by BLITZER, C. New York: The Bobbs-Merrill Company.

HARRISON, M. (1960). *Trade Unions and the Labour Party since 1945.* London: Allen and Unwin.

HARSANYI, J. C. (1956). 'Approaches to the Bargaining Problem before and after the Theory of Games'. *Econometrica,* 24, 144–157.

HARSANYI, J. C. (1963). 'A Simplified Bargaining Model for the n-Person Co-operative Game'. *International Economic Review,* 4, 194–220.

HART, H. L. A. (1961). *The Concept of Law.* Oxford: The Clarendon Press.

HEARD, A. (1960). *The Costs of Democracy.* Chapel Hill, N.C.: University of North Carolina Press.

HOBBES, T. (1946). *Leviathan.* Ed. OAKESHOTT, M. Oxford: Basil Blackwell.

HOMANS, G. C. (1961). *Social Behaviour: Its Elementary Forms.* London: Routledge and Kegan Paul.

HOMANS, G. C. (1962). *Sentiments and Activities: Essays in Social Science.* London: Routledge and Kegan Paul.

HOMANS, G. C. (1967). *The Nature of Social Science*. New York: Harcourt, Brace & World.

HOTELLING, H. (1929). 'Stability in Competition'. *The Economic Journal*, 39, 41–57.

HUGHES, H. S. (1959). *Consciousness and Society: the Reorientation of European Social Thought*. London: MacGibbon & Kee.

IRELAND, T. (1967). 'The Rationale of Revolt'. *Papers in Non-Market Decision-Making*, 3, 49–66.

JOHNSON, H. M. (1961). *Sociology: A Systematic Introduction*. London: Routledge and Kegan Paul.

KEY, V. O., JR. (1961). *Public Opinion and American Democracy*. New York: Alfred A. Knopf.

KEY, V. O., JR. (1966). *The Responsible Electorate: Rationality in Presidential Voting*. Cambridge, Mass.: Belknap Press of Harvard University Press.

KLUCKHOHN, C. (1958). 'Have There Been Discernible Shifts in American Values during the Past Generation?' in MORISON, E. F. (ed.), *The American Style: Essays in Value and Performance*. (New York: Harper & Brothers.)

KORNHAUSER, W. (1959). *The Politics of Mass Society*. Glencoe, Ill.: The Free Press.

LANE, R. E. (1959). *Political Life: Why People Get Involved in Politics*. New York: The Free Press. Page references to the Free Press paperback edition.

LASSWELL, H. D.; LERNER, D. (eds.) (1965). *World Revolutionary Elites: Studies in Coercive Ideological Movements*. Cambridge, Mass.: The M.I.T. Press.

LATHAM, E. (1952). *The Group Basis of Politics: A Study in Basing-Point Legislation*. Ithaca, N.Y.: Cornell University Press.

LEISERSON, M. (1968). 'Factions and Coalitions in One-Party Japan: an Interpretation Based on the Theory of Games'. *American Political Science Review*, 62, 770–787.

LEISERSON, M. (forthcoming). *Coalitions in Politics*, New Haven: Yale University Press.

LIPSET, S. M. (1959). *Political Man*. London: Heinemann. Page references to Mercury Books paperback edition.

LIPSET, S. M. (1964). *The First New Nation: The United States in Historical and Comparative Perspective*. London: Heinemann.

LIPSET, S. M. (1967). 'Political Sociology', in SMELSER (1967), 435–499.

LIPSITZ, L. (1968). 'If, as Verba says, the State Functions as a Religion, What Are We to Do Then to Save our Souls?' *American Political Science Review*, 62, 527–535.

LOCKARD, D. (1959). *New England State Politics*. Princeton, N. J.: Princeton University Press.

LOCKE, J. (1960). *Second Treatise of Government*, in *Two Treatises of Government*. Ed. LASLETT, P. Cambridge: Cambridge University Press. Page references to Mentor Books paperback edition.

LOCKWOOD, D. (1956). 'Some Remarks on the Social System'. *British Journal of Sociology*, 7, 134–146. Reprinted in DEMERATH (1967), 281–291.

LOCKWOOD, D. (1958). *The Blackcoated Worker: A Study in Class Consciousness*. London: Allen and Unwin.

LUCAS, J. R. (1966). *The Principles of Politics*. Oxford: The Clarendon Press.

LUCE, R. D. (1959). 'Analyzing the Social Process Underlying Group

196

Voting Patterns', in BURDICK, E., BRODBECK, A. J. (eds.) *American Voting Behaviour* (New York: The Free Press), 330–351.

LUCE, R. D.; RAIFFA, H. (1957). *Games and Decisions*. New York: John Wiley & Sons.

MCCONNELL, G. (1966). *Private Power and American Democracy*. New York: Alfred A. Knopf.

MACKENZIE, W. J. M. (1967). *Politics and Social Science*. Harmondsworth: Penguin Books.

MACPHERSON, C. B. (1966). *The Real World of Democracy*. Oxford: The Clarendon Press.

MACRAE, D., JR. (1958). *Dimensions of Congressional Voting: a Statistical Study of the House of Representatives in the Eighty-First Congress.* Berkeley and Los Angeles: University of California Press.

MACRIDIS, R. C. (1955). *The Study of Comparative Government*. Garden City, N.Y.: Doubleday & Company.

DE MAISTRE, J. (1965). *The Works of Joseph de Maistre*. Ed. LIVELY, J. London: Allen and Unwin.

MARX, K. (1869). 'The 18th Brumaire of Louis Bonaparte' (2nd ed.), in *Karl Marx and Frederick Engels: Selected Works*, Vol, I, 243–244. Moscow: Foreign Language Publishing House, 1958. (And in most collections of Marx.)

MEADE, J. E. (1965). *The Stationary Economy: Volume One of a Principles of Political Economy*. London: Allen and Unwin.

MEEHAN, E. (1965). *The Theory and Method of Political Analysis*. Homewood, Ill.: The Dorsey Press.

MEEHAN, E. (1967). *Contemporary Political Thought: A Critical Study*. Homewood, Ill.: The Dorsey Press.

MILBRATH, L. W. (1965). *Political Participation: How and Why Do People Get Involved in Politics?* Chicago: Rand McNally & Company.

MILL, J. (1828). *Essay on Education*. London: J. Innes.

MILL, J. S. (1843). *A System of Logic Ratiocinative and Inductive*. London: Longmans. References are to new impression, 1961.

MILL, J. S. (1848). *Political Economy*. (Vol. III in *Collected Works*. Toronto: University of Toronto Press.)

MILL, J. S. (1859). 'Coleridge', in *Dissertations and Discussions* (1st ed.). Reprinted in HIMMELFARB, G. (1962), Garden City, N.Y.: Doubleday & Company. References to Doubleday Anchor paperback edition.

MILL, J. S. (1861a). *Considerations on Representative Government*. Reprinted with introduction by F. A. Hayek (Chicago: Henry Regnery Company, 1962).

MILL, J. S. (1861b). *Utilitarianism*. Edition with introduction by M. Warnock (London: Collins [Fontana Library], 1962).

MILL, J. S. (1873). *Autobiography*. In *Essential Works of John Stuart Mill*, ed. LERNER, M. (New York: Bantam Books, 1961).

MILLS, C. W. (1956). *The Power Elite*. New York: Oxford University Press. (Paperback edition by Galaxy Books [Oxford University Press]).

MITCHELL, W. C. (1962). *The American Polity: A Social and Cultural Interpretation*. New York: The Free Press.

MITCHELL, W. C. (1967). *Sociological Analysis and Politics: The Theories of Talcott Parsons*. Englewood Cliffs, N.J.: Prentice-Hall.

MONTESQUIEU, BARON DE (1949). *The Spirit of the Laws*, New York: Hafner Publishing Company.

MOORE, B., JR. (1966). *Social Origins of Dictatorship and Democracy:*

Lord and Peasant in the Making of the Modern World. Boston: Beacon Press.

MOORE, B., JR. (1968). 'Thoughts on Violence and Democracy'. *Proceedings of the Academy of Political Science*, 29: 'Urban Riots: Violence and Social Change'. 1–12.

MURAKAMI, Y. (1968). *Logic and Social Choice*. London: Routledge and Kegan Paul.

NAGEL, E. (1956). 'A Formalization of Functionalism', in *Logic Without Metaphysics* (Glencoe, Ill.: The Free Press), 247–83.

NAGEL, E. (1961). *The Structure of Science: Problems in Logic of Scientific Explanation*. London: Routledge and Kegan Paul.

NEUBAUER, D. E. (1967). 'Some Conditions of Democracy'. *American Political Science Review*, 61, 1002–1009.

NISBET, R. A. (1966). *The Sociological Tradition*. New York: Basic Books.

NORDLINGER, E. (1967). *The Working-Class Tories: Authority, Deference, and Stable Democracy*. London: MacGibbon and Kee.

NOWELL-SMITH, P. H. (1954). *Ethics*. Harmondsworth: Penguin Books.

OAKESHOTT, M. (1962). 'The Moral Life in the Writings of Thomas Hobbes', in *Rationalism in Politics and Other Essays* (London: Methuen & Co.), 248–300.

OLSON, M., JR. (1965). *The Logic of Collective Action: Public Goods and the Theory of Groups*. Cambridge, Mass.: Harvard University Press.

OLSON, M., JR. (1967). 'The Relationship of Economics to the Other Social Sciences: The Province of a "Special Report"': a Paper Delivered at the Annual Meeting of the American Political Science Association.

OLSON, M., JR.; ZECKHAUSER, R. (1966). 'An Economic Theory of Alliances'. *Review of Economics and Statistics*, 48, 266–79.

OPPENHEIM, F. E. (1968). *Moral Principles in Political Philosophy*. New York: Random House.

PARSONS, T. (1937). *The Structure of Social Action*. Glencoe, Ill.: The Free Press. Page references are to the Free Press paperback edition, 1: 1–470, 11: 473–775.

PARSONS, T. (1951). *The Social System*. New York: The Free Press. References are to Free Press paperback edition.

PARSONS, T. (1954). *Essays in Sociological Theory: Revised Edition*. New York: The Free Press. References are to Free Press paperback edition.

PARSONS, T. (1960). *Structure and Process in Modern Societies*. New York: The Free Press.

PARSONS, T. (1963). 'Rejoinder to Bauer and Coleman'. *Public Opinion Quarterly*, 27, 87–92.

PARSONS, T. (1966a). 'The Political Aspect of Social Structure and Process', in EASTON (1966), 71–112.

PARSONS, T. (1966b). *Societies: Evolutionary and Comparative Perspectives*. Englewood Cliffs, N.J.: Prentice-Hall.

PARSONS, T. (1967). *Sociological Theory and Modern Society*. New York: The Free Press.

PARSONS, T.; SHILS, E.; NAEGELE, K. D.; PITTS, J. R. (eds.) (1961). *Theories of Society: Foundations of Modern Sociological Theory*. New York: The Free Press.

PLAMENATZ, J. (1958). *The English Utilitarians*. (2nd revised edition). Oxford: Basil Blackwell. (Reference to 1966 'reprint with minor corrections'.)

PLAMENATZ, J. (1968). 'Some American Images of Democracy', in HUTCHINS, R. M.; ADLER, M. J. (eds.), *The Great Ideas of Today* (New York: Praeger).

POLSBY, N. W. (1960). 'Towards an Explanation of McCarthyism'. *Political Studies*, 8, 250–271.

POLSBY, N. W.; DENTLER, R. A.; SMITH, P. A. (eds.) (1963). *Politics and Social Life: An Introduction to Political Behavior.* Boston: Houghton Mifflin.

POOL, I. DE S.; ABELSON, R. P.; POPKIN, S. L. (1964). *Candidates, Issues and Strategies: A Computer Simulation of the 1960 Presidential Election.* Cambridge, Mass.: The M.I.T. Press.

PRESTHUS, R. (1964). *Men at the Top: A Study in Community Power.* New York: Oxford University Press.

PYE, L. W. (1962). *Politics, Personality and Nation Building.* New Haven, Conn.: Yale University Press. (Available in paperback.)

PYE, L. W.; VERBA, S. (eds.) (1965). *Political Culture and Political Development.* Princeton, N.J.: Princeton University Press.

RAPOPORT, A. (1960). *Fights, Games and Debates.* Ann Arbor: University of Michigan Press.

REX, J. (1961). *Key Problems of Sociological Theory.* London: Routledge and Kegan Paul.

REX, J.; MOORE, R. (1967). *Race, Community and Conflict: A Study of Sparkbrook.* London: Oxford University Press.

RIESMAN, D.; GLAZER, N. (1955). 'The Intellectuals and the Discontented Classes', in BELL (1955), 105–136.

RIKER, W. H. (1962). *The Theory of Political Coalitions.* New Haven, Conn.: Yale University Press. (Also in Yale paperback).

RIKER, W. H.; ORDESHOOK, P. C. (1968). 'A Theory of the Calculus of Voting'. *American Political Science Review*, 62, 25–42.

ROGIN, M. P. (1967). *The Intellectuals and McCarthy: The Radical Specter.* Cambridge, Mass.: The M.I.T. Press.

ROSE, R. (1967). *Influencing Voters: A Study of Campaign Rationality.* London: Faber & Faber.

RYLE, G. (1949). *The Concept of Mind.* London: Hutchinson University Library.

SCHELLING, T. C. (1960). *The Strategy of Conflict.* Cambridge, Mass.: Harvard University Press.

SCHLESINGER, J. A. (1958). 'Political Party Organization', in MARCH, J. G.; SIMON, H. A. (eds.), *Handbook of Organizations* (New York: John Wiley & Sons), 764–801.

SCHUMPETER, J. (1950). *Capitalism, Socialism and Democracy* (3rd edition). New York: Harper & Row. Reprinted in Unwin University Paperbacks with same pagination.

SHILS, E.; JANOWITZ, M. (1948). 'Cohesion and Disintegration in the German *Wehrmacht* in World War II', *Public Opinion Quarterly*, 12, 280–315.

SHILS, E.; YOUNG, M. (1953). 'The Meaning of the Coronation'. *Sociological Review*, 1, 63–68.

SHUBIK, M. (1959). *Strategy and Market Structure: Competition, Oligopoly, and the Theory of Games.* New York: John Wiley & Sons.

SJOBERG, G. (1960). *The Pre-Industrial City.* New York: The Free Press. Page references to Free Press paperback edition.

SKINNER, B. F. (1953). *Science and Human Behavior.* New York. The Macmillan Company (Free Press, paperback edition).

SMELSER, N. J. (1962). *Theory of Collective Behaviour*. London: Routledge and Kegan Paul.

SMELSER, N. J. (ed.) (1967). *Sociology: An Introduction*. New York: John Wiley & Sons.

SMITHIES, A. (1941). 'Optimum Location in Spatial Competition'. *Journal of Political Economy*, 59, 423–439.

SOMIT, A.; TANENHAUS, J. (1964). *American Political Science: A Profile of a Discipline*. New York: Atherton Press.

SORAUF, F. J. (1967). 'Political Parties and Political Analysis', in CHAMBERS (1967), 33–35.

STORING, H. J. (ed.) (1962). *Essays on the Scientific Study of Politics*. New York: Holt, Rinehart and Winston.

STOUFFER, S. E.; SOUCHMAN, E. A.; DEVINNEY, L. C.; STAR, S. A.; WILLIAMS, R. M. (1949). *The American Soldier: Adjustment during Army Life*. Princeton, N.J.: Princeton University Press.

STRETTON, H. (1969). *The Political Sciences: General Principles of Selection in Social Science and History*. London: Routledge and Kegan Paul.

THOMAS, K. (1965). 'The Social Origins of Hobbes' Political Thought', in BROWN, K. C. (ed.), *Hobbes Studies* (Oxford: Basil Blackwell).

DE TOCQUEVILLE, A. (1946). *Democracy in America*. London: Oxford University Press.

TRUMAN, D. B. (1953). *The Government Process*. New York: Alfred A. Knopf.

TRUMAN, D. B. (1959). *The Congressional Party: A Case Study*. New York: John Wiley & Sons.

TULLOCK, G. (1967). *Towards a Mathematics of Politics*. Ann Arbor: University of Michigan Press.

VAN DEN BERGHE, P. L. (1963). 'Dialectic and Functionalism: Toward a Synthesis'. *American Sociological Review*, 28, 695–705. Reprinted in DEMERATH (1967), 293–306.

VAN DEN BERGHE, P. L. (1965). *South Africa: A Study in Conflict*. Middletown, Conn.: Wesleyan University Press.

VAN DYKE, V. (1960). *Political Science: A Philosophical Analysis*. Stanford: Stanford University Press.

VERBA, S. (1965). 'The Kennedy Assassination and the Nature of Political Commitment', in GREENBERG, B. S.; PARKER, F. B. (eds.), *The Kennedy Assassination and the American Public* (Stanford: Stanford University Press), 348–360.

VIDICH, A.; BENSMAN, J. (1958), *Small Town in Mass Society: Class, Power and Religion in a Rural Community*. New York: Doubleday & Company.

WAGNER, R. E. (1966). 'Pressure Groups and Political Entrepreneurs': A Review Article (1), *Papers on Non-Market Decision-Making*, 1, 161–170.

WEBER, M. (1949). *Max Weber on the Methodology of the Social Sciences*. Trs. and ed. by FINCH, H. A.; SHILS, E. Glencoe, Ill.: The Free Press.

WEBER, M. (1963). *The Sociology of Religion*. Trs. by FISCHOFF, E., introduction by PARSONS, T. Boston: Beacon Press.

WILLIAMS, J. D. (1954). *The Compleat Strategyst*. New York: McGraw-Hill.

WILLIAMS, R. M., JR. (1961). 'The Sociological Theory of Talcott Parsons', in BLACK (1961), 64–99.

200

WILSON, J. Q. (1962). *The Amateur Democrat*. Chicago: The University of Chicago Press.

WINCH, P. G. (1958). *The Idea of a Social Science and Its Relation to Philosophy*. London: Routledge and Kegan Paul.

WISEMAN, H. V. (1966). *Political Systems: Some Sociological Approaches*. London: Routledge and Kegan Paul.

WOLFINGER, R. E.; WOLFINGER, B. K.; PREWITT, K.; ROSENHACK, S. (1964). 'America's Radical Right: Politics and Ideology', in APTER (1964), 262–293. Reprinted in DREYER (1966), 189–226.

WRONG, D. (1961). 'The Oversocialized Conception of Man in Modern Sociology'. *American Sociological Review*, 26, 184–193. Reprinted in COSER, L. A.; ROSENBERG, B. (eds.), *Sociological Theory: A Book of Readings* (New York: The Macmillan Company, 2nd ed., 1964), 112–122.

WRONG, D. H.; GRACEY, H. L. (eds.) (1967). *Readings in Introductory Sociology*. New York: The Macmillan Company.

YOUNG, M. (1958). *The Rise of the Meritocracy*. London: Thames and Hudson. Page references to Penguin edition.

YOUNG, O. R. (1968). *Systems of Political Science*. Englewood Cliffs, N.J.: Prentice-Hall.

YOUNG, R. (ed.) (1958). *Approaches to the Study of Politics: Twenty-two Contemporary Essays Exploring the Nature and the Methods by Which It Can Be Studied*. Evanston, Ill.: Northwestern University Press.

Subject Index